DOC

ZOO MEMORIES AND ANIMAL STORIES

To Barbara

[signature: Lee G. Simmons]

LEE G. SIMMONS DVM

The first edition of *Doc: Zoo Memories and Animal Stories* was published in 2018 in Omaha, Nebraska, USA

ISBN 978-1-7322000-0-5

Published in 2018 by Dr. Lee G. Simmons, Omaha, Nebraska

Dr. Lee G. Simmons, writer, Omaha, Nebraska

Wayne Kobza, Pencil to Press, publication design, Omaha, Nebraska

Published with the assistance of Legacy Preservation LLC, Omaha, Nebraska

Printed and bound in USA.

Cover Artwork: (front) Dr. Lee G. Simmons and wife Marie, holding a baby gorilla at the Henry Doorly Zoo; (back) Dr. Lee G. Simmons, holding a bobcat.

CONTENTS

CONTENTS

CONTENTS

Marie and Dr. Lee Simmons, up close and personal with a panda during their 2004 visit to China.

DEDICATION

TO MARIE, THE BRIDE OF 58 YEARS, who thought she was marrying a kid who was going to be just a plain, ordinary veterinarian. Without Marie's incredibly calm and always pleasant tolerance, coupled with her very active participation and encouragement in the activities of the last 58 years, much that we have accomplished in the zoo and the conservation world could not and would not have happened. In those early days when the effort had to be daylight to dark, 24/7, it was Marie who carried the family, even bringing the kids to the zoo on Sundays so we could all have a picnic lunch together. She also kept me fed no matter when I came home. In later years, she turned our house into a nursery for many zoo babies and a bed and breakfast for visiting scientists from around the country. She is a quietly determined workaholic, always with a smile and a gentle hand.

Yes—it is a little bit autobiographical, and for that I ask your indulgence. This started out as simply a collection of zoo memories and animal stories that I was putting together so our kids and grandkids would know a little bit about how it was back in the early days. Unfortunately, when it was suggested that these should be expanded into book form, a bit of history slipped in. The zoo world in those early days operated in a substantially different way than it does today. There were a number of larger-than-life individuals, both people and animals, and some who were just plain interesting, which I have tried to accurately depict here. There are a few stories that I would have liked to put in, but I had to restrain myself. These stories are not in strict chronological order but were written down as they surfaced in memory. My hope is that you tolerate the history and enjoy the memories and animal stories.

— LGS, 2018

Tucson, Arizona, 1939.

TUCSON

I was born on February 20, 1938, in the Storks Nest Maternity Hospital in Tucson, Arizona. We lived in the desert and foothills north of town, and I was joined by two younger sisters, Dorothy May (Dottie) and Marie Lynnette (Nett). Later, in Oklahoma, our family portrait became complete with the additions of Barbie Ann and Cindy Lee.

My father was born on a farm near Turkey, a town in west Texas. He had come to Tucson as part of the federal government's Civilian Conservation Corps (CCC) program during the Great Depression. Being tenant farmers, his parents and their eight children grew their own food, but they had no money to buy shoes or clothes. Dad sent most of his pay home as an allotment. He got $5 per month, and the government sent the other $25 of his salary to his parents.

My mother (Dorothy Esther Taylor) had been born in San Diego, California, and had come to Tucson in a covered wagon behind a team of four mules with my grandmother, grandfather, and her four older siblings (Clarence, Joe, Eva and Naomie). My grandfather, Alva Melvin Taylor, was extremely tall, apparently standing more than 6' 6," and worked as a barber. He was also a preacher in the Reorganized Church of Jesus Christ of Latter Day Saints. My grandmother, Myrtle May (Bates) Taylor, whom we always just referred to as "Mom," was only 4' 9." Standing side by side, they made a very interesting Mutt and Jeff picture in the family photographs. Some of the family pictures show my grandfather cutting hair in a Tucson hotel, and he simply towers over his customers. He was also known to sharpen scissors, and he made and sold vanilla extract. At some point before my parents were married my grandparents were divorced. As a result, my earliest remembrances were primarily of my grandmother and only occasionally of my grandfather, who died when I was five-and-a-half years old. I do remember him shooting birds in his garden with a slingshot.

Dad had been working for the CCC in the mountains on dams, reservoirs, and parks when he met my mother. At the time they were married he was working in private construction, driving a bulldozer in the Santa Catalina Mountains north of Tucson.

One of our family stories recounts an incident when Dad was driving a bulldozer on the side of a mountain and a rockslide occurred, causing the bulldozer with my dad on board to slide down the mountain and through a large patch of jumping cactus. Dad stood up on the bulldozer to protect himself going through the jumping cactus, but when the bulldozer finally came to a halt and he was still alive, he forgot himself and sat down on the seat that was covered with cactus. The family story is of him having to overcome his shyness so that both my mother and my grandmother could pull cactus spines out of his rear end with pliers. Jumping cactus spines have barbs on the end. They don't come out easily, and there were apparently a lot of spines.

Sometime after the cactus experience my father helped build Old Tucson, a movie set on the west side of the Tucson Mountains. After the construction was completed, they used fire hoses on the new adobe buildings to make them look old. Dad was lucky enough to get a job as a prop man on the set of "Arizona," a western starring William Holden. Dad told us that on another film he got to meet Gary Cooper, who was very friendly and polite to all the workers on the set.

My dad built three houses during our time in Tucson. The first two were Southwestern-style stuccoed adobes, one for my grandmother and one for us. The houses were next to each other, approximately five miles northeast of Tucson. The third house was a concrete block house across the street, with the only gabled roof in the neighborhood. He built that house after World War II, when

At three months old with my mother Dorothy.

I was old enough to help a little. My dad's younger brother Robert had helped build the first two houses shortly after moving out of the family home in Texas. A family story describes how two proselytizing Jehovah's Witnesses set up a gramophone on the front porch on a hot summer afternoon. My mother told them to go away because my uncle Robert, who had a night job, was sleeping. They refused and started playing their recorded sermon loudly. Robert jumped out of bed in his underwear and ran into the kitchen, where he grabbed a skillet full of hot grease and then threw the grease through the screen door onto the Jehovah's Witnesses. The gramophone stopped. Washing the grease out of the screen took much longer than getting rid of the unwanted visitors.

Somewhere along the way my father began working as an aircraft mechanic at Davis Monthan Air Force Base in Tucson. Dad was an outdoorsman who loved hunting and fishing. My mother was very artistic and made virtually all of our clothes. I'm not sure I ever had a store-bought shirt until after I was married and away from home. My mother made her own clothes and all of my sisters' dresses, copywriting some of the patterns to sell to other people. Most of my shirts and many of my sisters' dresses were made out of fabric from chicken feed sacks. In those days many companies deliberately sacked feed in high-quality cloth that could be reused for clothing. She also made furniture and did wood carving. Mother had a wicked sense of humor.

OREGON

When World War II started, my dad was exempt from the draft by virtue of his age and his profession—he was an aircraft mechanic, an essential job during wartime. The attack on Pearl Harbor bothered him and ultimately motivated him to volunteer for the draft, which meant that he would serve for the duration. He was assigned to a carrier group at the naval base in Portland, Oregon. My mother and younger sister Dottie and I traveled to Los Angeles by train and then by bus up Highway 1 to Portland, Oregon, to join my dad before he shipped

My parents, pictured here in 1944, during their time in Oregon.

out. It was a long and largely uneventful journey except for one incident. The busses in those days were of poor quality and often very crowded. Highway 1 was a winding road. Dottie had a problem with motion sickness. When my mother told the bus driver that we needed to stop, he just ignored her, citing the schedule he had to keep. We were seated directly behind the driver, so as Dottie began to feel sick, my mother held my sister up over the back of the driver's neck and she vomited all over him. Needless to say, he stopped, and from that point on, any time anyone on the bus said they were sick he was quick to stop and let everybody get out to walk around for a minute.

During our first year in Oregon we lived in one of seven small bungalows in a logging camp outside of Warrenton. Our time there coincided with my first interest in snakes. I caught a small water snake and brought it into the logging camp where it was promptly pronounced to be a cottonmouth water moccasin. It wasn't, of course, since cottonmouth water moccasins have never lived that far north. About this time, a grizzly bear was raiding chicken houses near the camp. A hunt for the bear was organized, and two teenaged boys decided to sneak out and joined the hunt with their .22 rifles. You can guess who found the bear; sadly this resulted in lethal consequences for one of the boys.

I saw trucks loaded with logs come out of the forest to be rafted down the Warrenton River to the sawmill. When my dad could get away from the Naval Base we stood on the log rafts and fished in the river. During our second year there we lived in the town of Warrenton, where I started the first grade. I remember walking to school on wooden boardwalks with slimy slugs crawling across. If you stepped on a slug you immediately went down. My dad never got to go out on the carrier, in part because of his training as an aircraft mechanic and probably in part because he was considered to be an old man. Instead, he was made an instructor to train young aircraft mechanics, but he always regretted not being able to go out on a carrier, despite volunteering every time one went out.

BACK HOME

After the war we moved back to Tucson, and my dad returned to work at Davis Monthan Air Force Base. At the time, Tucson was a great place to grow up. As a family we picnicked, explored and hiked in the desert, foothills and mountains. Dad and I fished in the lakes at Mount Lemmon and Sabino Canyon. I was too young to hunt on my own, but by 11 I was accompanying Dad on mule deer and javelina pig hunts. Dad was a good shot with the old 30-40 Kraig and rarely missed. I still have that family rifle.

While on a mule deer hunt in Browns Canyon in the Huachuca Mountains, we laid awake by the campfire one night listening to a jaguar, who had probably wandered up from Mexico, calling. Using binoculars we spotted him the

On a Boy Scout hike in 1949, I took this photo of a bobcat using an old Kodak box camera. It was my first exotic animal photograph.

next morning on the other side of the canyon. He was a long way off but clearly identifiable. A few days later he tried to take possession of a deer two hunters had killed and was shot.

The world was a different place then, and no one worried about two young boys taking their dogs and their bicycles to ride out into the desert for a full day of exploring, collecting lizards and snakes and coming home just in time for supper. Our church Boy Scout troop was a ragtag lot without a single uniform among us, but we spent more time camping in the desert and mountains than any other troop because we had a very good scoutmaster, Art Mills, who was an outdoorsman. Most of our meetings were out in the desert on his place. The first exotic animal photograph I ever took was in 1949 during a Boy Scout hike using an old Kodak box camera to shoot a bobcat on a rock halfway up between Sabino Canyon and Mount Lemmon. The bobcat had its front foot caught in the jaws of a steel trap. We decided that we would turn it loose, and I can still vividly picture John Mills, our assistant scout master, jumping high in the air, in fear of becoming a soprano, when the cat hung a claw in his inner thigh. We had neglected to tell the bobcat of our good intentions. We finally got a coat over the cat's head long enough for John to step on the spring and relax the jaws of the trap. The bobcat limped off. I still have that black-and-white photo.

Our family was the proud owner of a talking raven, a profane creature who was absolute hell on stray dogs' noses. We bought horse meat hamburger at a USDA-inspected horsemeat market to feed him. I was doing a lot of camping with the Boy Scouts and my mother would always make a couple of skewers of beef steak shish kebab to take along for the first night on our trips. My fellow scouts always wanted a taste, so out of courtesy I sometimes ended up with very little to eat. I told my mother about the problem, and she came up with a solution—a huge batch of shish kebab skewers with horsemeat tenderloin in between the onions, potatoes and tomatoes. The first night out, we put the skewers on the grill and invited everyone to help themselves. Even our scoutmaster Art Mills took up my offer. After everyone had eaten, he asked me how we could afford all of that prime beef. I told him that it wasn't beef but horsemeat from the market where we bought meat for my raven. After that, I never had any problems with my friends wanting to taste my meat.

My dad had helped build Sabino Canyon when he was in the CCC, and he knew a secret. There was an island in the middle of the lake connected to the shore by an invisible underwater causeway. If you knew which rock on the shore to start from and which rock on the island to walk straight toward, you could wade across in three feet of water. We spent many nights out on the island fishing for catfish and drinking black coffee boiled over a campfire while people on the shore wondered how we got there.

My dad, pictured here near the Tucson mountains, was an avid outdoorsman all his life.

We also had a little business that paid quite well, especially for kids our age. My mother and I raised tropical fish and found out that a single strand of seaweed cost a nickel at the pet store. It so happened that David Mills and I knew that at least three different species of freshwater seaweed grew wild in some of the cattle ponds at the edge of the foothills, so we'd go out on our bicycles with a foot tub strapped to the carrier and collect seaweed and sell it to local pet shops.

My dad was tolerant of my interest in snakes and herpetology, even though he did not like snakes. His father had been bitten in the shin by a rattlesnake in West Texas when my dad was 11 years old. When I was little, my cousins and I would pull up my grandfather's pant leg and put our fingers into the pit in his leg.

My mother encouraged my animal interests and was even an active co-conspirator in many of my later endeavors, including helping raise many of the baby animals that I brought home such as squirrels and skunks.

VACATIONS, APPENDICITIS, AND THE OIL RIG WITH DAD HAY

Our family would drive to Seagoville, Texas, just outside of Dallas, and then onto Osawatomie, Kansas, which was close to Kansas City, for vacations with my Grandmother and Granddad Simmons and Mom and Dad Hay. Dad Hay was our step granddad, but we regarded him as our real granddad since he had married my grandmother when I was six years old. We had a big old 1938 V8 LaSalle, a poor man's Cadillac, with big spare tire compartments in each front fender. These proved beneficial during wartime when sugar was being rationed since we could put the spare tires in the trunk and load up the wheel wells with brown sugar during drives down to Nogales, Mexico. Nobody ever bothered to check the wheel wells, and we were able to do a lot of canning and make cactus jelly. It was a great road car and would really go. On one vacation to Texas and Kansas, my sister and I got into a scrap in the backseat, and she threw one of my cowboy boots out the window. Neither of us had courage enough to admit to our parents what had happened until we were 100 miles down the road and had stopped for gas.

In the spring after I turned 11, we went on our usual circuit to Seagoville and up to Osawatomie. Along the way, my appendix ruptured. I ended up having surgery in a little hospital in Olathe, Kansas. Luckily the early crude penicillin was just available. I was deemed unsuitable for the long ride back to Tucson when my parents' vacation time was up, so Dottie and I stayed on the farm with Mom and Dad Hay for the rest of the summer until they could take us back to Tucson. In addition to having oil leases of his own, Dad Hay did contract drilling for other people. It was shallow well stuff with an old cable "spudding" rig. As soon as I was well enough I spent the rest of the summer going to the rig with him every day. It was a great summer. His favorite saying was, "If you keep your eyes and your ears open and your mouth shut you learn a lot more." A working oil rig is a dangerous but exciting place for a kid. We had wells that blew in unexpectedly and tools that got stuck down the hole and had to be fished out. Even at 72, Dad Hay was (perhaps) the strongest man I've never met. He was not very tall, but he was built like a bear. I saw him lock his hands under a 500-pound drill bit between his knees and lift it with his legs so that the crew could put an anvil under it for sharpening. Even with a bad hand, he could grab an oil-covered cable with his gloves on and go hand over hand to the top of the derrick. When we shot a well Dad Hay let me hold the long tin shot shell steady in the top of the well casing while the Nitro Man poured nitroglycerin in it. With all that nitroglycerin going into each shot, he reasoned that it wouldn't make any difference if I was holding the shot shell or standing halfway across the field. If an accident occurred, we'd all be just as dead. It was a different time and a different place. I also helped when the Nitro Man put a detonator in a fence post and then strung wire the length of the well depth out across the field to check that the conductivity of the wire was in working order. Some men on horseback came up just as we were getting ready to shoot a well and crack the oil-bearing rock strata at the bottom.

Dad Hay told them it might be a good idea to get off their horses and lead them out into the middle of the field because the ground would shake, and oil and water might blow out of the top of the well. Three of them followed this advice, but one of them stayed on his horse. Dad Hay didn't say anymore. We moved away a safe distance, and he gave the signal to shoot. When the Nitro went off, the man was no longer sitting on his horse.

At another well, Dad Hay was having problems with some loafers from a nearby town coming out at night, priming the gasoline pump, and then short stroking it to fill their cars. After the well was shot Dad Hay had the Nitro Man put a spoon full of nitroglycerin in a five-gallon gas can. He chained the gas pump handle 17 ways from Sunday so it was impossible to short stroke. When we came to work the next morning a 1938 Buick straight eight was halfway across the field with the engine blown. After that, the gas thefts stopped. No one ever said a word or retrieved the car. Today, of course the authorities would likely label Dad Hay a dangerous terrorist. Those times were simpler, and, I think, better.

While Dad Hay was unfailingly courteous and rigidly honest, he had a diabolical sense of humor. If he was approaching a piece of property with an electric fence and gate, one of his favorite tricks was to ask his passenger to get out and open the gate, then he'd pull up just far enough so that when the gate closed it would make contact with the rear bumper and electrify the car and the door handle. It was a big shock when you grabbed the door handle. Once when we were on the rig, some quail hunters asked permission to hunt. Dad Hay gave them permission and asked what shot they were using. The answer was "number-nine birdshot." He stepped into the doghouse of the rig and brought out a little single-barreled 410 shotgun, also with number-nine shot in it. One of the hunters made fun of it, doubted it could knock down a quail and remarked that for enough money he would step out a distance, drop his pants and give Dad Hay a free shot at his rear end. So the bet was made. The man stepped out a fairly long distance, dropped his pants and bent over. Dad Hay calmly reached over and picked up one of his buddy's 12-gauge doubles and blistered the man's rear end. Amazingly, the man's buddies could see what was going to happen and still let it happen. In today's world Dad Hay would probably be deemed a felon and put in jail. That summer was so much fun, Dottie and I convinced our folks to let us spend the next summer on the farm in Kansas.

Once at a small family gathering in Kansas, an uncle by marriage let his temper get out of hand and cursed his wife in front of my grandmother and everyone else. Dad Hay walked quietly over and informed him that cursing in front of women and children was not acceptable. This man stood six-feet, four-inches tall and was the marshal in a small town near Independence. He towered over Dad Hay. He threatened to kick Dad Hay's ass and approached with his fists doubled up. At 72, despite having two fingers injured from an oil field accident, he was extremely strong in the hands and arms. He grabbed the marshal's wrists and squeezed them so hard that the man fell to his knees. Dad Hay first made him say "uncle," then made him apologize to his own wife and to my grandmother and everyone else. He let him loose and asked him if there was anything else he would like to do. The guy wisely said nothing, turned on his heel and got in his car and left. We had to give my aunt and cousins a ride home.

That was Dad Hay: an honest, old-fashioned man who believed in keeping his word and was not to be fooled with. To say he was an incredible and influential role model for a young boy would be a gross understatement. He lived to 100 years old.

The second summer Dottie and I stayed on the farm in Kansas, we moved the rig to another lease and had loaded everything on trucks, including one truck, which carried drill bits and pipe. Due to the load the springs were almost bent backwards. During World War II a bomb bay door on a B-29 had fallen and hit Dad Hay in the head, damaging his eyesight. Years later on the oilrig, a tornado blew off the tin roof of the doghouse, hitting Dad in the head. Between the two traumas he had lost nearly all of his central vision. In retrospect, his problems may have been macular degeneration. The result was that they were one driver short and he wasn't fit to drive a truck. At 12 years old I was quite sure that I could handle the driving. I even thought I had everyone convinced, but it was decided that Dad Hay would drive the truck and I would ride shotgun as his eyes. Those roller coaster Kansas gravel roads were narrow and surrounded by deep ditches on both sides. Dad Hay could see the edges of the road but struggled identifying what was coming at us over the hill. We were doing great until the engine lugged down just before we got to the top of a steep hill. Dad Hay hit the clutch, downshifted and the rear axle snapped like a gunshot. Without the engine the brakes would not hold the overloaded truck, and we rolled backwards all the way to the bottom of the hill and part way up the next before rolling back down to the bottom again. Despite his limited vision, Dad Hay kept the truck on the road all the way down that hill until it stopped.

THE PAINTED UNDERWEAR

Mom and Dad Hay were about 60 when they married, both having lost spouses. After the ceremony in Tucson they were heading back to Osawatomie, Kansas on a honeymoon to see all the relatives. They spent their wedding night in a small roadside travel court somewhere in eastern Arizona or western New Mexico. My mother had a mischievous and sometimes ornery sense of humor, and she had been painting with a phosphorescent paint that glowed in the dark because it had radium in it. It was the same kind of paint used on the hands and dials of wristwatches. She opened Dad Hay's suitcase before the wedding and painted flowers and coiling vines and leaves on the front of his T-shirts and underpants. On their wedding night my grandmother put on her nightgown and slid under the bed sheet. It was summertime, and in those days air-conditioning was a rarity, so folks slept under a single sheet. Dad Hay went in for his shower and came out in clean underwear and turned off the lights. My grandmother immediately burst out laughing as he slid into bed beside her. This was not the way a new bride, even if she was 60, was supposed to act on her wedding night. Dad Hay was getting a bit put out until she told him to look down. There, glowing up through the sheet, were flowers and vines and leaves. Of course today, phosphorescent paint with radium in it would be totally illegal.

My mother never quite outgrew her ornery streak. When Marie and I opened our suitcases on our honeymoon, I found that the leg holes, armholes and neck holes of all my underwear had been sewn shut and there was a package of comic books in the suitcase. A note told us to break the seal in case we ran out of things to do.

My grandmother had grown up on a Kansas farm and learned to be a copper smith in Tucson during the Depression. She was a typical hard-working farm wife who let nothing faze her. She could kill, pluck, and butcher a dozen chickens or help in scalding, scraping and butchering a pig with no problem. But if a mouse surprised her, she came unglued. I remember one Sunday sermon when Mom Hay stood up on the seat of the front pew with a loud shriek after seeing a mouse run across the floor.

Once my dog Bongo, who was part Airedale, caught and killed one of Mom Hay's laying hens. She came charging out and grabbed Bongo by the collar with one hand and the chicken by the legs in the other hand and beat him with the chicken until he went submissive. She threw the hen down and went to find a piece of string so she could tie the dead chicken around his neck and make him wear it for a day; this was standard operating procedure in the country to break a dog of killing chickens. Before she could find the string, the supposedly dead chicken shook itself, got up, and staggered off. In the coming weeks, the hen continued laying eggs as if nothing had happened.

In retrospect, perhaps the most important experiences during my time in Tucson occurred while I was in primary school. I started school in Warrington,

Oregon, while my dad was in the Navy. It was a small, two-room school with multiple classes in the same room, and I spent most of my first two years there. Back in Tucson after the war we were in base housing, and the government had co-opted part of a private school for us military brats. Needless to say, none of us fit in really well. I failed to pass the third grade, they said, due to my reading skills. The family thought it was just because it was a highfalutin private school where military brats were not welcome.

My dad built a new house on the northeast edge of Tucson, and my sister and I switched to a different school. At the beginning of the fifth grade my English teacher called my mother and me in for a conference and told us, "He is smart enough, he is good in math, he remembers everything he hears, but he can't read a book or spell." A plan was devised where I would come to school a half hour early each day for tutoring. Also, my recesses and lunch hours were reserved for more tutoring, and I would stay a half hour after school. Sometime near the end of that school year, as if by magic, I could suddenly read. That summer I read everything I could get my hands on and have been doing so ever since. In those days, if your parents or teacher told you to do something, you just did it. Fifty years later I read an article on dyslexia and thought, "Holy smokes!" My sister and I tried to find my teacher to thank her for taking an interest in me, but the school records were gone. Without her extra care, my career path and lifestyle would likely have been dramatically different. However, I still can't spell.

OKLAHOMA

In the middle of October 1951 my parents and sisters Dotty May and Marie Lynnette and I moved to Oklahoma so our father could work at Tinker Field Air Force Base in Midwest City and stay active in live aircraft. In November, my sister Barbee Ann was born. She was premature and only weighed two pounds, 15 ounces, but managed to survive. The following March we bought a 14.5-acre farm halfway between Jones and Choctaw, 23 miles east of Oklahoma City. The

Baker farm was owned by a brother and sister. The brother had been a trick shot in the circus, and these two did not believe in electricity or modern amenities. The farm had no electricity, a hand pump in the yard, a large wood-burning cook stove in the kitchen, a potbellied stove in the living room, and an outhouse down past the barn. It took nearly two years to convince Oklahoma Gas and Electric to run electricity to the farm. We got to experience life as the pioneers did and actually studied by kerosene lamps. Dotty and I finished the last three months of seventh grade at State Center (a three-room school) and then the eighth grade before going to Jones High School.

My dad worked a swing shift from 3 p.m. to midnight at Tinker Field. After a few hours' sleep, he was able to put in a few hours truck farming our property. Saturdays were full workdays on the farm. We raised lots of sweet potatoes, green beans, sweet corn, and watermelons. We even supplied a grocery store in Harrah, Oklahoma. They kept a running account of what they owed us, and throughout the year we drew on that account for groceries and supplies. We settled up with the owner once a year.

My mother, in addition to making all of our family's clothes, canned large quantities of vegetables, jams, and jellies every summer. We always had a cow to milk and often a pig to butcher in the fall. I didn't mind planting and harvesting sweet potatoes, sweet corn, and watermelons for our own use, but I grew to absolutely hate picking green beans. Interestingly, a job that I really liked was building fence.

In high school I worked part time on a nearby dairy. We started milking at 3 a.m., finishing just in time to go home, get a shower, eat breakfast and catch the school bus. We milked 110 Holsteins, and once a week, being the youngest and skinniest, I had to get into the big holding tank and scrub it out after it was emptied. Immediately after school the cycle started all over again. I appreciated the job and the money, but I took a solemn oath that I would never again have anything to do with a dairy cow.

In those days, Oklahoma was a wonderful place to grow up. You could hunt and fish, and frequently my friends and I would hand over our rifles to the bus driver in the morning. They'd get stored in the principal's office at school, and we could pick them up in the afternoon to hunt our way home. The school bus driver would obligingly stop and let you off with your rifle wherever you wanted. In the summer we enjoyed hunting bullfrogs. My best friend George Seebeck and I hunted enough of them for both our families to get together for a big fried frog leg feast.

Many activities would today get you labeled as a juvenile delinquent; but back then ornery behavior was considered normal for a young boy. Pranks like putting three bull calves in the hallway of the high school over Halloween weekend or turning over outhouses were not considered terrible crimes. Nor was blocking the entrance to the high school with bricks from the construction site of a nearby church. Of course when you were caught you had to publicly un-brick the door in front of God and everybody. Upending the Christian Church outhouse while the preacher was inside was not met with so much favor, at least by the preacher.

Our physics and chemistry teacher Mr. Cossey was tolerant of some of these shenanigans. During Mr. Cossey's physics section on electricity we shocked each other with old telephone generators. My father had taught me how to charge a car condenser by letting the spark from a speak plug wire jump to it. One day we charged a condenser at lunch and carried it with much care into the science room and set it on Cossey's glass-topped desk. He saw it when he came into the room, and he looked directly at me as if to say, "Just how dumb do you think I am?" However, his curiosity, as to whether we actually had the guts to do it, got the better of him, and he picked it up and touched his finger to the positive wire. I'll never forget the noise of that condenser discharging and Mr. Cossey smashing his knees into his pencil drawer from the shock. Our whole class laughed hard, but nobody laughed harder than Mr. Cossey.

KAYAKING THE KYAMICHI RIVER

Along with truck farming our 14 acres we did a lot of rabbit, squirrel, deer hunting and fishing. George Seebeck had built an 18-foot open cockpit kayak. When we were in college we snuck away for a week on an isolated 50-mile stretch of the Kyamichi River in southeastern Oklahoma. Our ritual was to take enough food for three meals and condiments and coffee. Anything else, you had to hunt or fish for.

Once I was standing on the covered-deck portion of the bow, hunting frogs while George and Willard Webster (Marie's uncle) manned the paddles. I was sliding a .22 pistol back into the holster when the safety strap accidentally slid through the trigger guard causing an unexpected discharge. The bullet went down through the deck and put a hole the kayak. We paddled upstream through the rapids. In case someone became sick or injured it would be easier to bring them down stream through the rapids even if you were the only paddler. Later we came around a bend and saw a local hunter who had just killed a spike buck (out of season) with an old 30-30 Winchester. This man had the blackest teeth I'd ever seen. We just kept paddling easy, trying to mind our own business. I was standing on the bow deck with a 12-foot frog gig in my hands. As we pulled close to the hunter I said, "Howdy." He was wearing bibbed overalls that were to long for his legs; he had worn through the back of the legs from walking on them. He had a belt around his middle with an old Iver Johnson Sealed Eight 22-cal revolver tucked under it. He looked up and calmly said, "I thought gigging was illegal." We assured him it wasn't and we continued quietly upstream.

One September we were gigging big carp in a creek off of Lake Carl Blackwell west of Stillwater, just for the fun of it. We didn't eat boney carp. At noon we came around a bend and there was an older couple setting on a blanket with a bottle of Jim Beam. We said hello and they asked what we were doing and what we were going to do with the big carp we had gigged. We told them we planned to give them away to the men who were always bank fishing around the lake. The man said he was in the insurance business in Oklahoma City. He asked if they could have some of the fish, and we promptly put three very large carp in the trunk of his big black Cadillac and shut the lid. We went on up the creek and just at dark came back past them on the way to the lake. The bottle was empty, and they were both asleep on the blanket. We always wondered if this couple remembered the trunk full of fish the next day when they sobered up. Septembers in Oklahoma are hot and fish rot in a hurry.

AUNT MAGGIE AND UNCLE LES

My dad's aunt Maggie and Uncle Les Glass lived in the same area of southeastern Oklahoma, close to the Kyamichi River and not far from Antlers. They lived primarily off the land by gardening, hunting, and fishing. And they had a few head of cattle and pigs that ran free in the hills living off of acorns. As a kid it was a great place to go because there was hunting and fishing in heavily forested foothills and low mountains to climb. Aunt Maggie and Uncle Les were favorites, and their hospitality was legendary. The summer after Marie and I were married, we went with my folks to visit. We caught a nice mess of fish and a big long American Eel in Rock Creek, which ran through their property.

When we brought our catch up to the backyard to clean, Marie took one look at the eel and said it was slimy and looked too much like a snake to eat. Actually, eel meat is white and flaky and very tasty. At supper I watched as Marie very carefully selected two small bluegills with their heads and tails still on to avoid the eel. On a deer hunt I bagged a big male bobcat that had been preying on Uncle Les' young pigs.

THE OKLAHOMA CITY
REPTILE HOUSE, BOB JENNY, AND SNAKE COLLECTING

Early on I showed up at the reptile house of the Oklahoma City Zoo with a pillowcase full of native, nonpoisonous snakes. There I met Bob Jenny, the reptile curator. Bob became an early mentor, one of many along the way, and I spent all the time I could spare during high school and college around the reptile house and going on snake-collecting trips with Bob. We collected cotton mouth water moccasins in the cypress swamps and the Long Grassy Lakes near Broken Bow in Southeast Oklahoma and diamondback rattlesnakes in the Panhandle of West Texas, close to Turkey. Our hunts were, in a word, interesting. I recall once being in the middle of one of the long grassy lakes in an old wooden boat we had found on the bank when suddenly the boat split right up the middle. This wouldn't have been terribly serious except that we had a TV cameraman along with us who had a 30-pound battery pack strapped to his back.

The rest of us could have easily swam ashore, but the cameraman would have certainly drowned. However, serendipity and fate teamed up that night. Just as the boat was about to sink we ran into another boat floating free in the lake and transferred over. Later on that trip, while I tried to walk across the swamp on top of the cypress knees, I lost my footing and fell on top of a sack full of cotton mouths. Luckily the snakes were all just as traumatized as I was because a snake bite in the belly would have been difficult to treat. During our return from the hunt I drove Bob's Plymouth Fury station wagon while he slept. We had done well on the hunt, and the back of the wagon was loaded with full snake boxes. The Plymouth had a big V-8, and I had never driven a car that would run that fast. On the way down we had crossed the Kyamichi River Bridge and noticed some construction to one side but not being from the area didn't know what was going on. It was dark and I was cruising the Plymouth around 85 miles-per-hour when we got to the bridge. Suddenly, I saw through the headlights that the deck had been totally removed. A detour veered sharply to the right and then sharply left and disappeared down over the bank. I had no choice but to hit the brakes and steer hard right and then hard left. We were airborne as we went down over the bank. Below was a one-lane pontoon bridge. When we landed on the bridge it threw Bob up against the windshield facing me. The boxes flipped over and the lids came off, and Bob was plastered with snake sacks full of cotton mouth water moccasins. Bob's eyes were very wide while he was pinned up against the windshield. The pontoon bridge gave and sank as we slammed down, but luckily it rebounded and bucked us back up into the air at least two more times before we roared up the bank on the other side. Bob and the snake bags flew back onto the front seat. I managed to get us back onto the highway and onto the shoulder, where I stopped the car to help Bob get off of the snake bags. Luckily no one died and no one was bitten. Once I calmed down I asked Bob if he wanted to drive. "Why?" he asked. "You're never going to do anything like that again—but we're not really in a hurry." He got back in and went back to sleep.

Another snake hunt provided almost as much surprise. Bob Jenny and I were catching diamondbacks in West Texas one spring, along with Tom Thorne. Tom was four years younger and would one day become chief veterinarian for the Wyoming Fish and Game Department. We were catching diamondbacks as they came out of their dens to get some late spring sun; we had done very well, even bagging two of them that were over six feet long. But the weather turned bad—a spring norther—and it started to snow. We found an old line shack to hole up in, complete with a potbellied stove. We made ourselves a hot meal and slept in our sleeping bags. The next morning Bob Jenny was cooking breakfast when Tom and I went out to our Volkswagen van to check on the snakes. They were all limp, apparently lifeless, so Tom and I decided to skin the two largest snakes. We had laid them out on two old boards when Bob called us in for breakfast. While we ate the sun came out, and when we finished we decided to head back to our snakes. Tom and I each picked one up by their tails to skin when the snakes coiled around and tried to strike. They were not dead! Just cold. So we started the engine to warm up the van; shortly thereafter, all of the snakes came back to life and survived.

Career wise, at that point my goal was to become a herpetologist and a reptile curator at a zoo. I had become friendly with Julian Fraser, the zoo director at Oklahoma City, and decided it ultimately would be good to have some say in policy and management at whatever zoo I worked. As strictly a reptile curator, that might be difficult since only zoo directors have much say. This helped make the decision to switch disciplines.

CAPTAIN DICK CLEMENTS

The Oklahoma City Zoo was full of larger-than-life characters, including a circus big cat trainer known as Captain Dick Clements. For a period of time he left the circus life and settled in, doing a lion and tiger act at the Oklahoma City Zoo and at nearby Spring Lake Amusement Park. Dick became a good friend of Bob Jenny's, and I got to know him and watch him work. His cat act was good but not exceptionally exciting, except for the night he crowded an Asiatic black bear in the ring and was mauled. As a result, Bob filled in while Dick healed.

Dick drank a bit. Sometimes more than a bit. He was doing his act at Spring Lake Park, and it included a lion known as a "door bounce cat". A door bounce cat is trained to wait until the trainer is about to leave the arena and then charges at the door just as the trainer jumps through and pulls it shut. The lion then bounces against the door and claws at it as if trying to attack the trainer. One night Dick had been at the bottle a bit more than usual, and as he headed for the door, cueing the lion, he tripped and fell down. The lion came roaring off of his stand, ran right over the top of Dick and was clawing at the door in the usual manner. Dick got to his feet, staggered over to the lion, elbowed him aside and went through the door. The lion went back to clawing at the door. Amazingly, none of the other cats took advantage of Dick while he was on the ground in a vulnerable position.

Another time Dick was sharing his small travel trailer with three nearly-grown male lions. In the middle of the night the hot water heater exploded. The lions went beserk and destroyed the inside of his trailer while Dick hid under the mattress of his bed. I saw inside the trailer the following day, and it was completely shredded.

After Dick gave up his act, he started supplying horsemeat to the Oklahoma City Zoo and the Tulsa Zoo. Dick had an old flatbed truck with a winch on it, and he'd drive out to a farm with old horses to sell, shoot them in the head with a M1 Garand 30-06 rifle, winch them up on to the truck and cover them with a tarp while he drove home to butcher and box the meat for delivery to the zoo. One day Dick made a delivery to the Oklahoma City Zoo and heard that a handsome, but very old, full-maned male lion that he had donated to the zoo was having difficulty standing and would be euthanized. Dick asked if he could have the lion for its skin since it had such a magnificent mane. The zoo said yes, so they gave the lion a quadruple dose of succinylcholine and loaded him on Dick's truck. He covered the lion with a tarp and drove off.

Everything seemed to be going fine until people in cars started passing him, honking their horns and pointing to the back of his truck. Dick looked in the rearview mirror and saw his old lion standing up looking through the window with the wind in his face. The road was rough, the old shocks didn't work so well, and the lion had bounced up and down with every bump in the road. Succinylcholine is a short-acting skeletal muscle paralytic agent, and even though they had given the lion four times what they thought would be a lethal dose, the bouncing of the truck bed had resuscitated him long enough so he could metabolize the drug. Dick now had a real problem and a possible danger to the public. He pulled the truck into a shallow ditch beside the road, grabbed his M1 and ran around behind the truck. He then emptied a full clip into the lion, killing the animal. Ever frugal, Dick had been buying government surplus ammo, and he hadn't realized that the black-tipped rounds he was firing were actually armor-piercing machine gun ammunition. He had shot completely through the lion, and the cab and the engine of his truck. Dick was now stranded on the side of the road with a dead lion and an even deader flatbed truck.

SNAKE IN THE HOUSE

When I was about fifteen my father caught me rummaging around in the bottom of his closet. He wanted to know what I was looking for. I tried to be evasive but that didn't work. My dad was not someone you could lie to, so I had to confess that I was looking for a snake that was loose in our house. As you might imagine, this news didn't thrill him, but he didn't overreact. He asked, "How long has it been loose?" When I told him the snake was a little over 6 feet long and had been missing for 10 days he was, to say the least, not happy. He did not like snakes but had tolerated me keeping them out in the shed. He issued some rather firm instructions to "find the damn thing and get it out of the house." No longer having to work in secrecy, I turned the place upside down and found the snake, bagged it up, and put it in the shed. Then my father sat me down for a serious "Come to Jesus" discussion where it was decided that if I promised to never bring another snake inside, I could continue to live at home.

JONES, OKLAHOMA

Jones was a small town, and Jones High School was a relatively small school. My graduating class had just 36 students. But there were advantages for someone interested in math, science, or engineering. I had developed an early fascination with all things mechanical. Our school had a good agricultural program, welding shop and a solid wood shop. Our principal Mr. Looper was an excellent math teacher, and Mr. Cossey—who also delivered mail part-time—was a great chemistry and physics teacher. I tolerated the rest of the curriculum out of necessity. Many in our class went on to complete degrees in science and engineering.

Mr. Fowler, our shop teacher and church pastor, got me interested in joining the Army Reserve, and so at 17 my parents signed the permission form and allowed me to enlist early. After basic training I served in the 4050 as an MP for four years. Later I transferred to the Oklahoma National Guard, where I'd stay for four years as a medic. This proved to be a good decision.

In addition to snakes, I had also been collecting birds and mammals. We had a mini North American zoo in the backyard, and it included a Red Tailed Hawk named Babe that I had gotten out of a nest and trained to work as a falcon. Babe and I hunted cottontails together. She was usually successful, although from time to time I contributed with a well-aimed rifle shot. While working with an ex-U.S. Army Cavalry Veterinarian named Dr. Carlson, it occurred to me that veterinary medicine was probably a much better discipline with which to attack the zoo world.

SKUNKS

A number of years earlier I had caught a baby skunk, and Dr. Carlson deodorized it for us. He then taught me how to deodorize skunks mostly so he wouldn't occasionally risk getting smelled up. The technique required a steady hand so you didn't rupture the scent gland sack. We kept a supply of tomato juice and spirits of ammonia close at hand just in case I made a mistake. This led to three housebroken, deodorized skunks—Stinky, Fragrance, and Flower— living in our house with us along and our Pomeranians for many years. This grew into a small business where we'd catch, breed, and deodorize skunks to be sold as pets. I became known as the "skunk man," and if there was skunk a problem in our area I got called to solve it.

My most memorable skunk incident came when the pastor of the Methodist Church called a friend of mine because a skunk had tunneled under the slab of the parsonage sunroom. More than once it created a nasty stench in the parsonage, and the pastor asked George if we could come over and take care of the problem. We had a technique that worked on most houses, particularly if they were elevated off the ground. We would open ventilation holes on two sides and then pour a dish full of Highlife at the opening on the upwind side and light it. The fumes from the burning Highlife—a volatile liquid used for fumigating grain bins—would flow under the house and drive everything out into the open. Then the owner of the house just needed to board up all of the holes. It had worked well

My mom was incredibly supportive of my animal activities. She's holding "Stinky" and "Flower."

a number of times, so we took a can of Highlife with us and went to the parsonage. There was only one hole tunneling under the slab of the sunroom, so there was no way to get cross ventilation. We decided to use a hammer to tap the floor in the sunroom to determine the location of the tunnel and the den cavity, then drill a hole through the concrete into the cavity. Then we poured in some highly volatile Highlife. Then we did one of the most foolish things either of us had ever done. We rolled up a piece of newspaper, lit it, and touched it over the hole. The effect was like putting a match over the vent hole of an old muzzle-loading black powder cannon. There was an incredible thump, and the whole floor seemed to jump about two feet into the air (although I'm sure it was just a couple of inches). When it settled back down there were multiple cracks in the concrete running every direction. The pastor had a surprised look on his face, and so did George and I. George's father, who was very active in the church, told the preacher that if the cracks bothered him, they could simply pour another four inches of concrete on top of the floor. The preacher's skunk problem, however, had been solved.

One year we had a female barn cat who nursed and raised a litter of three baby skunks. The cat's presence saved us a lot of nighttime feeding. The summer before my freshman year in pre-vet I had an interesting run in with a stiff-necked, blue-nosed Boston Yankee at the General Motors Pavilion on the Oklahoma Fairgrounds. I was sitting in the back of a Cadillac limousine with a Powers Model, letting a baby skunk walk around on the keyboard of the first IBM electric typewriter I had ever seen. He seemed to think that did not fit the General Motors image. The skunk did not spell out anything remotely coherent on the typewriter, but I sold 13 baby skunks to those Powers Models. Selling deodorized baby "pet" skunks nearly paid for an entire year of undergraduate school.

I should also mention that I traded a baby deodorized skunk to my uncle John T. Harlan for an old Martin guitar, thinking I would take lessons and learn to play. There was a large dairy two miles from home where I had worked, and the manager was a good friend and played guitar in a country western band. Bill agreed to give me lessons and so we began. Unfortunately, after some period of time, one night Bill looked at me and said, "Wouldn't you just like to sell me the Martin and save both of us a lot of pain?" I took his advice, and that was the end of my musical career. The rumor that I couldn't carry a tune in a bucket is probably true, but I wish I still had the Martin. It would be worth a lot of money.

In front of my high school in Jones, Oklahoma, where I was honored with my own street in 2008.

A HOG NOSED SNAKE AND MY FIRST DATE

My fascination with snakes and skunks gave me some notoriety, but it didn't necessarily enhance my social life. Shortly after my 16th birthday, having gotten my driver's license, I worked up enough nerve up to ask a girl from the nearby dairy for a date. I planned to pick her up in my dad's car and drive to a drive-in theater, which was about 20 miles away. I was dressed and ready in a blue satin cowboy shirt with pearl snaps and button-down flaps over the pockets when my mother asked me to do her a favor and run an errand into town. Timing would be tight, but I wasn't about to say "no" to my mother, especially before my first date. Driving into town, I spotted a small hog-nosed snake crawling across the road and stopped to rescue it. I didn't have a snake bag with me, so I put it in the right-hand pocket of my shirt. I shoved the flap extension through the loop on the front of the pocket to secure the snake while I ran my mother's errand. I was rushing, time was tight, and I forgot about the snake. I picked up my date, and we headed west on a gravel road, driving about 65 miles-per-hour so we'd make the show. Along the way, the snake poked its his head out from under the flap and started to crawl out. When my date looked over and saw the snake, its head waving in the air, she screamed and tried to jump out the open window of my dad's '49 Ford. Exiting onto a gravel road at that speed would have been a disaster. I grabbed her by the belt and tried to pull her back into the car. Hanging onto the steering wheel with one hand, and her belt with the other hand, I tried to get the skidding car back under control and get it stopped. She continued screaming and grabbed a three-cell magnetic-based flashlight off the glove compartment door and nearly beat me to death with it as she swung at the snake. She later apologized, claiming she was only trying to hit the snake. Once I stopped the car and grabbed the flashlight, I gently tossed the snake out the window and into tall grass in the ditch. As you might guess, we never made it to the movie. That was the end to my first and only date with that girl.

During high school and undergraduate school I worked many jobs in the summer to make money. One summer I worked on a hay crew where I was the lightest weighing member of the crew and had to tie the bailing wire around the bales directly behind the hay pickup. This was the dustiest, dirtiest job on the crew. Another summer I went on the road over a three-state area with a crew selling ads for business and professional reviews in newspapers. Back then doctors, dentists, lawyers, and bankers could not or did not advertise, so a two-page business and professional review in the local newspaper was a way around this ethical prohibition. For me the money was good. My folks would sometimes call the office to see where I was and how I was doing. They were always given glowing reports about how much money I was making. I'll always remember the surprised look on my dad's face when I returned from the summer and he asked me how much money I had in my pockets. I told him $64. That was the summer I had discovered partying, so I had to sell a Guernsey heifer with a heifer calf by her side to help pay tuition that year.

I spent another summer on the road selling Brother sewing machines. The money was good, but the real coup de grâce was to sell a machine to a wealthy wheat farmer's wife in the Panhandle and then put it into a walnut sewing center that would cover one wall of the room. We made a 20 percent commission on the sewing machines and a 30 percent commission on the cabinetry.

PRE VET AT CENTRAL STATE

I had switched my focus to pre-veterinary medicine before I started at Central State College in Edmond, Oklahoma. Because of good high school grades, the school allowed me to take 21 hours during my first semester and 22 hours every semester thereafter. In my freshman chemistry class there was a girl who I met but didn't get to know until the next semester when we took a life-saving class together because the state "unreasonably" required physical education even for pre-vet students. Marie Annette Giem was taking the class because she had a job lined up as a lifeguard the following summer. Marie was nicknamed "Corky" because she could float on her back with her toes out of the water, despite her slender figure. Later we took a water safety class at night. The rest, as they say, is history. Marie would one day be my wife.

Four of us from our high school class in Jones commuted 25 miles each way to Edmond every day in two cars. Sometimes an impromptu race would break out, which, on one occasion, resulted in the car I was riding in swerving out of control, rolling, and flipping off a small cliff and landing in a gully. The driver Gilbert and I both survived with cuts and bruises, and I'll never forget how everything shifted into extreme slow-motion. I can still visualize the rocks and dust and my big black leather briefcase, which all seemed to be slowly floating around inside the car. My briefcase seemed to push me gently in the face, but afterwards all my front teeth were loose.

OLD MAN MARTIN

Around this time I met one of the more colorful characters in central Oklahoma, Old Man Martin, who had a place on County Line Road halfway between Edmond and Guthrie. He had a large collection of antique guns and Western paraphernalia that we bought or traded for when possible. He was also one of the most notorious moonshiners in the entire state. When you drove onto his farm there were huge piles of empty whiskey bottles in all shapes and sizes along with a half dozen steam-threshing machines and tractors. Old Man Martin was a favorite in the annual Eighty Niners Day Parade in Guthrie. He'd fire up a few of his steam machines and drive them in the parade. At any given time, when you drove up, you never quite knew what the reception would be. Sometimes he would greet you like a long-lost brother and invite you in to trade guns, while other times he would politely order you off his property, usually while holding a 30-30 Winchester. It all depended on whether the ATF agents had been after him that week. I later discovered that Old Man Martin was extremely well-known to the federal agents who targeted moonshiners and bootleggers. His was an interesting household. He rarely was clean shaven and probably bathed just a couple times a year. He fingers were the size of thick sausages but could pick up, manipulate, and repair even the smallest part of a gun. His house was divided up: one half for him and the other for his wife, an extraordinarily prim and proper woman who wore long dresses straight out of the 19th century. She wore black stockings and a bonnet whenever she was outside. Other than her delivering food to his table in the gun room, there seemed to be very little trespassing in that household. He had a double barrel German muzzle-loading rifle that I wanted bad. Unfortunately, I was unable find the Quackenbush rifle he wanted in trade.

A friend of mine in the Oklahoma National Guard was a race car mechanic and claimed that the racing engine in Old Man Martin's battered GMC panel truck could outrun anything in the state.

More than a decade later at Cascio's Restaurant in Omaha, Nebraska, I was dining with a group of ATF agents. One of them was a very long-haired, bearded redhead whom I had not before met. My friend Dick Curd warned me not to read anything into his appearance because the man had been working undercover in Oklahoma on County Line Road. Before I could think I spoke up and said, "You must be after Old Man Martin." Everyone at the table was in shock, so I had to explain how I had come to know Old Man Martin when we were students at Central State College. It's funny how serendipity comes full circle.

MEETING MARIE'S FOLKS

Shortly after Marie and I began dating she invited me to Guthrie to meet her folks. In addition to operating a hardware store on the east side of town, they had a hatchery and laying hens. It's a wonder our romance didn't end in a hurry, considering my involvement in a bet with a group of buddies at Central State. It was customary there, for any man who could, to grow a beard for the Eighty Niners Day parade. A number of us had grown beards, and somebody decided that we'd all put $5 in the pot and the last guy to shave his beard off got the pot. In

Marie was a crack shot with a .22 pistol during one of our first dates along the Cimarron River.

1958 $40 was a lot of money, and I was determined to win it. So when I showed up to meet Marie's parents I had a full beard and mustache along with a flat top haircut. It's a wonder her dad didn't run me off.

Shortly after we began dating, her family held a reunion in Oklahoma City, where I would meet her extended family. Marie had told me the history of both sides of her family, including the fact that they were all teetotalers. I also knew that her grandmother Webster, who had been an elementary school teacher for nearly 30 years, was a hard-shell Baptist who took no prisoners. Two other former rogue vet students had married Marie's aunts, and they were not teetotalers. Al Bradley was a vet in practice in South Dakota and Norman Cotner would ultimately become an MD in Grove, Oklahoma. As we came into the room where everyone was gathered the first person Marie led me up to meet was her Grandmother Webster. Just before we got to her, Al's big booming voice rang out from a doorway across the room. "Hey Lee, what kind of beer do you drink?" he asked. Before I had time to think, I said, "Falstaff, if I can get it." Just like magic, a can of Falstaff came flying through the air, across the heads of all of the gathered family and into my hands just as Marie introduced me to her grandmother. So there I was with a can of Falstaff in my hands in front of Marie's teetotaling hard shell Baptist Grandmother. I'm sure she thought, "Oh God, not another one." The two scoundrels were laughing like crazy. I think it was three years later when she finally spoke to me again after Young Lee was born and she came to live with us to help while Marie taught school.

PISTOL SHOOTING AND MIDNIGHT ON THE ROOF

On one of our first dates I took Marie pistol shooting on the banks of the Cimarron River. I fancied myself a pretty good shot and threw some sticks in the water and then proceeded to make them bounce with a .22 pistol. Then Marie took the pistol and proceeded to outshoot me. When I got the pistol back I had to bear down hard to restore my honor. I later learned that for much of her childhood Marie had been going out on the banks of a pond with her dad and shooting sticks in the water with a Colt Woodsman. Years later a professor of mine would say that you should always take a woman with a pistol in her hand seriously because they are inherently better at pointing than men and will shoot you dead. I married a very good shot, but I'm still alive.

One night driving back from Woodward, Oklahoma—up in the Panhandle —I got lost in a rainstorm. I was too stubborn to just pull off the road, so I continued driving by watching the centerline and the side of the road. When the rain finally let up I realized I had missed the turn for Oklahoma City and was instead headed for Guthrie. I drove into Guthrie about midnight and decided there was no use going 39 miles home only to turn around and drive back when it got daylight, so I decided I'd stay with Marie and her parents. The problem was how to get in their house. Because of their business, Marie's folks kept everything locked up tight at night. By this time in our courtship I had my own assigned bedroom in the Giem home on weekends. So a little after midnight I was standing on the roof outside Marie's bedroom, tapping on the window, when her parents' bedroom window flew open and a voice demanded, "Who's out there?"

I knew her father slept with that Colt Woodsman on his nightstand. In what has to be one of the most inane answers ever, I said, "Me."

Then Marie's father hollered, "Marie, for crying out loud, get up and let him in so we can get some sleep." I wasn't dead, but the incident served as an omen that my single my life was about over.

COPPERHEAD

Marie should have noticed an omen herself on an early date when we were driving a gravel road in the country and there was a copperhead moccasin in the road ahead. I slammed on the brakes, grabbed a snake stick and sack, and five minutes later it was in the trunk of my car. If she had been smart she might have called the whole thing off right then, but, happily, women often make allowances for things like that. Her tolerance of strange behavior would have a very positive influence on 58 (and hopefully many more) years of our eventual marriage.

At the beginning of our second year at Central State, Marie switched to Oklahoma State University in Stillwater so she could pursue a vocational degree in home economics. By enrolling in 22 hours each semester, I was able to finish my pre-vet requirements in just two years. I was in a hurry!

VET SCHOOL INTERVIEW

My pre-vet grades were good. I made application and was accepted to interview for vet school in the summer of 1959. Happily for me, Marie's uncles, both of whom had formerly been at the OSU School of Veterinary Medicine, pointed out that no one in the history of the school had been admitted with a beard. I showed up for my interview freshly shaved (my cheeks and chin looked like the belly of a beached whale), and when asked what my goals and intentions were I said that I intended to go into the zoo world and become a zoo veterinarian and director. I think my interviewers weren't sure what to make of me, so they asked a few questions about giraffes and camels and elephants and snakes and then welcomed me into the class of 1963.

Early that spring, Marie and I decided to get married. On September 6, 1959, six days before school started, we had a large church wedding and then went on a short camping honeymoon, which required a bit of innovation since Marie's younger brother had removed all of the camping gear and food from the trunk of our car. Our first joint purchase as a married couple was an enameled diaper pail at a little country store by a lake, but not for the usual reason.

OKLAHOMA STATE VET SCHOOL

Marie began her last two years in Vocational Home Economics, and I started my first year in the Oklahoma State School of Veterinary Medicine. We lived in a 22-foot trailer that Marie's father had bought. We saved a lot of money by having to only pay $10 per month for trailer space rental. We'd park the trailer at my folks' place or her folks' place in the summer and can vegetables, which meant that our only food costs were for beef, bread, fresh vegetables, milk and coffee. We had chicken and eggs in abundance since Marie's folks had thousands of laying hens and raised a lot of fryers.

Marie woke early on that first morning in the trailer and cooked a huge breakfast that would've fed a football team. I staggered out for a cup of coffee and nibbled on a hot biscuit. After a few days, Marie decided that if I wasn't going to eat breakfast, she wasn't going to cook it. Things went smoothly after that.

That first year of marriage was an interesting one. Just before Thanksgiving I woke up in the hospital, having passed out one morning as I stood up getting out of bed. I had bled out during the night from a hemorrhaging ulcer. After a couple of weeks of transfusions I returned to school, only to be told that I would be better off to drop out and start the year over. I was in a hurry and objected to this idea.

Happily, the dean and my professors acquiesced. We worked out a plan for me to spend Christmas vacation and the semester break in the anatomy lab catching up. I worked hard to make this work, although I must admit I've never had a solid grasp of the anatomy of the head of a cow.

Ulcers had been a problem since I was 14 and followed me all through school and beyond. If I noticed that my fingernails were turning white I would swing by the blood lab in between classes and run quick hematocrit and hemoglobin tests. Then I'd check the results after my next class. If my hematocrit and hemoglobin got down to half of normal, I would go home to spend a couple of days horizontal, drinking nothing but half and half and whole cream. Despite this, those were good times. Newlyweds don't really need a lot of space, and we both had studies to keep us focused. We didn't have or need much money but always managed to keep $100 in a little tin box nailed inside a closet. At the end of the month we

Our wedding day: September 6, 1959.

might be down to spaghetti and meat sauce. Sometimes George Seebeck would bring over a bottle of wine, and we'd have spaghetti, meat sauce and wine. Marie always baked great fresh bread and rolls.

OKLAHOMA NATIONAL GUARD

I had spent four years in the Army Reserve as an MP, later becoming a medic in the Headquarters Company, 179th Infantry Brigade, 45th Infantry Division of the Oklahoma National Guard. Being a medic was a better fit for a vet student. No matter where your home company was, if you were in school you could make up your meetings at the closest guard armory. For a college student the National Guard was a great program because you could report in, spend two hours studying with other college students in a room at the armory and get a full day's pay. By then I was a Sergeant, so a regular day's pay for two hours of study plus the pay for two weeks at summer camp helped considerably with tuition. In the summer I attended drills at our armory in Edmond, Oklahoma and went to summer camp. After eight years in the Reserve and Guard I decided that all kids should serve in the military, even if only for a short time. Military service teaches discipline, responsibility, teamwork, and respect for country. I completed basic training at Fort Hood, Texas that first summer and then completed my summer camps at Fort Sill in Lawton, Oklahoma over the next three summers. When I switched to the Oklahoma National Guard, I spent summers in camp at Fort Polk, Louisiana; Camp Chaffee, Arkansas; and finally back to Fort Hood, Texas.

Military life provided lots of valuable life experience. I recall at 19 being handed a Winchester 97 pump-action shotgun and a duffel bag with $127,000 cash in it (which I had to sign for) to take to the Fort Sill paymaster and stand guard. And there was the time I was assigned to inventory and catalog a collection of captured World War II German concentration camp 16-millimeter films. Watching black and white film of countless naked, emaciated bodies being thrown into a big pit will change your perspective considerably.

In the 45th we hosted high-stakes poker games because the aid station had all the luxuries (ice, tents, generators, cracker box ambulances) needed to host a diverse group of serious players. Everyone took off their rank when they sat down around the poker table, so there would be sergeants and captains and bird colonels all sitting around the table. The rest of us played nickel—dime – quarter poker. I also learned to handle explosives during war games. It was a good education.

UNIVERSITY MEDICAL CENTER IN OKLAHOMA CITY

I worked as an electrician at the University Hospital Medical Center in Oklahoma City during summers and holidays for three-and-a-half years. This was a substantial source of our income back then. I applied for the electrical shop, and by the time my bosses found out that I wasn't actually an electrician, I was. The Med Center was user-friendly to students, and since no one else really wanted the weekend duty they let me work seven days a week during the summers for three years. The weekends were paid time-and-a-half.

Most of the wiring was so old and chaotic that we had to work everything "hot" because when you pulled a fuse you never knew exactly what was being turned off. Some of the wiring was still bare wire on porcelain posts. Two of the other electricians in the shop were taking outside contracts at the Med Center, and I was able to join them. Every other week we would work our usual five-day, eight-hour shifts, grab a quick bite to eat, and then work an additional eight hours on projects the hospital needed done. Marie also worked at the Med Center one summer. During that time we rewired most of the University Hospital, the doctor's quarters, the Med School, and the Children's Hospital.

OPEN HEART SURGERY

The wiring in Children's Hospital was also old and unreliable. They had just started doing the first open-heart surgeries, and the possibility of a power failure was unacceptable. For two summers (on Thursdays when surgeries were scheduled) I arrived at Children's prior to the start of surgery and tied heavy jumper cables to the mains on the fuse panel with king-sized alligator clamps on the other ends. That way, if a fuse blew during surgery, you could simply "hot jump" around it. I wore a cap, mask, and gown—just like a surgeon—but underneath I had an electrician's tool pouch on each hip and heavy rubber electrician's gloves. This strategy also meant that during surgery there were three large, bare, energized alligator clamps hanging out of the open panel box. Thankfully the fuses never blew, and I was able to watch early day open-heart surgeries. It was an incredible experience for a young vet student.

The first year-and-half at Oklahoma State was challenging, even beyond my ulcer problem. It's during that first year that medical, dental, and veterinary schools try to weed out students who are not going to make it through, so everybody was a bit paranoid. Our biggest challenge was organic chemistry. The chair of the chemistry department, who was not a veterinarian and didn't like vet students, insisted on teaching the class himself. I think he wanted to make sure that organic chemistry had the highest failure rate of any first-year course. When the midterm grades came out that first semester, half of the class had Ds or Fs. Luckily, Dean Holmes intervened to stop the massacre, and Dr. Peterson, our anatomy professor, opened a supplementary organic chemistry class. Dr. Peterson had a wide-ranging "garbage can" mind and frequently offered supplemental courses when he thought students weren't being taught adequately. I'm sure that did little to endear him to the other professors, but he had the students' best interests at heart and was good at anything he started.

During my four years I acquired two nicknames: Sleepy Number One (when my blood count was low, I frequently nodded off) and Tinker Toys (because I was always building something or repairing a piece of equipment around the school).

The personalities and characteristics of our vet school professors were interesting. Some of them were brilliant, larger-than-life icons. Others were not. I recall a pharmacology professor, Dr. Leslie McDonald, who unfortunately had a speech impediment and had difficulty pronouncing the letter "l." It was our opinion that he really didn't like students or teaching.

Pharmacology involves a fair amount of math. Math had always come easily for me, but the same could not be said for the professor, who had a set of very involved and sometimes convoluted calculations to determine drug concentrations and dosages. In our study group, it occurred to me that most of this could be greatly simplified by using simple ratio and proportions. Before one exam our study group adopted and practiced using ratio and proportion. On the exam the next day we all got all of the answers right, but since you had to show your work Dr. McDonald said that it was impossible to get a right answer using our methods. This left us with a much lower score, and I asked if we could come in after class and prove to him that ratio and proportion was a valid mathematical protocol. I led the way, and five of us went into his office. In those days I printed all of my notes with a Rapidograph drafting pen, which used India ink. I was making our argument with a considerable amount of zeal when my pen clogged up and stopped writing. Standard operating procedure was to shake it vigorously up and down so that the little weighted stylus would reopen the ink channel. I did so but with a little too much vigor, and the damn thing exploded. Permanent India ink sprayed all over the professor's desk and his white shirt. This ended the discussion and I think my classmates wished they didn't know me. We were absolutely right but lost the argument.

I found some vindication at the end of the semester. There were only two As in the class, and I earned one of them. As Dr. McDonald walked around handing out final grades he announced your grade aloud. He handed me mine, and looking at me in front of the whole class said, "I don't know how you did it. You're just not smart enough to get an A in my class. I know you're not cheating because I have been watching you, but you're just not smart enough to make an A in my class." I took that as one of the greatest compliments I had ever been given.

I recall once when our class was supposed to be doing a large animal clinical exercise in pharmacology but Dr. McDonald didn't show up. We were all standing around with our hands in our pockets waiting when someone speculated about whether or not cows would really exhibit an excitation type of Cat Reaction under the influence of morphine. The discussion went on and since McDonald had still failed to show up the next thing that happened was that we rounded up a nearly grown heifer and injected her with morphine. We found out fairly quickly that cows can in fact go a bit crazy and exhibit a Cat Reaction. She charged and had one of our classmates pinned against a board fence trying to bore a hole in his belly. A number of us charged her and knocked her over, and Della Baker (who was my surgery partner for two years) came charging in from behind like she was sliding into home base at a baseball game. She put her heels on the hock of the lower leg and grabbed the upper leg and tucked it back under her arm and stretched the heifer's legs out. Unfortunately, she had slid right through a big pile of, sloppy, cow manure so that her skin tight white pants were a mess. It was at about this time with Della hanging on for dear life that Dr. McDonald finally showed up. His first words were, "Miss Baker you can't hold that cow all by yourself." Della looked up at him and said, "I wouldn't have to if you'd quit standing there with your thumb up your ass and help." McDonald turned red in the face, spun on his heel and walked away. Class was over for that day. Della had a reputation for saying it like it was.

Between my junior and senior year in vet school I worked for a vet practice in Guthrie to get more hands-on experience in large animal surgery and practice. It was a mixed animal practice, and the experience was invaluable. I learned under Dr. Ed Detjen, an old cowboy who did things his way, and Dr. Jim Sewell, who had recently graduated from Oklahoma State and practiced more modern methods. I recall an incident when a young housewife brought in a Rat Terrier.

Dr. Sewell was very shy around women, and the dog didn't want to be up on the table. He was fighting hard to get away and turned upside down on his head as she hung onto him. The first kick of his hind legs opened all of the buttons on her blouse. The second kick shoved her bra right up around her neck. Dr. Sewell tried to help but didn't quite know what to do with his hands. The woman finally shoved the dog across the table and said, "If you'll take the dog I'll handle everything else." Jim's face was red as a beet. I was no help because you can't laugh that hard and be of much help.

Even though he technically taught poultry pathology, my vet school adviser Dr. Malle worked at instilling good economic practices into the class because he said that most failures were because of bad management and not bad medicine. Dr. Malle's informal economics lectures would serve me well later. Malle was also partly responsible for keeping me in school. We had a bacteriology instructor who, despite being a good bacteriologist, was not so good when it came to students. During the course of a semester he gave four 100-point exams and then a final exam that was worth the same as the other four. He also had a 100-point fudge factor that he apportioned on the basis of whether or not he thought certain students had a good attitude, worked hard or were lazy, or if he just didn't like you. It was totally subjective and depended solely on how he felt about you. Unfortunately, I was experiencing repeated gastric hemorrhages due to my ulcers. When my hemoglobin count was low I simply dozed off in class. However, I maintained a high B average on my exams. Not realizing that the professor hated my sleeping in class, a small group of my classmates decided to play a prank. They went down to the first aid station and borrowed a cot to put in my assigned seating space. The professor went absolutely livid but didn't say anything else until the midterm grades came out. At that point, I had an F in his class. That meant that at the end of the semester I would be out of vet school. One F and you were finished. He was so angry about my dozing off, he refused to even talk to me. I took my problem to Dr. Malle, and he advised me to work hard and make sure that I aced the last two exams and the final and leave the rest to him. I did well on the exams, even high pointing the final by 10 points. But I was still worried, because unless the professor relented in applying his fudge factor, I could still be out of school. Dr. Malle finally lured the teacher into his office and locked the door from the inside. Despite the teacher's rants and ravings, Dr. Malle kept him locked in his office until he finally calmed down and would talk about the problem. It might be worth noting that Dr. Malle was the school money lender, meaning that if you were on staff and wanted to buy a house or car he would give you a loan. Many of the staff owed him money. When the final grades came out, I had a D. It was my only bad grade in four years, but it meant I was still in school.

Years later that professor and I bumped into each other at a vet meeting in Chicago. He apologized and marveled that I would even speak to him.

CRESCENT, OKLAHOMA

In June 1961 Marie graduated and earned a teaching certificate. She took a job offer to teach in Crescent, Oklahoma, home of Donkey Basketball. Young Lee was born July 15, and Marie's teaching duties started in August, so that summer we stayed with her folks in Guthrie, about 10 miles from Crescent. When Marie went into labor with young Lee I was working 35 miles away at the OU Med Center in Oklahoma City. When the call came, I said I would be there right away but was told not to hurry because the first one usually takes some time. I swung by the house, grabbed my camera, and hurried to the little Catholic hospital in Guthrie to watch our first child come into the world. On seeing my camera, the little nun in charge of the maternity ward let me know in no uncertain terms that if I even thought about raising the camera before she had washed his face, combed his hair, and wrapped him in a blanket, death would be instantaneous. Later, both of our girls had their pictures taken almost immediately after birth and then again after they were cleaned up and their hair combed.

When we moved into a two-bedroom garage apartment in Crescent, Marie's Grandmother Webster came with us. She was a retired elementary school teacher, so Lee was read to almost from the moment he was born.

It was 43 miles to Stillwater, but luckily a graduate student in marine biology, whose wife was also teaching in the same town, was taking our parasitology course at the vet school. We carpooled for two years and drove the 86-mile round-trip on alternate days. On Saturdays I had half-day classes at the vet school, so I drove myself. By two o'clock every Saturday we would be packed up to visit Marie's family or my family. We had traded our 1951 Studebaker Champion with 140,000 miles on it for a used 1960 Rambler American with 6,000 miles. And the miles piled on. Marie taught junior and senior high school Vocational Home Economics at the Crescent schools for our last two years in vet school.

GRADUATION FROM VET SCHOOL

I was the only one in my class to graduate without a job. Having made up my mind that I absolutely wanted to work in a zoo, there were simply no veterinary positions in any zoo in North America then or in the near future. This frustrated my instructors, Dr. Malle and Dean Holmes. As graduation approached, professors were constantly dragging me into their offices and introducing me to veterinary practitioners who were looking for help.

I was also considering enlisting in the Air Force for four years. A bird colonel was even sent to talk to me since I already had eight years of active reserve and guard time, which would have counted toward pay and retirement. They offered to start me as a first lieutenant with a promotion to captain after nine months. This was guaranteed in writing. Plus, I'd have my choice of a duty station and I could take my family. I could have picked Spain as a duty station, which, at that time, was a great place to collect old guns. But it would have been an economic trap. It would have meant kicking out after four years and then starting over, at the bottom of a zoo vet's salary scale. Additionally, the Air Force would likely have been dangling the rank of major in front of you to reenlist with only eight more years to serve until retirement.

A SAINT LOUIS JOB

The St. Louis Zoo had a position that was going to open up. They planned to switch from an on-call veterinarian to a full-time staff position. I went to St. Louis to interview with Director Dr. George Vierheller. I arrived early and first met with Henry Sanders, the curator of birds, who had a wicked sense of humor. Sanders asked me if I would like to see their walrus. They don't have walruses in Arizona or Oklahoma, so I said sure. He led me into a holding room with a very large, friendly tuskless male walrus named Charley, who promptly pinned me into a corner with his chest, explored me with his mouth and whiskers and slobbered all over me. Henry just laughed. When I finally met with Dr. Vierheller, a very formal zoo director of the old school, I looked disheveled and was slimed from head to shoulders in walrus slobber. The job was not going to open for eight to 12 months, and we were pretty much addicted to eating regularly.

ALTUS, OKLAHOMA

I had heard about a position as mammal's curator at the Zoo in Columbus, Ohio, and made arrangements to drive up for an interview. In the meantime, Dean Holmes introduced me to a veterinarian from Altus, Oklahoma, and we agreed to drive down and interview immediately after taking the national and state boards. We got away very early on a Saturday morning and drove to Ringling, Oklahoma, to visit by dad's Uncle Henry and Aunt Thelma Bachhoffer, who had 14 kids. We arrived in Altus before noon and had lunch with the vet and his wife (a very nice couple in their mid-50s). We looked at the practice. It was a very good, mixed practice. He had had a partner who had gone back into the Air Force. The job came with some very nice perks, including a three-bedroom brick house and a new car. The starting salary of $13,000 per year would have made me one of the highest-paid graduates in my class.

We stayed at their house that night, and over breakfast the next morning we discussed starting the job, and if we still liked each other after two years they would offer a partnership. Economically it was very tempting, but I told him that I was going to look at a position at the Columbus Zoo in Ohio. If that failed to pan out, I promised him I'd make the two-year commitment. Only Marie knew that the position in Ohio paid just $5,100 per year with no perks. I'm convinced luck plays a greater part in finding a life partner than smarts, because when we discussed the options Marie said, "You're the one who has to be happy with your job. I'm going to raise kids." It would be another seven years before we approached that salary. Marie wanted five kids, but it was still a quiet ride home.

COLUMBUS, OHIO

I drove the 1,000 miles to Columbus straight through in 20 hours, stopping at the house of our family doctor's mother early on a Saturday to shower and put on a suit. She kindly fed me breakfast, and then I went to the zoo. I showed up at eight o'clock, and Steve Kelly, who had just been appointed director, arrived at 11. Steve had an interesting background. In addition to being Irish and a spitting image of the actor Peter O'Toole, he was formerly the mammal's curator. His whole family was theatrical, starting with his uncle Emmet Kelly the Clown, and his father Bev Kelly, who managed the St. Louis Opera.

After touring the zoo and having lunch we went back across the road, to the Wyandotte Inn, about two o'clock that afternoon, and we stayed there drinking for almost 12 hours. When Steve learned I didn't have a hotel, he promptly invited me to come home with him. It was an offer I couldn't turn down, considering I had a full tank of gas and just $19 in my pocket. I was planning to sleep in the car.

I awoke early the next morning, found the bathroom, showered and shaved and was reading the Sunday paper in the breakfast nook when Steve's very surprised blond wife came down the stairs in a nightgown. We introduced ourselves and Joan asked if I would like some coffee and breakfast. After the night I just had, I said yes. I continued reading while Joan fixed bacon and eggs. Just as she put them on the table in front of me, a cat that I had not seen came down across the counter and made a dive for my bacon and eggs. Before I could think, my reflexes kicked in and I hit the cat with a right cross that sent him spinning across the room. She screamed and someone gasped. I looked over to see the zoo director in a bright red pair of bikini underpants standing at the bottom of the steps looking fairly horrified. Guys from Oklahoma didn't even know men wore such things.

I remember thinking, "Boy, you better eat these eggs fast because this job just went down the drain." Steve Kelly hired me anyway, and I agreed to start in two weeks. I drove straight back to Guthrie. A full tank of gas and $19 could take you the 1,000 miles home in a little Rambler American if you didn't eat, at least in those days.

Marie and I packed up and headed for Ohio. The trip went smoothly, except for losing a wheel and hub off of our homemade trailer. Finding a 1934 Ford hub was interesting. We got lucky; years before, an old farmer had bought out a bankrupt Ford dealer. Columbus in those days was very political, and the zoo was directly under the auspices of the mayor and service director. Starting as mammal's curator in June, things evolved quickly, and by the late fall my position was as staff veterinarian and assistant superintendent. This made me one of only about 12 veterinarians who had full-time paid jobs in the zoo world.

Despite the fierce partisan politics, Columbus was a great training ground because I got to do just about everything. At one point I was staff veterinarian, assistant superintendent, mammal's curator, acting curator of the aquarium, and in charge of overseeing the birdhouse. My official title was "staff veterinarian," thanks to some very good advice: that title was a professional appointment from which I couldn't be fired unless convicted of a felony or my license was revoked. This was the result of some neat legislation that had been passed by the city attorneys, who included doctors and veterinarians so they wouldn't seem self serving, back in the 1800s. This meant that after 10 months at the zoo, my new position was virtually untouchable. And, I have to admit, I pretty much operated as an untouchable. It probably wasn't very fair because all the other staff positions were at risk on a month's notice.

Among the partisan practices in Columbus, the city had a "flower fund" (make that the mayor's slush fund) that all city employees were expected to contribute to in fixed amounts every two weeks. At Christmas they came around with a large loose leaf book that listed every city employee's name and an amount they were expected to contribute toward a "TV" for the mayor. My contribution was supposed to be $75. I refused, the collector left, and very shortly Jim Savoy, the new Superintendent, came down and said he had just been told that if I didn't give my share he would have to give his and mine. His job could be on the line, but I still refused.

He went back upstairs and told them that I was uncontrollable, and he couldn't do anything with me. Needless to say, I was not well liked down at city hall. Columbus was a great training ground, if you could survive long enough to leave of your own free will. That job equipped me to handle just about any zoo position. I also began to realize that the knowledge gap in medicine and husbandry between what you really knew and what you needed to know was huge. A zoo where you got to take on any and all problems was a great place to learn and fill that gap.

TB IN GREAT APES

In Columbus, "Colo," the first captive bred gorilla in the world, was born. The great ape collection was one of our claims to fame. Unfortunately, just before my arrival human tuberculosis has been discovered in a gibbon, and a substantial portion of the zoo's guerrillas, orangs, and chimpanzees tested positive on the intradermal TB test. This was the first time that anyone had attempted to treat a tubercular outbreak in a great ape or primate collection. Previously, the standard procedure had been to euthanize the collection.

With Colo, treatment was the only option. They had the whole collection on isoniazid, rifampin & PAS (para-aminosalicylic acid) with streptomycin early on in some cases. In order to monitor the collection using x-ray, gastric lavage, and pulmonary cultures, we had to immobilize them once a year. In 1962 they had given oral Phencyclidine Hcl (Sernylan) to immobilize the great ape collection, but the dosage had to be very large and the effects lasted for three days or more. We switched routes in 1963 and, for the first time, used injectable Sernylan in a great ape. Phencyclidine Hcl was a brand-new experimental dissociative drug, which would later become known as Angel Dust on the street. By injecting the drug our results were much better. Induction times were 7 -10 minutes, down times were 45 -60 minutes, and recovery times were short and smooth. While immobilizing the great apes for TB testing, chest x-rays, and gastric lavage, Millie, our oldest female gorilla and Colo's mother, sat up, stretched her arms, and pounded on her chest. There was panic and a mass exodus of MDs and vets who had crowded into the room, but Millie just looked at us and dropped her arms. We then injected her with more Sernylan.

Maggie, our adult female orang, ultimately died of Pulmonary TB, which had invaded her spinal column. She had vomited on me from the top of the exhibit shortly before she died. As a consequence, my next TB test was positive but unexpectedly and unexplainably, six months later, I was again negative. I have continued to remain negative since then.

ANGEL DUST

One day there were representatives from the Park-Davis Drug Company visiting my office, discussing this new drug. Their consensus was that 3-5 mg was better than three martinis, plus there was no hangover. I didn't realize it, but Lloyd, our 55 year-old hospital administrator, an atypical zoo employee who had retired early from his job as distribution manager for the *Cincinnati Inquirer*, had been listening to the conversation. Despite a financially successful career in news, he had always wanted to work with animals and decided life was too short not to do what made him happy. Lloyd's wife was an executive at the big Sears store where, coincidentally, Marie taught sewing for two years. After lunch that day I noticed Lloyd was acting strange. He admitted that he had listened to us talking about Phencyclidine and was curious, so he had taken a little. When I asked him how much he had taken he confessed that he was unsure. Turns out he had just opened the bottle of dry powder and ran a damp finger around the rim before putting it in his mouth.

Lloyd was normally as straight laced as anyone I've ever known. We couldn't send him home in that condition, so we just sat down and talked to him for five hours. He was a weightlifter and in very good shape, so he did a little ballet for us up on his toes. He said he felt so strong he could bend iron bars but didn't want to because he loved the whole world. It was an interesting five hours. When he began acting normal again, I locked up the Sernylan and drove him home. We had a serious talk the next morning, and there was never a repeat performance.

MIKE JULY AND BONGO

In the early days both in Columbus and in Omaha we worked inside the exhibits very closely with many animals that zoo staff and keepers don't do today. This was partly because of our facilities and partly because we didn't have the safe immobilizing drugs that exist today. I think it was actually better for the animals that way. This process allowed us to conduct daily examinations and treat wounds and illnesses easily and quickly.

We were always careful with animals considered extremely dangerous, but it was an expectation that we'd get occasional bumps, bites, and bruises. Colo (whose main vice was spitting) and her companion Bongo were young adult gorillas who had been raised and socialized with keepers, and we had few problems going in close to work with them. Given their strength and size (Bongo weighed aproximatly 300 pounds), we avoided roughhousing and kept things civilized. Well, most of us did. Mike July was an ex-Marine and former boxer who weighed 220 pounds and was the only keeper big enough and strong enough to wrestle with Bongo. They'd square off in the exhibit like a couple of football linemen and charge each other. Stopping Bongo was like stopping a locomotive. Bongo usually won, and after they were tired they'd lean against the wall and share a Coke. One day while Mike was leaning against the tile wall, Bongo grabbed Mike by both ears and whacked his head against the wall. The impact knocked Mike momentarily unconscious. Bongo exhibited concern for his well-being, and after Mike regained consciousness we decided it was time to stop being up-close and personal with Bongo.

AOUDADS

Shortly after I arrived in Columbus a keeper failed to close a gate quickly enough, and our herd of 18 aoudads, or Barbary sheep, stampeded over the top of him. They spread out in every direction, some as far as the center of Columbus. We had to dart them using Sernylan. We eventually captured 17 of them after three months of nearly round-the-clock hunting. The last old buck was shot by a farmer near Plain City. He was angry about the possibility that the buck might have bred some of his sheep and had threatened to sue the zoo. He butchered the animal, and put it into his freezer. We opted not to call the authorities because we thought he'd get what he deserved when he tried to eat that smelly, tough old buck.

HIPPO WATER BOWLS

I had never been the boss of a large staff. I had been raised and mentored to always ask people to do things politely rather than shouting and giving orders. This worked well most of the time but not always. A small faction of the keeper staff resented having a kid fresh out of college from Oklahoma running the show. This was particularly true of one longtime keeper who thought he really should have had my job. Subsequently, early on there were some practical jokes and other gestures not so funny. Once, another keeper solemnly declared that he really didn't want to rat anyone out, but he felt obligated to tell me that Eddie (the longtime keeper) was shirking his duties and hadn't put a water bowl in with the hippos for two full days. I had already decided to have it out with Eddie, so I was halfway across the zoo with a bone in my teeth when it hit me that the damn hippos were swimming in a 10,000-gallon pool of water and the whole zoo was watching. I pulled up, chuckled to myself that I had been had, and then went back to my office. I read the civil service employees manual and the union rulebook. I let the two manuals digest for about a week and then reread them again. By then most of the staff had accepted me and things were going well. Still, a few malcontents were beating me to death with the rulebooks. They knew how to get out of doing almost anything they didn't want to do by quoting a rule or regulation. The only solution I could come up with was to pick out two of the worst offenders and simply frame them. They were guilty of countless offenses; however they were totally innocent of the two offenses I used to suspend them.

I called Eddie into my office and asked him if he had seen what just happened. He said yes, and I asked him how long he had worked at the zoo. "Eighteen years," he said.

I then told him that the way things were going there was no chance in hell that he could make 19 years. At this point, I had established that I could read and be just as devious as they could. Eddie took the hint and decided to call a truce. I agreed, and the next three years were peaceful. Eddie even became a friend.

LOU PISTOIA

Louis Pistoia was probably the best reptile curator I have ever met. At a time when others bragged about 10 year longevities Lou would show you F1s, F2s and F3s. He was more than just a little suspicious of veterinarians treating reptiles, and in those days rightfully so. However, perhaps because of my association with Bob Jenny, he seemed to regard me as an exception to this rule. Lou had apprenticed under Carl Kauffeld from the Staten Island Zoo, who had long held the record for the most rattlesnake species, until Lou built his collection in Columbus.

Lou began bringing in native local snakes with little subcutaneous tumors that felt like a pea just under the skin, to be removed. After I had operated on half a dozen, he asked me to come to the reptile house where he had another snake with those little tumors that needed removal. I told him to bring it over to the hospital, but he said he'd rather do it in the reptile house. I put together a wet pack. When I got to the reptile house I asked where Lou was, and someone told me that he was in the public aisle. This was a little odd, but I didn't think much of it. When I went into the public aisle I found Lou, but there was no public. He immediately wrapped a chain around the door handles to lock them shut and put the key in his pocket. I saw that the other doors were also chained and padlocked.

I asked what was going on, and Lou said we better do the surgery here where we wouldn't be bothered by the public. There was a large flat snake box on the floor, and he pulled the top door open with his snake hook. Out came a very hacked off nine-foot black tree cobra. Most cobras are by nature slow and fairly laid-back, but tree cobras are fast and very aggressive. For the next 45 minutes, Lou and the cobra and I danced and played "ring around the rosy" in that locked hallway. I kept asking Lou for a snake hook to defend myself with but he was afraid I might hurt his snake. Every time he would get the snake pinned, it would struggle and he'd release it so he wouldn't hurt it. He finally pinned it and grabbed it behind the head. I got out my surgical wet pack and somewhat shakily removed three small tumors.

It turned out those half-dozen common snake surgeries had just been Lou's way of testing my skills. The cobra was my proving ground. After that, Lou and I got on very well.

At one point we noticed Lou acting strangely. He was arriving at the zoo before daylight and staying late into the night. We were worried he might have cancer or some other terrible problem, but when questioned he said he was fine. This pattern went on for more than three months. He finally came to coffee one day and admitted that he had a cobra loose in the back of the reptile house, and it had gotten down a floor drain. He had been trying to catch it by placing lab rats out for bait, hoping he could catch the snake and put it back where it belonged. Lou had been afraid to tell anyone because he knew our solution would be to fumigate the sewer system and kill his snake. Lou only came clean after he caught the cobra. To Lou, snakes were more important than people. The fact that the sewer system connected the whole zoo campus didn't matter.

Lou had the largest poisonous snake collection in the world, but 90 percent of it was off display, behind the scenes. He was a perfectionist. There was a right way, a wrong way, and Lou Pistoia's way. And you had better do it Lou's way.

PAT BURCHFIELD

Pat Burchfield, now director of the Gladys Porter Zoo in Brownsville, Texas, had a wicked sense of humor. One day, while another keeper was cleaning the window of the python exhibit, Pat made faces at the keeper through the window. The exhibit housed three large reticulated pythons, and to clean it without removing the snakes, keepers would take a snake hook and put three to four layers of burlap sacks over them to defeat the heat-sensing pits in their noses so they wouldn't detect an intrusion. Then you'd go in quickly, clean the windows, get out and remove the sacks. Pat waited until Jack, who was cleaning the exhibit, was out before he said, "You missed a spot in the lower right-hand corner of the window, and you know how Lou is."

Jack couldn't see the spot, but he figured he could give the corner a quick polish with a hand towel and get out before the snakes noticed him, so he went in. Pat promptly locked him in the cage and then went around to the front window and pounded on it. Jack backed into a corner with his knees up and a tea towel in front of him for protection. Finally, Pat unlocked the cage and left for his two days off. When he returned he expected Jack to take revenge. What he didn't fear was Lou because he assumed nobody would have the courage to tell Lou about pranks involving his snakes. Nothing happened. Jack never said a word and went on like it never happened. Six months later, in the middle of December, Jack came into the reptile house—a converted public restroom—before daylight. Entering in the dark, you had to open the door and feel your way down the back aisle behind the exhibits to the light switch, which was located behind the hot water heater. Jack first took our 14-foot king cobra out of its exhibit, put him into a perforated metal garbage can and secured the lid. Then he moved the can to a secure part of the building and proceeded to set a diabolical trap. The exhibits on that side of the building had been built by Lou on legs about 30 inches off the concrete floor. They didn't extend all the way to the ceiling. Jack started making carefully balanced stacks of cans and buckets next to the wall and on top of the exhibits and then bridged them over the top with more cans and buckets. The result was delicately balanced arched stacks of garbage cans and buckets. He then opened the door to the king cobra's exhibit, turned out the lights, crawled under the exhibit and waited. When Pat came in he felt his way down the aisle until he hit the open door. This could only mean one thing, something was loose. Jack gave Pat time to think "1-2-3 king cobra" and dug his fingernails into the calf of Pat's leg. Pat went crashing into the first stack of cans and all hell broke loose. Jack crawled out from under the Exhibit and out the door and left Pat writhing around on the floor in the dark under stacks of cans and buckets thinking there was a very large King cobra under there with him. Lou came in and found a situation that Pat couldn't possibly explain without admitting to his previous horseplay. Sometimes revenge is particularly sweet.

BOB AND THE TAPIR

When I think of Columbus I'm reminded of a bird curator who decided to become a TV star. There was only one regular TV slot still available, and none of the rest of us wanted to do it. It was called *Lucy's Toyshop*, and Lucy personified all the stereotypes about so-called "ditzy blondes." The cameramen hated *Lucy's Toyshop*. The bird curator started taking birds on the show, and one day he came into my office to ask about the young bald eagle we were treating for a broken wing. He was, (he said) after all, the bird curator. I finally said, "Bob, do you want to take the eagle on *Lucy's Toyshop?*" He said he did. We loaned him a gauntlet and the cage, and off he went. In those days the Wyandotte Inn right across the road was a favorite place to eat lunch or, in some cases, to drink it. Some of us were there at the Wyandotte watching TV when Bob came on the show. Lucy said, "Well Bob, what have you got today?"

Bob replied, "Well Lucy—and boys and girls—today I've got a bald eagle," at which time the eagle struck out and drove the talons of one foot through both sides of Bob's nose. It was a live show. Bob fell to the floor, with a considerable amount of screaming, and both cameras followed him down. With no one to help him, Bob finally got the eagle under control and pried its talons out of his nose. With the only two cameras on the set fixed on him the director had no other options, just the screaming curator with an eagle attached to his nose. By the time he got back to the zoo his nose had swelled to three times its normal size. If he expected sympathy, it was not to be.

Thus, Bob was nicknamed "Old Eagle Nose." For the next three months while his nose healed, a familiar refrain around the zoo was, "Real men don't scream" and "When are you going to take another eagle on the show?" The next time he went back on the show he took another raptor, a sparrow hawk. Again, we were all at the Wyandotte Inn. Bob didn't take a glove because sparrow hawks are the smallest of our raptors. As Lucy's introduction was finishing, the sparrow hawk sank its talons into Bob's finger. He wasn't going to scream this time and pried the talons out of his finger. Holding the flapping little bird by the legs with one hand, he looked up at the camera and said through clenched teeth, "Look boys and girls, that's real blood."

Sometime later Bob again came shuffling into my office, this time asking to borrow a mammal. Bob and I really didn't like each other, and I was about to say no when I looked up and saw two of his keepers behind him nodding their heads up and down. I figured I should take their hint, so I asked him what he had in mind. He told me he heard we had a tame tapir. We did in fact have a very calm, large male tapir. What Bob didn't know was on days when there were groups of girls in front of the exhibit, the keepers would hand feed him loaves of bread. The tapir had acquired a conditioned response to being fed: he got an erection. Pound for pound, tapirs are probably the best endowed of all male mammals. Bob told me his keepers had volunteered to load him and our department wouldn't have to do anything. I agreed.

When the day arrived, it seemed like half the zoo was there to see him off. He didn't suspect a thing. Just as he was about to drive off, one of his own keepers casually walked up and with a straight face handed him two loaves of bread and said, "Here Bob, sometimes he gets a little excited. Just give him one of these before you start and he'll calm right down."

That noon, a $100 bill wouldn't have bought standing room at the Wyandotte. When the show started Lucy opened with the usual, "Well Bob, what have you got today?" Bob said, "Well Lucy—and boys and girls—today I've got a tapir."

Just as the keepers pulled up the crate door, the big male walked out. Bob started into his recently learned speech about tapirs and threw a loaf of bread to the tapir.

Lucy's eyes got very wide, and before she could think she pointed and said, "My God, what's that?"

Both cameras fixed on the tapir. Without thinking, Bob said, "That's his d**k Lucy." Then he added, "Surely by your age you've seen a d**k before."

The TV screen went black, and that was the end of Bob's TV career. The Wyandotte was chaos. Beer mugs were flying, people were rolling on the floor, and I saw a bird keeper bang his head against the bar until it bled.

HAULING ANIMALS TO CANADA

After a zoo conference, the director of the Wasaga Beach Zoo in Ontario, Canada, who was quite a colorful character, came through Columbus and purchased a male lion and some stump tail macaques from our zoo. Wasaga Beach is about 450 miles north of Toronto on Hudson's Bay. The deal included that we would transport the animals, and he would reimburse all expenses. I had never been farther north than Niagara Falls so it seemed like a good opportunity to see Hudson's Bay and some of Canada. The trip was planned for the first part of February, and a hospital keeper and I were going to drive them in a little Corvan. Just before leaving he called and said that he had bought a male aoudad from the Cleveland Zoo, and he asked if we could pick it up on our way. Foolishly, we agreed. We made arrangements to pick the aoudad up at midnight in the zoo parking lot in Cleveland. The folks in Cleveland crated him up and left him at a designated spot. As the sun came up Friday morning we pulled into Buffalo, New York, had some breakfast, washed up and went to the Buffalo Zoo, where we met Clayton Freiheit. Clayton gave us the grand tour of the zoo, including his two favorite animals, a pair of huge gaboon vipers. He also fed us lunch. Then we headed for the Canadian border at Niagara Falls.

There we met a Canadian customs and agriculture agent who'd never heard of an aoudad. He asked for another name, something unscientific. I explained that they came from the Atlas Mountains in North Africa and some people called them Barbary sheep even though they weren't really sheep. Then things went downhill rapidly.

It seems Canada had just had a scabies mite outbreak, and all sheep, whether true sheep or not, had to be dipped and certified clean by a USDA veterinarian. It was Friday afternoon, and no animals were allowed across over the weekend. We scrambled back to the zoo and found Clayton. He called their USDA vet, and convinced him to please bring some concentrated chlordane sheep dip and the paperwork to the zoo. The clock was ticking, and we were panicking. Plus, there was no tank to dip the aoudad in. The zoo dug up a 55-gallon barrel and we filled it with diluted chlordane, pulled the 300-pound male out of his crate and somehow stuffed him backwards into the barrel. His horns were wider than the barrel, so his head, ears and horns were above the rim. Then we poured more of the solution over his head and ears and rubbed it into his horns.

The hard part was pulling this 300-pound male out of the barrel and back into his crate. We were up against a tight deadline to get back to the border by five o'clock. During all of this Clayton was very helpful, standing well out of the splash zone, chain-smoking cigarettes and offering advice. By the time we got the animal back in the crate, there was as much sheep dip on us as there was on the aoudad. There was no time to jump into the shower. We raced to the border, presented our certificate and crossed over. We headed north, and when we got to the far side of Toronto we were hungry and stopped at a bar and grill. The bartender immediately said we had to leave. I apologized for our smell and asked if they could just make us some sandwiches to take with us. The bartender told me he didn't care how I smelled. The problem was we were on the couples-only side, and if we would just go to the other side they would be glad to feed us no matter how we smelled. It was still a long drive to Wasaga Beach, and we were still covered in dried sheep dip. When we got there we unloaded the animals and headed to our motel for a bath. Our motel turned out to be a summer cottage on the beach with a small bathroom heater that wasn't even lit. Even though the cottage was well below freezing, the water in the shower was hot. We desperately needed to get clean. When I stepped out of the shower and put my foot on the linoleum floor, it momentarily froze there.

STINKY

Columbus had acquired a young Jaguar named Stinky who had been bottle-fed. His diet was apparently deficient, and his permanent teeth came in with no enamel on the distal half. Soon after he grew into an adult his canines had eroded down and the root canal was exposed, causing pain. He tried to relieve the pain like a baby chewing on a pacifier; he began chewing on his paws and tail. We tried all kinds of nasty tasting things on his tail and paws to stop him, but nothing worked. The tail became infected, and we had to amputate part of it. The third time this happened we decided it was time for drastic action. Otherwise it was only a matter of time before we would have an ascending infection of the spinal cord. My first inclination was to cut the canines off and do a root canal, and we

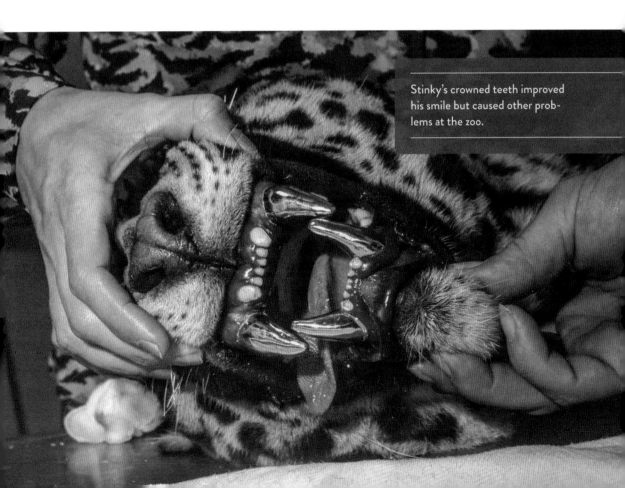

Stinky's crowned teeth improved his smile but caused other problems at the zoo.

sought advice from a local dentist. He suggested that we put crowns on his teeth. We anesthetized Stinky, made molds of his four canines and sent them off to the lab. Back came four shiny, chrome vitallium crowns. We anesthetized Stinky again while we cemented them in place. When he woke up he had the shiniest chrome smile in the world.

Unfortunately, Stinky's crowns were much harder than natural teeth. He promptly learned to strip paint off the bars and bite holes in things that otherwise would be impossible to bite through. He became a nuisance with a pretty smile. One of our hospital keepers had developed a strong bond with Stinky and sometimes would put his face up to the bars to let stinky lick his face and hair. We told the keeper repeatedly not to do this. Eventually Stinky would turn into a Jaguar. I even ordered him not to do it, but he didn't listen. One day, over the noon hour when no one else was around, Stinky grabbed him behind the ears with the claws of both paws. He pulled his head up to the bars and used his rough tongue to rasp a two-inch hole through the skin on top of his head, almost to the bone. Stinky then turned him loose. We never had to warn that keeper again.

This same keeper also had a habit of raiding lunch boxes for cookies and cake. We told him to stop, but again he wouldn't listen. We asked our dietitian to grind up Purina Monkey Chow biscuits. We mixed the powder with ripe bananas and patted balls of the mix into cookies and even put crossed fork marks on them and then baked them. For a week we salted lunch sacks and boxes with Purina Monkey Chow cookies while the whole zoo looked on and chuckled. Someone finally spilled the beans, but it stopped the cookie stealing. However, I must admit that I tried the cookies for myself, and they tasted pretty good.

A JAGUAR WITH CEREBRAL EDEMA
AND A HARROWING CAR RIDE

During my time in Columbus, one of our Jaguars slipped and hit his head while running in circles about eight feet off the ground, around his outside en-

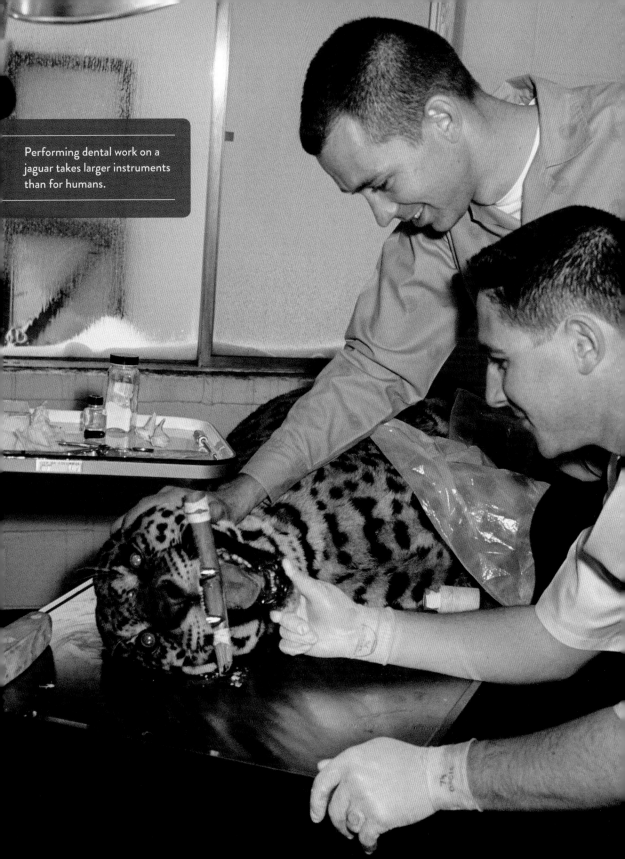

Performing dental work on a jaguar takes larger instruments than for humans.

closure, similar to a motorcycle rider in a hippodrome show. By the time we got to the exhibit he was exhibiting an ascending paralysis in his hind legs which progressed forward until he was completely down. We checked to make sure he was truly unconscious before we went in with him. His respiration was almost undetectable, and he had a nodal heart rate.

We decided he likely had a severe subdural hematoma and wouldn't survive. However, if he had any chance of living, it would be at the vet school 18 miles south of the zoo. We loaded him straight into my car without taking time to get any medical gear or immobilizing equipment and drove straight to the school. Two keepers were pumping his chest in the car, and we got him inside so they could do an EEG. There was no evidence of a subdural hematoma, and we assumed he probably had cerebral edema. We started giving him IV Ureaphil and 50 percent glucose while we rushed him to radiology to see if there was a skull fracture. While he was being X-rayed, what seemed like half the vet school came in to watch, attracted by a visiting Jaguar. As they crowded around, the Ureaphil and glucose began to work, reducing the edema. Suddenly the Jaguar started regaining consciousness, and the radiologist instructed us to "get that animal the hell out of here immediately."

This was no small feat. We had to clear the room and doorway of the large crowd that had bottlenecked at the door. We had no ropes, nets or other immobilizing equipment with us. The three of us took our belts off, placing one around his neck and the other two on his legs. Then we rushed him back out to my car, a Plymouth Fury V8, a retired Interstate police car with a big hemi engine. The drive back to the zoo was a winding road alongside the Scioto River. The Jaguar lay on the back seat with two keepers in the front seat leaning over to hold him down. We discussed among ourselves that if he became uncontrollable, we'd drive the car into a ditch, jump out, shut the doors and try to find some fence wire to tie the doors handles shut until we could get a ride to the zoo and get the capture equipment. Thankfully, the keepers were able to control him all the way to the zoo. And the jaguar ultimately regained full function with no impairment. Reflecting on that 18-mile drive along the Scioto River, with the speedometer well over 100 miles-per-hour, we were probably in more danger from the car ride than the Jaguar. That big hemi could sure run, and we had plenty of incentive.

MAGGIE AND JIGGS AND A KEEPER NAMED SKIP

The Columbus Zoo had a pair of adult orangs, Maggie and Jiggs. Jiggs was a large Bornean male with huge facial plates. Maggie, the female, was much smaller and slimmer, with long dark hair. She liked to collect pockets off uniform shirts.

Both orangs were easy-going and friendly with keepers. We were treating them for TB, and we tried everything to disguise the horrible taste of PAS. Orangs are very intelligent apes, and they outfoxed us every time. One day out of pure frustration I dropped a half dozen enteric coated PAS tablets into Jiggs' outstretched lip. Then we waited for him to suck through the sweet enteric coating and get down to the horrible tasting green core of the tablet. When his lips began to turn green we realized he liked the horrible taste. He was a true orang contrarian. After that, giving them medication was easy. They held out their lips, you dropped the pills in, and they sucked on them until they were gone.

One Sunday afternoon an excited visitor rushed into my office and said the orangs had grabbed a keeper and were tearing his clothes off. I rushed over to the ape house with a dart gun. The crowd was so large, I had to literally fight my way through the crowd into the front keeper's aisle. There I saw Skip, the keeper, with his back to the crowd, stark naked except for his shoes and one sock. He was squirting a high-pressure hose at the orangs. I asked what happened and he said the orangs had grabbed him and torn his clothes off.

I said, "I can see that, but they don't have you now and you're stark naked in front of hundreds of people."

"They've got my wallet and $300 of my money, and they're eating it," he said.

"Those people have been looking at my front side for half an hour, and they can damn well look at my backside until I get my money back."

Skip proceeded to hose his wallet and what was left of his money out through the back scuppers. Later I asked Skip how it happened, and he said that our uniform company had sown the shirt pockets on extra tight so that when Maggie grabbed it she pulled him up against the bars. Then Jiggs ambled over and grabbed him by both arms. The two of them cooperated to turn him around facing the crowd, and Jiggs held him while Maggie methodically split his clothes off. He had a hole in the toe of one sock, so she pulled it up his leg and split it off. Thankfully, the orangs didn't hurt Skip. They just wanted his clothes.

THE ELEPHANT HOUSE WALL

In Columbus we had two old rogue female Asian elephants named Cincy and Tanzy. Neither was workable, and they did whatever they wanted to. At one time they had apparently been good working elephants, but when their old keeper retired he had not trained a replacement and the zoo lost control. The keepers had solved the problem of being able to move these two old girls around as needed with food. When they wanted the elephants to go outside they put a pile of day-old bread in the outside exhibit, and when they wanted them to come inside they put a pile of bread in their inside quarters. It was a simple system.

In January the keepers noticed the elephants were showing signs of respiratory problems and coughing. I couldn't examine them properly because of their aggressive behavior. From a distance, the keepers seemed to be right. And one of the elephants seemed worse than the other. We put oral tetracycline hydrochloride in their water. In those days it was horrible-tasting orange stuff, so we tried to disguise it with honey or grape juice but to no avail. They drank it because they had no other choice, but any keeper who came close got an orange shower.

I surmised the problem was caused by the elephants standing outside in the cold every morning. I jumped the keepers about this, and they said the elephants opened the door and went out themselves. I told them they should lock the door and even threatened to fire the next keeper who left it unlocked. The Columbus keepers in those days were nearly as rogue as the two old elephants, and they politely neglected to tell me they left the door unlocked because the elephants liked it that way. That night, they locked the door as instructed, and in the morning when the elephants tried to open the door and go out, it wouldn't open. One (or both) of the elephants solved the problem by charging the door and knocking it out, along with the concrete block wall on each side of it. When I arrived we had an elephant house with a gaping hole in the east side and two elephants outside, just like they wanted. We had to get a team of very nervous city masons to the zoo to rebuild the wall while our keepers carried pitchforks and bullwhips

Tanzy and me at the Columbus Zoo, 1964.

to keep the elephants back. The elephants continued to open the door and go out whatever they pleased, and eventually they recovered from their respiratory problems.

These two old rogues were responsible for developing one of the best bird keepers we ever had in Columbus. Dick was an elephant keeper, and one day while cleaning the inside quarters he wasn't paying attention and Tanzy slowly backed up to him. She swung a hind leg up and pinned Dick to the wall with her foot in his stomach. She didn't hurt him but held him there while Cincy ambled over and tussled his hair and examined him all over with her trunk. After the elephants turned him loose, he came into my office to report what had happened. He claimed to have been held against the wall for at least an hour, but I suspected it was likely just a few minutes. Dick declared that if he had to go back to the elephant house he would quit. So he became a bird keeper—and a very good one. Tanzy would later grab a visitor's Leica camera and crush it, the first Leica I had ever seen.

Another recurring pachyderm experience at the zoo came via our black rhino male. Male rhinos practice retro-grade micturition, which means that they urinate straight backwards, great volume and distance. A four-foot chain-link fence separated our outside rhino pens from the public. The male had learned that when a crowd gathered he could back up to the bars, scrape his feet two or three times and let fly. Everyone would run and scream. Babies in strollers were particularly at risk and often came away wet and smelly. On afternoons at coffee break, watching the rhino was a favorite keeper pastime.

V.D. RIDER AND THE HYENA

The Columbus Zoo had a large spotted hyena named Joey. He had been hand raised by the keepers and seemed very amenable most of the time. However, if you tried to clean his exhibit while he was in it he became excitable, and it became very clear why spotted hyenas are called laughing hyenas.

The keepers' solution was to enter Joey's enclosure with brooms and shovels, then they would hold out their wrist. Joey would grab a keeper by the wrist with his teeth, and the keeper would lead him out of the enclosure and into an empty stall. Once his enclosure was cleaned, they would reverse the procedure and lead Joey, with his jaws around a wrist, back into his enclosure. A few times I even did this myself. One day Joey became curious about a padlock with a cast-white metal body and crushed it between his molars, effectively popping the lock open. I had read that hyenas would routinely crush the leg bones of animals like the Cape Buffalo to get after the marrow. Seeing him crush this lock led us to change our methods.

I felt it was counterproductive to have just a male, and decided we should get Joey a mate and breed them. I contacted an animal dealer named V.D. Rider and ordered a female. When she arrived and we uncrated her, she looked like a smaller version of Joey. I phoned V.D. to ask why he had sent us another male. After a long silence and a chuckle on his end of the phone, he said, "You're pretty new at this aren't you? You don't know much about hyenas, do you?"

I admitted this was the first spotted hyena I had ever worked with, but I was still insulted by his remark. V.D. then told me that telling a male from a female—unless she was old and had pups—was almost impossible with the naked eye. Both sexes looked like well-endowed males. He also told me that if we didn't like the one he shipped we could send it back and he would send us another one, but it would look exactly the same. I asked him how he could tell them apart. He happily shared with me his technique. He said to take a silver dime, drill a small hole through one edge, tie it to a silk thread and hang it over the center of the animal's back. If the dime turned one direction it was a male, and if it turned 90 degrees it was a female. Sadly, I no longer remember which orientation meant which sex. Sure enough, I went back to the books, which confirmed what V.D. told me. I had been reading about the power of hyena jaws, but I hadn't gotten to the part about the morphology of their external genitalia looking exactly the same. We ultimately had to rename Joey "Josephine" since he (make that "she") got pregnant and had a pup. I watched the birth, and it was interesting to say the least. Even more interesting was the fact that unlike virtually every other carnivore species whose offspring are born blind and nearly helpless, spotted hyena pups are coal black when they are born with their eyes wide open and a mouth full of teeth. Within 20 minutes, it was up and exploring around and ready to bite!

ABE THE CHIMP

During my time in Columbus, a couple who owned a large book store on the Ohio State campus inquired about donating a young male chimp to the zoo. They had bought the animal on a trip to Africa, but he was becoming more and more aggressive. We said we would take him, but they weren't quite ready to bring him to the zoo.

After numerous phone calls to the zoo over the next six months, they finally made an appointment and brought the chimp, named "Abe," to the zoo. He looked to be between four and five years old, and from all of the crying on the part of this couple, it was obvious that he had become a surrogate child. It was also obvious that he had become aggressive and unruly. Both the man and woman had scars and fresh bite wounds on their arms and hands. There were hugs and kisses and tears that seemed to go on forever. The couple also had an African American maid with them who, it appeared, took care of Abe when they were at work. She wore a short-sleeved summer dress, and there was not a single scar or bite wound on her. If Abe got out of hand, she simply cleared her throat or gave him the eye and he folded up and became civilized.

Abe drew blood from both surrogate parents before they got out of my office, and he made several aggressive passes at us. I managed to get the maid aside, and she told me that the first time the animal bit her she smacked him and didn't let him get away with things like that. So much for the Walt Disney love and togetherness theory.

Once these people finally left the zoo we took Abe in the back room for a discussion. Like the woman had said, he became a very civilized little chimp. If you know anything about chimp behavior, in the wild the only individuals they show affection for are those who are dominant to them. If you are subordinate you are going to get thumped and probably bleed a bit. We would take Abe for coffee break and gave him a dime to get a Coke. He brought the Coke back to you. We continued giving him dimes until all of us had a Coke. The last dime was his, and he would take it over to the concession stand and drink his Coke in one gulp and then shove the cup back in to be refilled. He did this repeatedly until he was completely full of Coke. As long as you were there to back him up he would take on any keeper "to protect you."

YOUNG LEE AND THE TIGER CUB AND OTHER TV PROBLEMS

The Columbus Zoo was a good training ground in many ways, including a few forays into television. I became a regular on a couple shows where I would come on with an animal for a 10 or 12-minute spot. One of them was broadcast during the day, but it taped in the evening. I would frequently take an animal home with me, eat dinner, put on a coat

Young Lee made an easy target for a young tiger I brought home for a television show.

and tie and go do the show. One day I took a young tiger home, and as I got out of the van and started to clip a heavy leash to the tiger's harness he bolted away straight across the grass in front of our apartment to where Marie and young Lee were standing on a neighbor's porch. As predators always do he went straight for the smallest prey. Young Lee was a toddler and luckily still wearing a thick diaper. The tiger cub grabbed him by the rear end and put four nice scrape marks on his rump. It was some years before Lee really warmed up to tigers.

Six months later that same tiger went wild on a live TV show. We had the first segment, and a group of Hawaiian dancers wearing hula skirts and parading around grass huts and palm trees were to follow us. As our segment finished, the tiger went berserk and tore down their whole Hawaiian set, leaving them no way to do their bit.

Another time, a young lion got nervous on live TV and emptied his bowels on the small table we were standing behind. The table had a two-inch raised rim, so he was sitting in an inch of smelly, liquid, brown goo. I got control of his tail so he couldn't paint us with brown stripes. The blond-haired hostess started turning green and couldn't talk for fear of throwing up. As you might, guess, the rest of the interview became a monologue.

A TIGER IN YOUR TANK

We were approached by the Humble Oil Company to train a tiger for their "Tiger in Your Tank" commercial. The company led us to believe that our participation could ultimately lead to a contribution toward building a new zoo hospital. With that kind of a carrot dangling we couldn't refuse.

For a year we campaigned a good sized male Bengal tiger at meetings, banquets and on TV. This would likely be considered insane today, and surely no insurance company would allow it. When it was all finished, whatever monetary payment there was went to the mayor and the service director. Humble tried to compensate those of us who had trained and worked the tiger with coupons for a tank full of gas. We tore up the coupons. When it came time to ship the tiger to another zoo, we planned to put a shipping crate in a Belen cage and let him in. I was going to just take him by the scruff of the neck and lead him into the crate. My body language must have given me away; he refused to enter the crate and tried to eat me. He might have succeeded if not for a quick-thinking keeper who tossed me a broom stick. One good crack on the nose and he turned back into a friendly cub. That episode taught me to be careful about handshake deals, even with large, "respectable" companies.

ARTIFICIAL INSEMINATION IN CHIMPS

We nearly became the first zoo in the world to successfully artificially inseminate a chimpanzee. Willy Kubler, a German chimp trainer with the Ringling Brothers Circus, had given us a large male chimpanzee, Moroc, who had been acquired as a youngster in Morocco, North Africa. He had been raised in a French bawdy house and thought he was more human than chimp. I had previously operated on Moroc, draining a large abscess in his sub guttural sac and establishing a permanent stoma. At 150 pounds he had gotten too big and too tough to work in a circus, so Willy gave him to the Columbus Zoo.

We had a female chimp named Mary who cycled regularly and showed every sign of being a good reproductive candidate. We put Moroc and Mary together, and it was obvious that she was highly receptive. The problem was Moroc showed no interest, even at the peak of her estrous cycle. His time spent in the bawdy house had humanized him. However, he showed interest in a couple of our keepers and would present to them through the bars while they were cleaning. Since he liked Skip best, we planned to have Skip don a pair of surgical gloves and collect a semen sample to evaluate Moroc for fertility.

The first collection went fine, and the quantity and quality were good. We recorded Mary's estrous cycles and practiced the insemination procedure on Mary to be able to inseminate on exactly the best day without anesthesia. We were eagerly looking forward to a baby chimp and a great publication. Unfortunately, on the morning Skip was going to collect semen, after he had put his gloves on, there was a noise at the window. Somehow the word had gotten out, and what seemed like half our zoo keepers were plastered against Moroc's window, making faces and being obnoxious. Skip took one look, handed me the tube and said. "If you want that damn sample you're going to have to collect it yourself."

Unfortunately, the zoo vet is the guy with the dart gun and therefore usually the most hated person in the zoo. Moroc only wanted to throw feces at me. And that is how we lost our chance at international fame.

GRANDMOTHER WEBSTER AND MOROC

There is a backstory on Moroc worth sharing. Willy Kubler was in Columbus preforming with the Circus when he called me to ask if I could look at one of his chimps who had a large swelling at the base of his neck. After the circus closed, Willy his wife and small baby were staying at a friend's place, so we went to see them. On examining Moroc it was evident that he had a sub guttural sac infection. All great apes and many other primates have an interconnected series of subcutaneous air sacs that communicate with the respiratory tract through an opening in each side of the larynx. These sacs are between skin and the muscles and in some cases extend back under the armpits and around over the shoulder blades nearly meeting at the backbone. In many primates these pouches are inflatable and greatly assist in adding resonance and volume to their territorial calls. They are lined on the inside with mucosal cells much like the trachea. If an animal gets an infection in one or more of these pouches, they won't drain and are difficult to treat. The bacterial-laden exudate can get into the trachea and cause pneumonia. The best treatment is to surgically establish a permanent stoma or opening at the bottom of the sub guttural sac immediately below the larynx. This allows for any fluid exudate to drain out and for the sac to be flushed with antibiotics.

We scheduled the surgery, and upon arriving I set up my surgical pack while Willy opened the cage door (inside a semi-trailer) containing all the chimps and led Moroc out by hand. Things were going fine until I pulled out a syringe full of phencyclidine. Moroc took one look and bolted. Marie and young Lee were standing off to one side, and Marie's Grandmother Webster, an 80-year-old retired schoolteacher, was standing in the narrow space between the semi-trailer and the house. Grandmother Webster always wore long ankle-length dresses, and as Moroc charged toward her she grabbed her skirt on each side, spread it wide and assumed a football lineman's blocking stance. Moroc was intent on escaping, not hurting anyone, and he charged through her skirt like a bull through a matador's cape.

"Moroc," one of Willy Kubler's chimps.

Willy chased after Moroc and grabbed him by the hand, but Moroc wasn't coming back. Willy hollered at his wife in German, and then the second amazing thing that day happened. Willy's wife, carrying their small baby, went up the steps into the semi-trailer, opened the door to the chimp cage and handed the baby in with 11 chimpanzees. They included another large adult male, a number of adult females and some youngsters. Marie, her Grandmother and I were totally amazed. Then Willy's wife took Moroc's other hand and together they led him back to me. With the two of them holding on to him and talking sternly, I injected him. Meanwhile the chimps were passing the baby from adult to adult, smelling her, licking her, taking a finger and gently opening her mouth and exploring her hair. Willy said not to worry because the old females would not let anyone get out of hand or do anything rough. After about 10 minutes, Moroc was down and I proceeded with the prep and surgery.

It was difficult concentrating on the surgery while watching those chimps out of the side of my eye, passing the baby around amongst themselves. Within 90 minutes Moroc had recovered consciousness, Willy's wife retrieved the baby and Moroc—with the new opening in his neck—replaced her in the chimp troop's curiosity.

MAJOR THE AFRICAN GRAY

Another animal character at Columbus was Major, the African gray parrot. We didn't know how old he was, but he had been at the zoo a long time. African gray parrots have perfect pitch, exact pronunciation in their mimicry and the ability to repeat very long sentences and songs. Major did a perfect imitation of a female bird curator, who was long since dead, with a very distinctive, irritating voice. There had been a litter of puppies in the birdhouse kitchen, and Major could do all of their voices at once. He did the ping of a hammer hitting a hard-concrete nail, the sound of a crock bowl sliding across the floor and many other things. He had also learned a lot of profanity over the years, thus he could not be put on public display. But he was a favorite in the birdhouse kitchen.

Shortly after I arrived, a contest developed to see who could teach Major the most obscene things to say about the zoo director. After work one day, Terry Strawser the bird curator and Dave McKelvey were trading for birds with a fellow named Frank Farmer. Frank was a talented engineering consultant who was into exotic birds and antique guns. I was waiting for a chance to trade guns with Frank and decided to participate in the contest. Major was a quick and easy pupil. You just took a small stick, tapped on his cage half a dozen times and repeated your sentence. With a very few repetitions Major would have it letter perfect complete with an exact replication of your voice. However, I can't repeat my phrase in civilized company.

While I was teaching Major, the director walked quietly up the back aisle and caught me in the act. He didn't say a word but just glared, turned on his heel and left. The next day we were waiting for the fallout, but it never came. A few days later, at the zoo's Christmas party, he made the mistake of taking the wife of the council president for a behind-the-scenes tour. When they came into the birdhouse kitchen she said, "Oh my, what a beautiful bird." And Major began reciting what he had been taught. I'm sure she heard words and phrases she had never heard before.

The next morning we got word that Major was to be off the grounds by sundown. Dave McKelvey had long wanted Major and gave the zoo $100 and an old refrigerator for him. Since I was credited with being the straw that broke the camel's back he gave me a huge longhorn steer horn.

Dave and his wife Diane (a very talented artist) then rented an apartment just behind us and brought Major with them. In the summertime when everyone had their windows open, the mothers in our apartment complex wouldn't let their children play between those two buildings because of the things that Major recited. Guests came to the McKelvey household just to hear Major. There was no difficulty recognizing which person had taught him each ditty. The final twist is even more interesting. An evangelical preacher moved into the apartments. His wife was a nurse, and Marie had made the mistake of offering to occasionally babysit for free. This became a regular thing, and when the preacher would come to pick up his kids he never lost an opportunity to proselytize. I was near the end of my patience when fate took a hand. The preacher decided to save Dave McKelvey's soul, which may have been an impossible task. He began visiting the McKelvey apartment regularly, and after about the fifth visit Dave quietly got up and let Major out of his cage. Major did not like strange men. As Dave related it, Major hopped down off the counter and clackety clacked across the floor into the living room and just as the preacher said, "What a pretty parrot," Major sank his beak into the preacher's Achilles tendon. The preacher screamed, jumped up, caught his shins on the coffee table, fell over it and broke his nose on the floor. He never came back to Dave's house or ours.

THE SHOTGUN AND THE TV

For a long time I had been an amateur gunsmith. I had a workbench with a small lathe in a closet of the apartment. One of the guys at the zoo had asked if I could make a new firing pin for the right-hand barrel on a double 12. The pin was sticking down after firing, and when he opened it and loaded a new shell it would fire immediately on closing the breach.

Marie had taken young Lee to Oklahoma to see her folks, so one night I had some time to spare and turned a new firing pin. I installed it and checked it out to make sure it was no longer sticking. About midnight, not thinking as clearly as I should have been, I snapped both triggers, opened the breach, stuck two shells in the chambers and snapped the breach shut without checking to see that neither the right or left firing pin was stuck down. The left barrel immediately fired, blowing our old black and white television set to kingdom come. It was summer, and since we didn't have air conditioning, all of the windows in our apartment were open. Rose, the same neighbor who had been standing on the porch with Marie and Young Lee when the tiger bit him in the rear, heard the shot and rushed across the lawn in her nighty. She came running into the living room expecting to find me dead or wounded and promptly stepped in the glass from the television. She screamed loud enough for everybody in the apartment complex to hear. I picked her up out of the glass and backed over to the couch. A few minutes later her husband came through the door, and he found me sitting on the couch with Rose in her nighty, sitting across my lap while I pulled shards of glass out of her feet.

Had there been no shotgun blast, blood and a blown up television, a husband could have easily drawn the wrong conclusion. As it was, he sat down on the couch and helped pull the glass out of her feet. That night an urban legend in our apartment complex was born. Before Marie and young Lee got home I went down to Sears and bought a new color TV.

LEONARD THE SPARROW HAWK

We acquired a young sparrow hawk or kestrel from a keeper named Leonard Bernstein and so named him Leonard. He was a great little bird and flew free in our living room. He would come down on your hand and take grasshoppers, small mice or bits of meat from you. We have a great picture of Leonard sitting on Young Lee's fist. One day I foolishly thought, "he's a sparrow hawk, why not give him a sparrow?" I went outside and caught one and turned it loose in the living room. He caught it immediately and took it up on top of the valance over the front window. I went into another room and came back to find out that he had meticulously plucked all the feathers off the sparrow before eating it. Marie will attest that there are at least 4 bushels of feathers on a single sparrow. From then on it was grasshoppers and mice.

FLOOD AT THE ZOO

The first winter we were in Columbus the ice froze very deep on O'Shaughnessy Lake at the zoo. During the spring thaw an ice dam formed against O'Shaughnessy dam and water, complete with big ice flows, backed up into the zoo grounds. We made 10-foot tall stepped pyramids of hay bales for our hoofed animals to climb up on. Our experienced keepers made a sandbag dam across the top of the ramp going into the basement of the Wagner building, an old WPA facility housing hippos, tapirs, hyenas and other midsize mammals. It had an old steam boiler in a pit in the basement that had been converted from coal to oil. When our little dam broke, the ice-cold water rushed down the ramp and hit the red-hot boiler. It was pretty spectacular, and luckily no one got hurt. We had to use kerosene salamanders for temporary heat until a new boiler could be installed on a raised slab.

FISHING WITH ART HEGADUS

The zoo's assistant dietitian was Art Hegadus, who lived across the lake from the zoo. Art was a rabid fisherman and had been named Ohio Fishermen of the Year four times. Art kept a small Jon boat at the zoo, and we would frequently fish in the morning before work and in the evening after work. Art had grown up beside the deep valley, which now formed O'Shaughnessy Lake, and had memorized all the underwater structure like the palm of his hand. Thus, fishing with Art for white crappy and bigmouth bass was generally very good.

Art had two quirks when it came to fishing. For one, no one was allowed to use live bait in his boat. Second, while Art might not mind if you got skunked, he absolutely refused to come in until he had caught at least one fish. He claimed never to have been skunked at fishing in his whole life, and I believed him. The lengths to which he would go to catch at least one fish were extraordinary. If all else failed he would row back in to the zoo, put on a small outboard motor and putt putt seven miles up the lake to an old dairy farm that had been submerged when the lake filled. Art would center us over the top of an old underwater silo. If you lowered a jig down into the middle of the silo you were guaranteed to catch fish. The only drawback was that the State Girls Industrial School was located on the bank close to the silo, and getting too close to the bank with your boat was absolutely forbidden. The matrons had biceps bigger than Olympic weightlifters.

JIM SAVOY AND THE RACCOON

One of the things that fell under my purview as mammals curator and zoo veterinarian was to respond to calls for help from the public. If there was a wild animal in someone's house or a problem in the area we would load up our nets, dart guns, ropes and live traps and head out with a small crew to solve their problem.

One such call came into the office, but Jim Savoy, the director who had replaced Steve Kelly, decided to handle it himself. The call came from the publisher of the *Columbus Dispatch* newspaper. It seems that there was a raccoon tail hanging down from the smoke box in their living room fireplace. Jim decided to make some brownie points by going alone, but he failed to get any of the equipment or keepers to help.

Sure enough, there was a raccoon tail hanging down off of the smoke shelf, obviously attached to a live raccoon on the other end. Jim decided to get a pickax handle, which he had in his car, to grab the raccoon by the tail and jerk it off the smoke shelf. Then he'd just run outside with the animal and hit it in the head with the pickax handle. Unfortunately, it didn't quite work as planned. Jim jerked the animal out of the fireplace, but then things went awry. As he started for the door the raccoon grabbed his leg and bit the hell out of him. Jim went down but didn't turn loose of the pickax handle, thus chopping an antique coffee table in half. Then he rolled around on the snow-white carpet with the sooty raccoon still biting his leg. Soon their carpet was covered with blood and fireplace soot. Nearby sat broken fragments of the antique coffee table. The raccoon finally broke free and ran out the front door. The zoo didn't win any good brownie points with the *Columbus Dispatch* that day. However, the incident reaffirmed that Murphy's Law works quite well.

ROPING A TAPIR AND A NIGHT WATCHMAN

One night in Columbus the night watchman called and said that a big male tapir had gotten out of his pen in the Wagner building. I got dressed and went into the zoo. When I arrived I saw the tapir was leisurely exploring the zoo grounds. In those days I didn't know of anyone who had chemically immobilized a tapir. The dart gun didn't seem like a good option, and the tapir, self-confident and stubborn, was in no mood to be herded back into the building. I was fairly good with a lariat and decided that if I threw a big loop over his neck and then let him step through it with one front leg I could suck the loop up around one shoulder and the opposite leg. However, I failed to factor in two critical pieces of information. The tapir weighed approximately 600 pounds, and, of course, there was no way he would remain calm and docile with a lariat pulled around him. The roping went perfectly. The tapir stepped through the loop just as planned, but when I sucked the rope tight he took off like a thunderbolt. I held on tight and dug in my heels, but the worst was yet to come. As he roared past the night watchman he changed course and circled him twice, neatly putting a double loop around both of his ankles. He then took off for the lake at O'Shaughnessy Dam with the night watchman screaming and bouncing behind him like a ragdoll and me on the end of the rope trying to dig my heels in and stop him. I thought about turning loose of the rope but since the tapir had circled his ankles twice I wasn't sure the loops would relax. Tapirs are aquatic, and I feared he would dive into the lake and drown the night watchman. I charged forward to take the tension off the rope so that the loops around his ankles would slip off, but they were locked tight. Neither the nightman's weight nor my frantic 128 pounds slowed him down in the least. Finally the tapir passed close to a small tree. I lunged ahead to get a wrap around the tree. We now had a 600-pound tapir tied to a tree, frantically trying to get to the lake with a night watchman in between screaming that his legs were being cut in two by the lariat rope.

The tapir finally calmed down, and I was able to get the nightman free. I sent him to the diet kitchen to cut up some apples and bananas. I probably should have done that in the beginning. Then we quietly led him back into the Wagner building, eating apple and banana slices out of our hands. It was an early and valuable lesson in the Law of Unintended Consequences.

MONKEYS AND MUSHROOMS

In Columbus we had a monkey Island exhibit with Patus monkeys. The prevailing wisdom was that Patus monkeys didn't swim, but we found out the hard way they did swim—just underwater. One day they all went into the moat, and as the first monkey surfaced at the outer wall a thoughtful visitor put his arm down to save him. The monkey grabbed the visitor's arm and held on while all the other monkeys surfaced. They climbed up the startled visitor's arm and escaped onto the zoo grounds. The first monkey was the last one to exit.

We rounded up the crew and gathered every net we could find and went after them, across the highway and onto a golf course. I was in hot pursuit of the troop when I looked back and realized none of the keepers were behind me. I doubled back and found out that as we had come through a patch of forest the keepers had noticed a huge crop of morel mushrooms under some elm trees. They abandoned the monkey chase, took off their shirts and frantically started filling them full of mushrooms. I had never seen a morel mushroom but soon had a shirt full myself. It took us about two months to capture all the monkeys. They hung around the edge of the zoo, and a few of them climbed up onto a shake shingle roof and pried up the shakes looking for beech nuts. We had to pay for this man's roof repairs. Battered, pan fried morels are the very best.

DIARRHEA EPIDEMICS

Six months after I arrived in Columbus an epidemic of diarrhea struck almost every animal in the Wagner building. We took fecal samples and culture swabs from all of the animals and went to the Ohio State School of Veterinary

Medicine in Columbus for help in diagnosing the causative agent. By the end of the following day all the animals were back to normal, but we had not come to any conclusions. Two weeks later the same type of epidemic occurred and we again did fecal samples and culture swabs, still to no avail. This sequence continued at exactly two-week intervals for the next two months. It drove me crazy, and it really drove the vet school clinicians and bacteriology department crazy. Fortunately the animals always recovered.

We didn't solve the mystery until a group of keepers came in early to go fishing in the lake before starting work. After they got back from fishing one of them came into my office and said, "I think there's something you should know."

A few months before, the zoo director had gotten a call from the mayor's office saying that an old friend of the mayor's who had worked in another city department would like to work at the zoo. With the zoo being directly under the mayor, such a request is hard to turn down, even if the person is past retirement age. We put this man, Roscoe, to work in the Wagner building since the work there was not terribly strenuous. After he had settled in for a couple of months Roscoe decided to take a hand in animal management. He was apparently independently wealthy and only wanted to work at the zoo because he liked animals. Every payday he would take his paycheck and load the trunk of his car full of milk. He came to the zoo at 6 a.m., before the rest of the keepers arrived, to take all of the feeding pans down off the wall and give every animal in the building all the milk they could drink. Then he'd gather up the pans, wash them, and hang them back on their pegs. When the rest of the keepers came in at 7:30 he would be reading his paper and drinking coffee, but by nine o'clock we would have another diarrhea epidemic of unknown etiology. Since he was a friend of the mayor's, we couldn't fire him, so we put him to work making wire monkey cages in another part of the zoo. Our epidemics never recurred.

It's worth noting that Roscoe's personal lunch diet consisted primarily of iceberg lettuce, peanut butter and lots of milk. When I confronted him about feeding the animals so much milk, he simply stated, "You young college guys don't know anything about nutrition."

BARBITURATE POISONING

We had an incident where two of our cats, a Bengal tiger and a cheetah, were found one morning unconscious in their outside exhibits. We took them to the zoo hospital, pulled blood samples and took stomach content samples. The results indicated high levels of phenobarbital in both sets of samples. Since there was no reversing agent for this drug, our only recourse was to try to remove as much stomach content as possible and to medically support them until they could metabolize the drug. We set up an IV drip on both animals and put together a keeper schedule for round-the-clock care and monitoring. This included monitoring their blood values and hydration and turning them over every half-hour 24-hours-a-day to avoid developing dependent edema, pneumonia or pressure sores.

The tiger woke up after three days, but the cheetah was unconscious for two full weeks. In retrospect it was amazing the animal survived and didn't develop any fatal complications.

We speculated that since none of the other animals in the collection had shown any signs of barbiturate poisoning that it must have been a deliberate act. Since the outside enclosures for the big cats were close to our perimeter fence along the highway it would have been fairly easy for someone to insert capsules of phenobarbital in chunks of meat, throw them over the fence onto the top of the exhibit where they could fall through the bars and in with the cats. We sent samples of the rest of our meat supply to the lab, talked with the police and other zoos around the country but came up with no answers. We could only suspect that someone deliberately and maliciously poisoned the animals.

About six months later at the annual zoo and aquarium conference in Washington, D.C., we were at the National Zoo in the old cat house when the subject of our poisoning incident came up. The director of the Cincinnati Zoo

immediately disagreed with our conclusion and said that he thought it was probably from our horsemeat supplier euthanizing horses for slaughter with phenobarbital. I said it that if this was the case there should logically be a lot of large cat
poisoning cases around the country. Then he immediately started a very spirited
discourse on why this wasn't so. He was leaning with his back against the public
rail in front of the tiger exhibit, an old-style setup with a raised floor and iron bars
at the front. A big male tiger backed up to the bars, swished his tail back and forth
and then raising it over his back, made several scratching motions with his hind
feet. Everyone in the crowd of 30 standing in front of this man knew that these
actions were a precursor to the tiger urinating. Tigers practiced retrograde urina-
tion like rhinos. Since I was on the opposite side of what had become a somewhat
heated discussion, I was not inclined to warn him but figured that someone in
the crowd surely would. As it turned out he either didn't have any friends in the
crowd or they were all friends with a mean sense of humor, because nobody said
a thing. The big male let loose, hitting him in the back with the stream of urine.
As the pressure quickly built up, the stream climbed up his neck, sending urine
around his collar and over his tie and then over the top of his bald head until it
ran down and cascaded off of his eyebrows. He jumped out of the way, and, to
his credit, pulled out a handkerchief, mopped his head and face and continued on
with his argument on why my theory was wrong. I figured that I really won the
argument because it is hard for an audience to pay attention to what someone is
saying when they are laughing that hard.

CIRCUS PRACTICE

As any zoo veterinarian will tell you, when the circus comes to town you
frequently get asked to diagnose, treat or help with a circus animal problem.
Over the years in Columbus (and later in Omaha) the zoo was asked for assistance countless times. Just as our knowledge base has grown and animal care
has evolved and become progressively better and more sophisticated in the zoo

world, so has it evolved in the circus world. Keeping animals who may easily travel 50,000 or even 100,000 miles a year requires a lot of attention to detail and effort. One of the problems that circus trainers frequently ran into in those days was food. Liberty ponies or elephants were generally not a problem since hay and grain is readily available in almost any town. The problems arose when big cats such as lions or tigers were involved; a good supply of affordable raw meat was not always readily available. For small circuses the cost of grocery store beef could be more than they wanted to pay. Frequently big cats and bears were fed what was available or affordable, which sometimes meant chicken necks and wings or even hog necks.

In Columbus we got a call from a circus trainer who said a tiger had gone off feed and was losing weight. He brought him out to the zoo and we immobilized the animal, drew blood and X-rayed him. It was quickly apparent that there was the cervical vertebra of a pig lodged in the jejunum with the dorsal vertebral spine penetrating into the abdominal cavity. Despite this foreign body penetrating into the peritoneal cavity the animal did not have a roaring peritonitis as you would expect. His white count was only slightly elevated. There was only one solution and that was immediate surgery to remove a section of jejunum and do an end to end anastomosis. The surgery went well, but the recovery was slow and hard since the animal had actually stopped eating three weeks earlier. Its gut motility was compromised. It was a testimony to animal's immune systems and resistance to infection that the tiger was still in relatively good condition. We kept him on fluids for nearly a week and slowly coaxed him to take more and more liquids and then gruel by mouth.

In Columbus we built up a substantial circus practice which then followed us to Omaha in 1966. In addition to Willy Kubler's chimps we treated the Kirby chimps, the Klouser bears, Gunther Gable Williams elephants, cats, liberty ponies and many others with a predominance of big cat acts. Willy Kubler even gave Omaha a big male chimp named Mickey who had grown too tough to work in the act.

Marie and I developed a number of good friends in the circus world who would visit us in Columbus or Omaha in between engagements. We were also invited to a lot of circus parties where the performers—both human and animal—put on special acts for each other. These were usually after the last act of the day and went long into the night. A lot of good natured parody, fun poking and new acts could be expected. At the first one we attended we couldn't figure out why young Lee had lost interest and just wanted to sleep until we realized that it was 2 a.m., well past his bedtime.

Once we were visiting the Kirbys in their motorhome, specially built by the Greyhound bus company. This was before motorhomes were common. It had living quarters for Andrew and Marie upfront and quarters for eight chimpanzees in the back with separate heating and air-conditioning. Another veterinarian who worked on circus animals and his wife from Kentucky had come up to see the show and visit on a Sunday. We started out eating and drinking before the matinee and continued on until the evening show. Andrew was a Scotchman and therefore drank scotch. I was drinking Jack Daniels, and the other vet was drinking beer. Our three wives were being somewhat tolerant. What we failed to realize was that every time the Kentucky veterinarian went back into the animal quarters to get another beer from the cooler, he was also handing out beer to the chimpanzees. By the time the evening performance came around none of us was feeling much pain, including Andrew. What we didn't know was that the chimps were also drunk.

As part of the act an adult female chimp would ride a bicycle across a high wire over the ring with two other chimps hanging onto it. They fell off the high wire and three chimps and a bicycle smashed Andrew, our drunken Scotsman, to the ground. Marie was a fiery red-haired Texas girl with a temper. In this case her temper was in full flare, and as she moved and whirled through the act in her long sequin-covered gown, waving a sequin-covered wand, it was apparent that she was more than a little angry. Every time she got close to one of the drunken chimps or Andrew she would make a very elegant motion with the wand and tap them on the head. What the circus people knew but the audience didn't was that that wand was actually a steel bar covered with cloth and sequins. The act turned into the most incredible comedy those of us in the know had ever seen, and the other circus performers were rolling with laughter. The audience was also laughing but for a different reason. They thought it was a deliberate comedy act. By the time the act was finished both Andrew and most of the chimps had lumps and goose eggs on their heads where Marie had tapped them with her magic wand. For a finale, the big adult female chimp drove a Suzuki motorcycle with seven other chimps in front and behind her on the bike. Even as a drunk driver she managed to circle the ring once, but on the second trip around Andrew didn't get out of the way and she ran right over him with the motorcycle. The audience howled, the circus people howled, and Marie waved her wand making more lumps. Luckily Monday, Tuesday and Wednesday were moving days.

INJURIES AND MORE

Animals sometimes attack and injure cage mates or worse. They also sometimes injure keepers. Usually this is the result of misjudging their intent or letting your guard down around dangerous individuals. There are very few wild animals that will not bite or make you bleed if given the chance or handled the wrong way. The difference is that a six-ounce Marmoset or small owl will make you bleed a little, but a chimpanzee will bite off a finger or worse. Species such as the bears and large cats are known predators and generally given respect and caution. However, there are animals that people generally think of as benign that can also be dangerous.

Such was the case of Jack Tuller and the camel. Most people don't know that male camels have an incredibly powerful jaw and long canine teeth. In the days of camel transport it was not uncommon for a town in Asia or the Middle East to have laws that required camels to be muzzled. One day Jack Tuller, the patriarch of an extensive, longtime family of zoo keepers, was walking by the dromedary camel pen when a big male reached over the fence, grabbed him by the top of his head and shook him like a ragdoll. He peeled the scalp nearly off of his head. The camel could just as easily have crushed his skull and killed him so being scalped was the lesser of two evils. Happily, after some medical attention he recovered.

In Columbus there was a nightman who had developed a rapport—so he thought—with an adult male chimpanzee. Every night while making his rounds he would stop in front of the chimp cage and hold out one hand and the chimp would take it. Then, very carefully, the chimp cleaned under his fingernails with his teeth. He would then hold out the other hand and the chimp would clean under the fingernails on that hand. He was told not to get close to the chimp. Unfortunately, as is often the case when people don't listen, he paid for it. One night the chimp cleaned the fingernails on the man's first hand and then bit off the index finger on his second hand.

I once lost focus while trying to observe how a female tiger cared for her newborn cubs. I backed too close to a leopard cage and ended up with a leopard attached to my left side with the claws of one paw. A nearby keeper grabbed me, and a tug-of-war ensued which kept the leopard from digging the claws of his other paw in and pulling me within range of his mouth. Animal bites and claw wounds heal slowly and almost always get infected. My scars are still visible.

In Columbus we kept a bite book. Half of it was for injuries suffered by the public. For example, there was the time when a drunk climbed over the guardrail and tried to pet a black leopard (with very bad results). The other half of the book was for bites and injuries to zoo keepers.

The king of the bite book was a keeper named Jim, a tall lean former basketball player. Every other entry seemed to have Jim's name on it. Every species he worked with seemed to bite him. When Lou Pistoia talked to Jim about coming to work in the reptile house, I felt compelled to call him in for a serious Dutch Uncle talk. I pointed out that Lou had the largest collection of poisonous snakes in the world and his probable life span in the reptile department would be less than two months. Jim said that Mr. Pistoia had assured him that he wouldn't have to work with any poisonous snakes until he was well trained and ready to do so and that he really wanted to become a herpetologist. Jim was probably the mildest, most polite keeper at the zoo. No one had ever heard him even utter a swear word, and he was so shy and bashful around girls that we were quite sure he had never had a date. With one exception—the time the reptile keepers set him up so a three-foot black caiman grabbed his hand—Jim escaped getting bit and didn't die.

In about two-and-a-half years he became a very good herpetologist and applied for a curator's position in a small southern zoo. Jim had agreed to start work right after Christmas. The director asked him if he would like to come over to their house for Christmas dinner. He arrived in his suit and tie, carrying a bouquet of flowers for the director's wife. When the door opened he got the shock of his life. While the zoo world generally knew that the director and his family were reputed to be nudists, we didn't know for sure, and none of us had thought to warn Jim. When the door opened there stood a stark-naked zoo director who promptly grabbed Jim by the arm, welcomed him and drug him inside. He was introduced to the director's wife and two teenage daughters who were also stark naked.

Jim came back to Columbus for New Year's, and over a number of beers at the Wyandotte Inn told us how difficult it had been to hand a bouquet of flowers to a naked wife and eat Christmas dinner sitting across the table from two naked teenage girls.

He did, however, turn out to be a good reptile curator.

OKLAHOMA CITY ZOO JOB

In 1965 the director's position at the Oklahoma City Zoo came open. By then I had realized that Columbus was a great training ground but not a place where you could spend the rest of your career and accomplish much, unless, of course, there was a dramatic change in management. The politics were just too fierce and corrupt.

I applied for the Oklahoma City job, was shortlisted and went in for an interview. It seemed like a near-perfect match since my parents and Marie's parents both lived within 35 miles of the zoo. I had done my undergraduate work at Central State in Edmond and had gone to vet school at Oklahoma State, 75 miles away. I was pretty much regarded as a hometown boy. The Oklahoma City Zoo and its reptile house had been my first zoo, and I had connections.

The daylong meetings and interviews with the zoological society, staff, mayor and city manager all seemed to go well—so well, in fact, that as we got ready for the last interview of the day the president of the Oklahoma Zoological Society was settling on a salary and making arrangements for movers to transport our furniture. It was technically a city job but the society had a great deal to say about running the zoo. He said that this was a small group, and it would be a short interview. As we came into the room I noticed that it was a different kind of group, considerably older and with a lot of gray hair. After the introductions and comments by the society president about how well things had gone and the fact that I had accepted the job, a blue-haired lady at the end of the table said, "Well, Lee, tell us about your politics."

I didn't quite understand what she was asking but finally figured out that she wanted to know what political party I belonged to. Having been subjected to two-and-a-half years of Columbus, Ohio's politics I had developed strong negative feelings about politics and politicians. It probably didn't help that for two years I had been lucky enough to be in a position to ignore politicians. With a professional appointment, it was hard for me to be fired. I stood up got on my soap box and politely but firmly informed them in no uncertain terms that in my opinion politics and politicians had no place in a zoo unless they paid their admission, obeyed the rules and stayed on the sidewalk. It got very quiet in the room. The board president looked like he was going to have a heart attack, and then the next questions were about my family, a few trivia questions and the interview was over. The instant we got out the door the society president began to profusely apologize for not having briefed me in advance. These were the political heavyweights who actually ran things behind the scenes. All I would've had to do was smile, say I was an independent, that I didn't really pay much attention to politics and everything would've been fine. He had just assumed that since I had spent so much time in Oklahoma I would have instinctively known who these people were. He hadn't counted on the fact that politically I was still a country boy. He apologized profusely all the way back to the hotel but the interview was over and he knew, so was the job. While it was a disappointment to go from making moving plans to returning home empty-handed, again fate had stepped in.

Subsequent history for zoo directors in Oklahoma City proved that not getting the job was one of the best things that could have happened. It also was a very useful lesson on doing your homework and knowing when to keep your mouth shut.

OMAHA ZOO

In September 1966, while attending a zoo conference in Washington D.C., Warren Thomas, the director of the Henry Doorly Zoo in Omaha, Nebraska, approached me. I knew Warren from his time at the Oklahoma City Zoo, before he had moved to Omaha in 1965. He asked if I would be interested in a staff veterinarian position in Omaha. Since I had decided that politics would impede significant progress in Columbus, I was interested. Plus, moving to Omaha would put Marie, young Lee, and me much closer to our parents in Oklahoma. Warren Thomas had already developed a reputation of not staying hooked very long in one place, and I sensed a potential opportunity to become a director, so I agreed to come out and look at the zoo.

On October 1, Marie and I drove into Omaha after a short stop in Avoca,

Iowa, to talk with a highway patrolman (his idea, not mine). The zoo in Omaha was in a very pretty park with an old 1920s and WPA-era municipal menagerie. Plus, the construction of a "new" zoo was underway. The red barn and bear grottoes were completed, and the gorilla and orang buildings were nearly complete. An old open-air picnic pavilion had been closed in and converted into offices, and a large open space—which we later used as a museum—later still as a reptile exhibit and finally as our first aquarium. We learned about future plans for the zoo, met with a couple of board members, and ultimately decided that it would be a good move. I agreed to start in Omaha on December 1. We then spent two days looking at houses in the Westside School District before settling on a small house 10 miles west of the zoo at 10315 Wright Street (we still live there today). We then headed back to Columbus, stopping briefly to talk to that same highway patrolman—I am a slow learner—where I submitted my resignation at the zoo. We later wondered if that highway patrolman might have been an overlooked omen.

I made arrangements to get paid for my accumulated compensatory time, vacation time and retirement, which would take three months to receive. Over the next two months I put things in order at the zoo and made provisions for veterinary care to bridge the gap until the folks in Columbus could hire someone new.

We arrived in Omaha on December 1 to close on the house. We made a hefty down payment with money we had temporarily borrowed from Marie's parents until Columbus paid us for time owed and retirement. Two days later we drove to Oklahoma City for an exotic animal pathology conference, returning a few days later with a used gas anesthesia machine in a small trailer. On December 8 Warren Thomas called me into his office and said he was leaving the next day on an expedition to the Amazon River in Peru and I would be in charge of the zoo for two months. This was a surprise since no mention had been made of a pending trip.

At that time the zoo had 10 employees and a budget of $100,000 per year.

About three days later a group of five sober-looking men in suits and ties showed up at the zoo looking for Thomas. They seemed surprised to see me and even more surprised when I told them that he was in Peru. They asked who I was and what my duties were and how long I had been in Omaha. I introduced myself and answered their questions and they went away. I was a bit puzzled because they had not introduced themselves, but I guess I was still a somewhat naïve country boy. Later I found out that they were the executive committee of the zoo board. Years later, I would learn that they had come to the zoo that day to fire Warren Thomas. I should have suspected something when they had asked me how much I was being paid. They came back two more times in coming years with the same intent, each time finding Thomas out of the country, until President Ben Morris showed up unexpectedly on March 3, 1970, and I was suddenly acting director. Mr. Morris and three of the board later took me aside, and Ben, in his usual gruff ex-Marine fashion, said, "Look boy—we want you to succeed, so whatever you do, balance the damn budget, and we'll probably let you do any damn thing you want. I'm not going to tell you how to run the zoo but if you need help, all you have to do is ask." Happily that's pretty much the way it turned out.

FIRST YEAR AS DIRECTOR

The Henry Doorly Zoo in those days consisted of two sections. The first was the old Riverview Park facilities, including an 1899 round rock bear pit divided into two cages, three WPA-era large cat cages, six 1920s-era chain link cages and the old monkey house, plus two Behlen corn crib cages for small monkeys. A five-room, two-story, red granite park caretaker's house had been built in 1900. The second part consisted of a Museum with the Elgin Gates Collection of Heads and Horns, the offices, the new red barn area, the new bear grottos, small mammal house and the gorilla and orang houses plus some minimal hoofed stock pens. Including me and the secretary there were 14 employees and a budget of $350,000. It turned out that there was also a substantial amount of debt owed to International Animal Exchange for animals that the board hadn't known about.

I sat down with secretary Jan Thompson and looked at the 1970 budget plus the income and expenses from the previous year. Jan handled many zoo responsibilities and was someone to trust. Given my instructions to "balance the damn budget," we were very cautious about the expenditures in the beginning. By summer it became apparent that the budget was doing well. None of the keeper staff had been given a raise in three years, so we gave them one and bought three unbudgeted pieces of equipment. When I reported this at a monthly board meeting, Mr. Johnny Becker, our previous board president and managing partner of Pete Marwick and Mitchell Accounting, raised an objection and said, "He can't do this; we can't afford it." Ben Morris quietly raised his hand and said, "Mr. Becker I'm not going to tell Lee how to run the zoo. If, at the end of the year the books don't balance, it's his ass."

I guess you never quite get over being a Marine.

I'll admit: it was an interesting experience having the head of a big six accounting firm tell us we couldn't afford to do something and my board president telling the rest of the board that my job was on the line if the books didn't balance at the end of the year, but I was pretty sure of the numbers and of our economic trend.

There are some days you remember for the rest of your life. One of these came at a board meeting the following January when we passed our audit out to the board members. Our numbers showed that we had finished the year in the black for the first time in the history of the zoo and had a surplus of $40,000 in the bank. Everybody seemed happy except Johnny Becker, who again raised his hand and said, "Wait a minute, this can't be. There is something wrong here."

Ben Morris reminded him that it was his firm that had done the audit. Looking at me, he said, "Dr. Simmons, would you like to explain these numbers to Mr. Becker?"

Ben had a Cheshire cat-grin on his face and leaned back with his hands folded over his stomach. I stood up and said, "Mr. Becker, do you remember when I took over as director I asked for an interim audit (I had gotten some good advice) and said that I would be responsible for everything after that line in the sand and that the board was responsible for everything that had happened before that line? Well I'm willing to be responsible for everything that has happened after March 3 last year." I stood there watching comprehension slowly sweep across Mr. Becker's face and glancing at Ben. I thought his face was going to break, his grin was so wide. No one said anything more.

Another one of those days to remember occurred three board presidents later after an annual meeting when our newly elected president asked me if I could come to lunch. So I met George Mazanec, who was with Northern Natural Gas, at the Omaha Club. George ordered a drink and I did likewise and then he said, "Dr. Simmons, I've been watching the way things work on this board and we're going to make some changes." In the back of my mind I was thinking, "Holy smokes, what's going to happen now? Did I misjudge this guy?" Then he told me that the zoo board president was no longer going to co-sign all those small checks. If a purchase cost less than $10,000 (unless it might get us into trouble) he didn't need to know about it. And if he didn't need to know about it, no one else needed to know about it until they saw it on our financials. I remember thinking, "Wow, there is a God, and he lives in Omaha." Up until then, some board presidents had been used to examining and sometimes arguing about purchases as small as $5. Mazanec also agreed that four board meetings a year were enough. This set a precedent that, happily, was never reversed. Ben Morris and George Mazanec became two of my heroes for life.

For more than 50 years, Marie and I have had an interesting and great ride in Omaha.

OMAHA ANIMAL STORIES

In those days, restrooms for both staff and the public played a large part in our winter quarters management scheme at the Henry Doorly Zoo. The restrooms were heated, had running water, drains in the floor and could be easily cleaned, so many animals wintered in them. This worked since we were only open seven months of the year and had no need for public restrooms during the five months we were closed. For years, flamingos wintered in the women's public restrooms and alligators wintered in the men's public restrooms. Even the staff restrooms in the administration building were frequently put to use. One winter we had a very friendly young pair of mountain lion cubs start the winter in the women's restroom, but about two thirds of the way toward spring Jan Thompson, who in today's world would be called an executive administrative assistant because she kept the zoo operation glued together, said we had to switch them to the men's room because the wear and tear on nylons was just too expensive. They had grown rapidly and had become aggressively playful. Imagine sitting on the toilet when suddenly two pairs of clawed paws came snaking into the stall from different directions at your ankles.

One incident comes to mind involving a zebra duiker, perhaps the rarest of all duikers, wintering in the public restrooms connected to the administration building. One of our night watchmen was an old ex-packinghouse worker who spoke broken English and could barely say the animals' names but had that rarest of all innate abilities: the ability to observe, remember, and understand an animal's behaviors. In situations where the area keeper might have reported an animal dead or seriously ill at 7:00 a.m., he would call you up at midnight and say, "Doc you better come! That red thing or that black-and-white thing or that animal down in such-and-such building isn't acting right. You better come."

We quickly learned to heed his warnings. About two o'clock one winter morning, the phone rang, and when I answered he said, "Doc you'd better come. That little striped animal in the restrooms isn't right." I asked him what was wrong, and he said, "I don't know, but that animal always moves to a new spot twice by this time, and he hasn't moved. You'd better come."

I drove to the zoo, and we looked at the duiker through the door. He was curled up in a normal sleeping position. I could see his respiration but couldn't detect anything wrong. I whistled, tapped on the door and spoke loudly to wake him up without startling him. He didn't move so we quietly opened the door and walked softly up to him and touched him on the rump and he still didn't move. I then grabbed his head in case he woke up and took flight, and I could feel that he was rigidly frozen in a sleeping position. We lifted him out and rolled him over. Our examination revealed nothing except that he was unconscious and rigid. A more careful exam revealed a small red bite wound with two puncture marks on his neck. We pulled back all of the hay from around his sleeping site, leaving only a round bowl-shaped mound where he had been. As we slowly dismantled the mound we saw a black widow spider. Needless to say, a black widow spider bite on a 7-pound antelope does not have a good prognosis. Pathology confirmed the diagnosis.

Some people can develop the ability to see through long years of experience and some people are luckily born with it. This individual had no animal experience prior to coming to the zoo, and we had hired him primarily out of desperation. A night watchman was not a sought-after job, but he got us out of bed at night to deal with animal problems more often than all of the other night men put together in my career.

BIG BEN

Another of our Omaha characters was Big Ben, a Clydesdale gelding from the Budweiser hitch. We had acquired Big Ben in a trade with August Bush of Grants Farm in St. Louis. He wanted black squirrels so we trapped and traded 6 black fox squirrels for a Clydesdale. Pound for pound a bit lopsided but everyone was happy. Every morning he met the first visitors at the front gate and escorted them down into the zoo. He let the kids hang on his legs and crawl on top of him and do whatever they wanted. You could actually see him slide his feet across the ground when kids were nearby to avoid stepping on them. He never hurt a soul except an Air Force colonel who admitted to teasing him. Big Ben bit him. Ingrid Schmidt, one of our supervisors, used to ride him through the zoo on morning rounds. I tried it once, but he was too wide for me without a saddle.

LEROY AND THE GRIZZLIES

One morning while I was on my zoo rounds I pulled up in front of the grizzly bear exhibits in a little ragtop Jeep. We had two very aggressive older female grizzlies and a young 800-pound Stone Mountain male. Even though he was twice their size, the old sows ruled the roost. To my complete astonishment Leroy, the supervisor of the area, was in with the three grizzlies. The activity was

PHOTO COURTESY OF THE *OMAHA WORLD-HERALD*.

Big Ben—always a hit with kids.

fierce. The two females were frothing at the mouth with jaws popping like machine guns, making short charges at Leroy. Leroy would meet them halfway with an aluminum scoop shovel, banging heads right and left. Big John the male was standing up on his hind legs backed into a corner wanting nothing to do with the situation. The profanity coming out of the exhibit exceeded anything I had ever heard. Leroy was a large man, probably incapable of jumping the 10-foot-wide moat, and all I had with me was a single shot Stevens Favorite .22 rifle. Killing one, never mind two, angry grizzlies with a .22 was probably nearly impossible. If they got him down I planned to try for eye shots to penetrate those thick skulls. I popped extra .22 shells into my mouth where they would be handy and kept my rifle down out of sight so he couldn't see it for fear he would realize how much trouble he was in and try to run. I sat and watched Leroy meet every charge head on with his shovel, ultimately driving all three bears into the den. He then pulled the door shut and stuck the handle of his scoop through the bars to temporarily lock it.

I entered the den area and told Leroy how much danger he had been in. In those days, of our 14 employees, only four of us had prior zoo experience. The rest of the crew had come directly off the streets of Omaha. Leroy had little animal experience or knowledge but had figured out that the small sun bears and polar bear cubs were the easiest of the four bear exhibits to clean. He assigned the grizzlies and black bears to his two keepers. His keepers had called in sick that day with hangovers, and the whole area was his responsibility. He had never cleaned the grizzly exhibit but was used to going in with the small bears and shoving them around with the aluminum scoop shovel. He was simply treating the grizzlies the same as he did polar bear cubs and had no idea of the danger.

I put the rifle away and went down to the concession stand to get a cup of coffee. Once the adrenaline wore off I started shaking so bad that I couldn't get the cup to my mouth. I had to bend down and slurp a couple of drinks with the cup still on the counter.

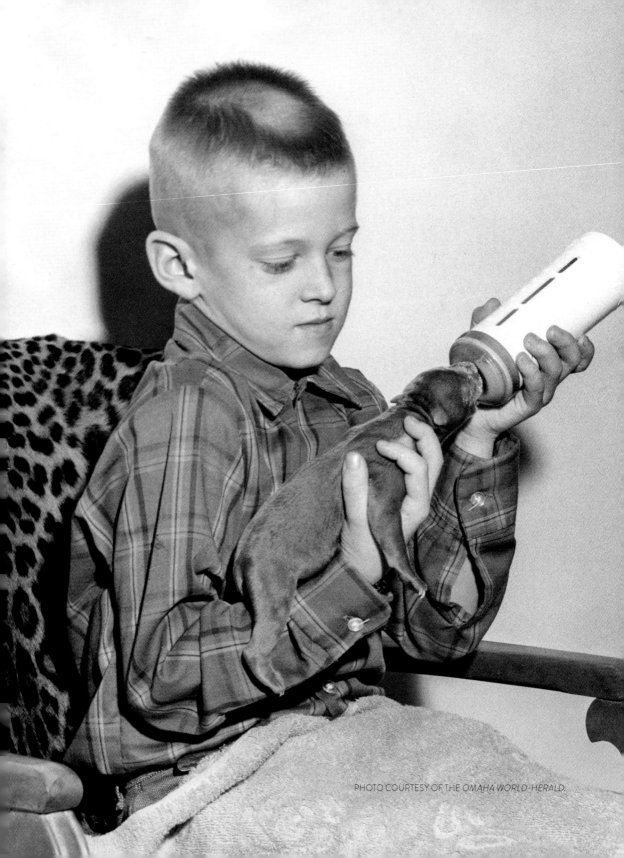

THE SEWER GRIZZLY

The two female grizzly bears were too old to get pregnant, but one did and produced a cub. Shortly after birth, the cub managed to fall down the floor drain in the den. The bears had previously ripped the drain cover off. We knew there was something wrong because we could hear the baby's howls as if they were coming out of a trumpet when he should have been snuggled up against his mother nursing. We separated the mother into a different den and looked down the drain with flashlights but couldn't see him. We didn't know how far down the cub was. This was long before fiber optic video cameras, but I finally had an idea. I called Marie at home and had her bring my shop vacuum with a long hose to the zoo. We hooked up the vacuum, turned it on, and

Facing page: Young Lee, feeding the sewer grizzly.

Right: The sewer grizzly became a regular member of the Simmons family. Marie even bathed him in our kitchen sink with our daughter Heather watching.

PHOTO COURTESY OF THE DURHAM MUSEUM.

fed the hose down the drain. At about 10 feet the pitch of the motor changed, and we quickly pulled the hose out. There was the eight-ounce cub stuck by the nose to the small end of the vacuum hose. We turned off the motor and took him home to an incubator where he stayed until he outgrew our house. This happened quickly because bear cubs double their weight weekly.

FU MANCHU

One of the more notable animal characters in my career was a Sumatran orangutan named Fu Manchu, who became a nationally famous escape artist. He

Fu Manchu, below, and Heavy Lamar, facing page.

came to Omaha in 1966 from an animal dealer in Louisiana. From the moment he arrived, it was clear he was very intelligent, curious, and sociable and friendly toward people.

He first escaped the old monkey house. He was in a chain-link enclosure and simply unbent the crimps at the top and bottom of a spiral of chain-link wire and unscrewed it to allow the opposing sides to fall back. Fu then went down the aisle, twisted off the all the padlocks, and let the other orangs loose.

Luckily, most of the other orangs were young and easy-going, except Tondalayo, a nine-year-old female who could be a handful. We put everybody

back in the rewired enclosure and shortly thereafter moved the orangs to the new building. The padlocks in our new building posed a major problem because the throw bolts locking the doors and exhibits were all exposed to the orangs. Fu simply popped the padlocks and let everybody loose. He never ventured far. He just waited outside the building until someone came to see what the trouble was. Then he'd put out his hand to lead you back into the enclosure or the exhibit. The other young orangs, of course, were all over the zoo. We bought bigger, heavier padlocks—to no avail. We then welded stainless steel plates on the doors to shield the padlocks, a tactic which worked for a while.

Fu then started a series of escapes that drove us nearly crazy. He continued twisting off padlocks. Padlocks are expensive, and sooner or later an orang was going to get in trouble mingling with our zoo visitors. The last straw came when Fu let Dennis the Menace in to the boiler room. Dennis had come to Omaha from the National Zoo in Washington, D.C., where he had escaped and destroyed a lot of equipment and microscopes in their hospital lab. Hence the name, Dennis the Menace. He was young, rambunctious, and innovative. Dennis simply pulled down all of the small pneumatic control tubing in the boiler room and rolled it up into a big copper ball. The Honeywell people took a month to fix it and charged us a fortune. We knew we had to do something. It was obvious that Fu was getting out through the door from the moat into the furnace room. That door had no handle on the outside and only a key would open it. We finally set up a blind and had people watching while Fu was in the outside exhibit. Jerry Stones finally solved the mystery when he saw Fu take a piece of wire out of his mouth, then bend it 90 degrees on each end. He inserted it in the space between the door and jamb and rotated it to push the bolt back and open the door. The lock did not have a secondary safety bolt to prevent the main bolt from being pushed back. The question was: where was this intelligent toolmaker getting the wire? We searched and could not find the answer. Another blind and hours of watching eventually answered the question.

We had acquired an old female nicknamed Heavy Lamar. She was horribly obese. We had her in a back enclosure since with her appetite she wasn't trustworthy to be with the large group and lots of food. We had her on a 1,200-calorie diet, which she hated. Heavy was breaking off pieces of wire from a light cage. Then, lying on her side, she would extend her arm into a small transfer chute, holding the piece of wire. Fu would do the same thing from the front exhibit with a handful of monkey biscuits. The trade would be made. Our mystery was solved.

From then on we searched Fu's mouth each time before he went outside. In retrospect, his willingness to be searched and give up his wire was amazing. We also changed the door lock.

This kind of intimate animal contact and management was just our standard operating procedure in those days.

Orangs in general, and Fu in particular, are natural born mechanical engineers. They are so intelligent that they usually refuse to participate in testing programs. It's common to use a puzzle to measure intelligence in chimps, gorillas and other primates, but orangs usually won't actively participate. They'll sit back and look at the puzzle, and when you've gone home and can't see them, they'll solve the puzzle. Fu was particularly adept at solving mechanical problems. In those days we worked in with a lot of animals—that is worked in close contact—that most zoo people would not work with today. If we were in the exhibit fixing something Fu would be looking over your shoulder, stealing tools out of your pockets and attempting to undo what you were doing. He knew exactly how to adjust a crescent wrench, use a pair of pliers or even a screwdriver. He usually concentrated on the door hinges or the lock mechanism. In those days the laminated windows in our exhibits had a thin coating of gold on the inside, which was electrified. We had a 10,000-volt weed-cutting fence charger hooked up to it. Fu's favorite stunt was to roll up a big ball of orang feces, stick it against the stainless-steel frame and then roll it over to short the glass out. The other orangs could then finger paint the window. Fu didn't finger paint but just made it possible for everyone else to do so.

Once we were examining a young orang with a snotty nose when Saul Kitchener, our primate curator, lost his balance, put his hand out and touched the glass and was promptly knocked to the floor. He was laying there making interesting noises while we laughed. Fu approached, carefully examined him, then helped him to his feet and took Saul's right index finger in both hands. He led Saul over to the window and swiped his finger along the bare strip between the gold plating and the stainless-steel frame. It was if he was saying, "See dummy, if you touch it there it won't shock you."

On another occasion, five or six of us were carrying a young, uncooperative orang out of the exhibit for treatment. Fu was doing his usual thing, exploring our pockets. He pulled Jerry Stone's mace canister out of its pouch. We were in a small vestibule between the exhibit and the kitchen when Jerry started shouting, "Fu, no no, no!" Fu maced the daylights out of all of us and himself and then threw the canister down and went back into the exhibit.

When it was time to immobilize everyone for annual physicals, Fu would grab an old tire or even a young orang and hold it over his rump where he knew we wanted to shoot him with the dart. When we finally managed to make the shot, Fu would pull out the dart and hand it back to us. Then he'd wait by the door until the drug took effect.

Fu's last big Omaha escape came when he dismantled a climbing apparatus we had built in the outside exhibit and made himself a ladder to the top of the building. He methodically tore all of the flashing off the parapet wall. When I came up, I made the mistake of saying, "All right Fu, what are you going to do now?" Fu calmly went over, ripped off a 200-pound chimney and threw it down. We put up a ladder, Fu climbed down, offered his hand and we went inside.

By this time Fu weighed more than 250 pounds. We had gotten some large government surplus parkas and given them to all of the staff. They were big but warm and the price was right. Fu's favorite pastime was to lift up the back of your parka, slide up inside it with his arms in the sleeves beside yours and then look over your shoulder and grab your wrists like a puppet. He would make you pat your head, rub your belly and slap yourself in the face. It was an interesting feeling to have an intelligent animal having so much fun at your expense. Even though Fu had never hurt a soul, even three times rescuing keepers being attacked by other orangs, we decided it was time to stop working in with him.

We had made a decision to concentrate our breeding program on Bornean orangs, and since Fu was Sumatran we sent him to Brownsville, Texas, to be with his favorite keeper, Jerry Stones, and six females. He died old and happy with 20 additional offspring.

BRIGGS: A DESTRUCTION MACHINE

When we decided to switch to only breeding Bornean orangutans we found ourselves in need of a breeding age male. In the hospitality suite at a zoo and aquarium conference one night I announced to everyone present, "Does anyone have a breeding age male Bornean orang they could loan us?"

Almost immediately, Jim Doherty from the Bronx Zoo stepped up and said they had a breeding age male named Briggs who was surplus and would be glad to loan him to Omaha. I inquired about age and health and the usual things, and then Jim laid out their requirements. We would pay for shipping and for a veterinarian to accompany the animal to Omaha to make sure that he was safe while en route. This cost more than I had anticipated, and so I said we really didn't have the money (nor see the need) to pay for a round-trip plus hotel accommodations while in Omaha. Jim immediately told me not to worry and they would take care of that expense. One problem still persisted: the only crate they had was a large, heavy one, thus they would have to airfreight the animal to Chicago and rent a truck and drive it to Omaha. Again, I pointed out that such an expense was more than we could handle. Jim again told me not to worry, the Bronx Zoo would pay for all the shipping expenses. Somehow it failed to occur to me that Jim was entirely too eager to pay for all of the expenses of getting Briggs to Omaha. I guess I felt that the Bronx Zoo, being a very large and wealthy zoo, was just being very generous.

When Briggs arrived in Omaha we were astounded by the size of the crate and the fact that the pipe bars were three inches in diameter. Still, I didn't trip to the fact that there might be something amiss. Only later did we find out that Briggs was probably the most destructive orang anybody had ever known. Orangs by their very nature and intelligence can be quite destructive because they think, plot, plan and are good at taking things apart. These traits in an animal that weighed more than 300 pounds and had fingers the size of big sausages made for an awesome destructive machine.

It turned out that the Bronx had built a whole new exhibit for their orangs and for Briggs that had an elevated grate floor which gave the illusion that the orangs were off the ground and in the tree tops. They had furnished it with indestructible steel plants and furniture so Briggs would no longer be displayed in an exhibit with four bare walls. Briggs methodically destroyed all of these supposedly indestructible furnishings until he was again in four bare walls, sitting on a steel grating above a keeper space. One day while eating a bunch of grapes, one grape fell down through the grate. When Briggs had finished the rest of the grapes he calmly found a weak seam in the grating, peeled it up, went down into the keeper space, picked up his grape and went back up into the exhibit. While he was down below the only thing between Briggs and the outside world was an unlocked man door.

Our zoo convention came shortly after this incident where I famously asked if anyone could loan us an orang. Briggs made our lives interesting. While our exhibit was orang proof, it wasn't Briggs proof. One day while Dr. Lindsay Phillips and I were immobilizing some Oryx, a keeper ran up and told us that Briggs had torn the door off one of the bedroom enclosures behind the scenes. Lindsay and

I had our capture guns and bags with us, so we rushed up to the orang house where we heard a terrible banging coming from the back aisle. The keeper in charge of the building was nowhere to be found. Another keeper told us that Marty Stumbaugh had been in the back when Briggs tore the door off. We didn't know whether Marty was dead, injured or what.

Lindsay and I loaded up our dart guns. He went around to the far end of the back aisle while I stationed myself at the near door. We planned for a keeper to call out "1-2-3," over the radio and on the count of three a keeper at each end of the aisle would jerk their door open and Lindsay or I would make the shot and immobilize Briggs. The last thing I said to Lindsay before we started the procedure was, "Let's try not to shoot each other with a dart full of Sernylan."

They counted "1-2-3," and the doors opened. There was Marty calmly watching Briggs with a heavy steel door from between two enclosures in his right hand trying to pound his way out through into the back aisle. Thankfully he was still safely contained. This incident led us to reinforce the weak spots in our exhibits and holding areas. Briggs made good Christians out of all of us since every time we were about to open a door to the back aisle we'd say a little prayer that he was still inside and contained. The moral of this story is never trade or acquire animals when you've had more than one drink, even with a friend like Jim Doherty. Briggs was however a very enthusiastic breeder.

TONDALAYO

Another famous orang in Omaha was a female named Tondalayo. Even though she had chewed up three zookeepers she was easy to handle and produced a number of offspring. We had made arrangements with the radiology department at Omaha's Clarkson Hospital for x-rays and ultrasounds, and we could bring immobilized animals to the basement garage where they would bring a machine down and do the work up. We would take Tondalayo by the hand and lead her out, put her in the passenger seat of my little Jeep and drive her to the hospital. She enjoyed the sightseeing and scenery, and we enjoyed the reactions from other drivers as we pulled up beside them. When we got to the hospital we would simply take her by the hand, lead her into the garage and have her lay down to be x-rayed. As long as you had her by the hand and were indicating to her that you wanted her to cooperate she was amenable to almost anything. She'd even put her arm through the bars of the gate and allow you to draw blood.

WOLF AND THE HOOF TRIM

Wolf, our first male gaur, a rare species of wild cattle from Southeast Asia, was a magnificent animal who stood nearly 7 feet tall at the shoulder. He was

Dr. Bill Russell proved my attempt at a practical joke to be an effective way to complete a hoof trim.

easy going but still a very large wild caught bull. His diet, which may have been a little too rich, coupled with captivity caused his front hooves to get a little too long. When Dr. Bill Russell, a new veterinarian, came on board, I mentioned that sometime in the near future we would probably have to trim Wolf's toes. We had named him Wolf because he had the habit of putting his nose in the air and howling like a wolf, a very un-cow-like activity. Immobilizing a large ruminant for any length of time is always a matter of concern, and when Bill mentioned this I said that we could probably do the job without immobilizing him. I told him that he could just put a pile of chopped apples and carrots on the edge of the moat and when Wolf came up to eat, he could just stand down in the moat and nibble away at his toes with the hoof trimming shears until the job was done. He looked skeptical, as he well should have, because I was just pulling his leg and having a little fun. We had never done anything like that with a wild hoofed animal.

About two weeks later I was making rounds when I came up to Pachyderm Hill, and there was Wolf standing at the edge of the moat eating cut up apples and carrots. Bill Russell squatted on the edge of the moat, slicing off small bits of his overgrown toes with the shears. At one point Bill took a bite of the hoof that was too big and tough, and Wolf held his foot up as if to help so that Bill could put full force on the sheer handles. I was totally dumbstruck. Luckily, I had my camera with me, so the procedure is documented on film.

When I walked up to the outer edge of the moat Bill said, "This actually works pretty well."

I just smiled and said, "I told you so."

Sometimes serendipity works, but I've often wondered whether Bill was just trying to pull my leg and Wolf fouled things up by cooperating.

ELEPHANTS IN THE PICNIC PAVILLION

Early on in Omaha we converted an old open-air picnic pavilion into a building by putting up plywood sides and a plywood ceiling. Using old telephone poles and bridge planks from the Union Pacific Railroad we built corrals for our three-year-old female elephant, an Indian rhino and a pair of white rhinos. A couple years later the Hunts had a semi-trailer loaded with 17 young elephants heading across country when one of the elephants went down. They called, and we agreed to do what we could.

By the time they arrived in Omaha the animal was dead in the front of the truck. We unloaded the other 16 elephants into the building. We now had 17 elephants and 3 rhinos in the Pavilion, and it was standing room only. After performing a necropsy on the dead elephant we examined the others to make sure they were healthy. Then we loaded 14 back on the truck. We kept a young male for Omaha and held a young female for the zoo in Madison, Wisconsin. As the elephants grew and developed tusks, keeping the corrals intact became difficult. It seemed like every night they ate their way out, and every morning we had repair work to do. We finally put up hot wires so they couldn't use their short tusks to splinter the bridge planks.

One morning after discovering they had dismantled part of the corral, Jerry Stones, our senior supervisor, said he thought the fence charger had shorted out. I was wearing crêpe-soled hush puppies and buzzed the wire with my finger. I could feel a faint tingle. I told Jerry the charger was okay and they had simply found a way around the wire. He tentatively buzzed the wire with his finger and didn't feel anything. He failed to realize was that he was wearing rubber boots, which provided too much insulation. I told him to try touching the wire with one hand on the ground and before he could think, he did just that. He made one of the most incredible sounds I've ever heard a human being make and curled backward in a complete circle before falling over on the ground. I'm not sure he ever totally forgave me for that.

UPSIDE DOWN HUMMINGBIRDS

Shortly after I became director in Omaha we developed a hummingbird exhibit in the small mammal building. Our husbandry knowledge, limited as it was, was actually quite good since we had hummingbirds who lived for as long as seven years in the exhibit. One winter morning, just after I came in, the supervisor of the area rushed down the hill with her hand inside her shirt underneath her parka and said we had a sick hummingbird. Even today a sick hummingbird is pretty much a lost cause because they are so small, their metabolism is so high and there is so little that we know about them. They are usually just found dead in the exhibit. In those days we had no hospital but kept a couple of small baby incubators hot in the office library. We put the hummingbird in an incubator. It was unable to fly or even stand, was upside down and obviously had CNS problems. We made up some sugar water and fed it every 10 minutes. Miraculously, after a while it was no longer ataxic, it could sit up, and finally it flew normally.

We fed it and watched it for a couple hours before deciding it must have banged its head. Then we sent it back to the exhibit. A week later we had a repeat performance with a different hummingbird, but the outcome was the same. This repeated itself a number of times. We examined diet, exhibit design and a number of other things. But the birds always recovered and seemed normal. Finally, early one morning the supervisor called me up to the exhibit and said, "Smell this." It was the hummingbird feeder, and when I sniffed it smelled like homebrew. Mystery solved. All of the incidents had occurred first thing in the morning on cold winter days when the building was kept very warm. Standard operating procedure was that just before the keepers left at the 4:30 p.m., they would refill the hummingbird feeders. In those days we didn't have the sophisticated commercial hummingbird diets available today. We mixed our own. The formula was a complex one and included sugar water, grape juice, orange juice, condensed milk, Gevral protein and vitamin powder. Last but not least was a generous handful of live mealworms. We put it all into a Waring blender and reduced it to a fine slurry, which we strained and fed to the hummingbirds. It was obviously a good formula since we did so well with hummingbirds. But if it had a flaw, it was certainly not sterile. Just before the night watchman turned out the lights at 7 p.m. the hummingbirds would tank up and go into estivation for the night. At about 7:30 the next morning the keepers would come back in, turn on the lights and then begin to mix up a fresh batch of hummingbird mix. In the meantime the hummingbirds would wake up and immediately go to the feeders filled the night before and tank up. All night long in the warm exhibit the hummingbird mix had been fermenting. If you wake up and drink as much homebrew as you can hold, you too would be immediately drunk. We changed our management so that the last feeding of the day was boiled sugar water in sterilized hummingbird feeders. Problem solved.

MALIKA THE ELEPHANT AND BLIND KIDS

In 1966 we had a three-year-old female African elephant named Malika who developed into probably the best elephant I have ever known. You could do almost anything with her, and for her entire 48 years on Earth she was completely trustworthy toward people.

As she grew into an adult we rode her and put our own children on her or anyone else who wanted to experience an elephant. She was so trustworthy that we regularly used her in a program for students from the Iowa School for the Blind. The students would get to "see" a number of animals with their hands such as large pythons, birds, rabbits and Malika. We would routinely take 30 or 40 blind kids and let them walk in with Malika in her sleeping quarters. Malika would move her feet carefully so as not to step on anybody. Her keepers would hold kids up who wanted to see her tongue and teeth by feeling around inside her mouth. We even put kids up on top of her to crawl around, and there was never an incident. This went on for a number of years until our insurance company got wind of it. Sadly, since that time none of the kids from the school have ever been able to "see an elephant."

Malika, pictured here with me, was incredibly popular with children.

ICHABOD AND MY FINGER

Shortly before Warren Thomas left for Brownsville, Texas, Omaha received a group of orangs from Malaysia, which were ultimately intended for Brownsville. One young male named Ichabod was one of the most aggressive orangs we had ever seen. He attacked other orangs and keepers. Sometime later, Jerry Stones was working with the group when Ichabod grabbed him and attacked his middle finger on the right-hand. The bite was severe enough that Jerry had to have the finger split down both sides and the bone scraped to get rid of an infection.

One day we were in the outside exhibit to examine a young orang when Ichabod cornered a new keeper while Jerry was up on a climbing apparatus to bring

PHOTO COURTESY OF THE DURHAM MUSEUM.

A young Malika— getting a foot trim.

down the young orang. Ichabod was in the process of closing to attack, so I went to rescue the keeper by threatening Ichabod with a post mall handle. Ichabod backed off while the keeper got out of the outdoor exhibit. That's when I made a tactical mistake. Rather than backing up holding my threatening position, I instinctively did a military about-face to walk off when Ichabod grabbed me by the ankles and flipped me upside down. He then grabbed me by the left leg and started working his way up my shin like it was an ear of corn until he was chewing on my knee. When he started biting into my knee I became afraid I would end up crippled. I grabbed him by the cheek pads with both hands and got him off of my knee. Then he wrapped himself around my left hand and proceeded to bite off the distal phalanx of my ring finger and generally chew up the hand.

The keepers came to my rescue, but being new and inexperienced they tried to beat him off with broomsticks. They were hitting me more than Ichabod. Jerry got down out of the tree and they grabbed Ichabod by the legs and me by the legs and just pulled us apart. A couple days later the mayor of Omaha received a letter from two little ladies who had witnessed the incident demanding that I be fired because I had used profanity during the attack. I don't remember using profanity, but I probably did. Ichabod chewed up and swallowed the piece of finger but spit out the fingernail.

Jerry Stones drove me to the emergency room at St. Joe's Hospital, just across the Interstate bridge from the zoo. A surgeon I had met before but whose name I can't recall was on duty. He was a large African-American and one of their top surgeons. He examined my ring finger and decided to give me a general anesthetic so he could properly debride and cleanup the wounds. I said "no" since I knew that if I was asleep and had no control over what happened, when I woke the ring finger would be completely gone back to the knuckle. The surgeon wasn't happy, but I told him that it was a foregone conclusion the bites would get infected and had to be left open. The end of the finger could only be partially closed so that it would drain properly. I told him I wanted him to block the arm and we would argue over every scrap of bone and tissue that he removed, or I would simply walk out and have Jerry take me to the Med Center where a board member was an orthopedic surgeon. He grudgingly relented, and it made for an interesting discussion during the repairs. When he finished, Jerry and I went back to the zoo and had an interesting discussion with Ichabod.

When I got home I screwed a hook into the ceiling above our bed so that I could sleep with the hand elevated above my heart. Otherwise every beat of the heart could be felt acutely. Even with heavy antibiotics, my hand became infected and over the next six weeks, a number of small bone chips worked their way out of the end of the finger. All of the bite wounds ultimately healed, and today I have a functional finger. Very few people notice the missing phalanx.

We ultimately shipped the orangs to Brownsville where Ichabod chewed up a number of keepers.

KING COBRAS AND GARTER SNAKES

Early on in Omaha we had converted the large open space of the old picnic pavilion into a museum for mounted heads, horns and animals from the Elgin Gates collection. A few years after I became director we decided to convert the center of the area into a reptile exhibit.

We put together a good collection of reptiles. The most impressive animal in the collection was a 15-foot-long king cobra who was very handsome. The snake was a good feeder with one unfortunate characteristic. Whenever he shed his skin he would not always shed his eye caps. This causes problems because the eye cap is, in effect, his cornea, and the unshed ones build up layer upon layer and become opaque so that the snake cannot see. In a poisonous snake this makes them very dangerous. Even an easygoing animal will become aggressive and strike blindly when he senses something he can't see.

Whenever the snake shed his skin we would soak him in his exhibit with water, hoping to cause the eye caps to shed. When that didn't work we brought him out on the floor and pinned his head to carefully remove the eye caps with thumb forceps. The king cobra is probably the deadliest of all snakes. Even though he was basically an easygoing animal, he didn't like being handled, and at 15-feet-long he could rear up high enough so that he was looking you in the eye and actually striking downward at you.

Every time we had to perform this procedure our adrenaline was up and there were knots in our stomachs.

Unfortunately, the cobra did not make old bones, and that was our fault. Near the end of a long winter two years later we ran out of other large native snakes to feed him. King cobras will generally only eat live snakes. We only had a few small nonpoisonous native snakes left and chose a local garter snake as his next meal since he had not eaten in over two months. The garter snake was not very large, but it would have to do until spring. We put the snake in and the cobra immediately struck it, killed and ate the garter snake. Then he rolled over and died within 30 minutes.

What we failed to realize was that garter snakes usually prey on toads, and toads have toxins in their skin glands that build up and accumulate in the snake's tissues. However, the toxins don't harm the garter snake. Even though this particular garter snake had not eaten a toad in more than a year since we had captured it, the toxins were apparently still there in high concentration. I called Lou Pistoia in Columbus and told him what had happened. He replied that it was totally to be expected. I told Lou I hadn't read that or heard about it from anyone. He said, "It's not published anywhere, but everybody knows it." Well, almost everybody.

Lou had solved a similar problem years ago. He was so protective and softhearted about snakes that he couldn't stand to feed even common snakes to another snake-eating snake. Instead he trained a young king cobra to eat shed snake skins that he had stuffed full of smelt, head to tail. In Lou's case, it worked pretty well.

SHARK ADVENTURES

When we started to design and build our first 70,000-gallon marine aquarium in the old museum space, we decided to loan all of the mounted specimens to Morel Hall at the University of Nebraska-Lincoln. We knew we wanted a shark exhibit. We struck an agreement with a well-known shark collector from the Florida Keys to collect brown sharks for us. As we got closer to our April 1984 opening date we kept in close contact with him. Everything seemed to be going all right, and then about three months from opening he quit responding to telephone calls and correspondence.

Panic set in, and after a month-and-a-half of trying to reach him I called a friend at Sea World in Orlando, Florida, who gave me his secretary's name. I called the secretary's number. An unfriendly male voice answered the phone and wanted to know who I was and why I was calling. After I explained our situation he explained that I had the right number but that she was not in. The man claimed to be her boyfriend and said that she no longer worked for our shark collector and that she didn't know how to reach him. After some considerable prodding and pleading he explained that our supplier was no longer in the country. Apparently, he had left just 20 minutes before a large group of federal agents had appeared and confiscated his boat, house and truck. The man explained that the collector likely wouldn't come back into the country for at least seven years. He also said that it was unrelated to income tax evasion.

It didn't take a lot of imagination to figure out that someone who operates boats out of the Florida Keys and who ships large boxes full of live sharks and sea water all around the U.S. and the world might have the opportunity to do something illegal.

This left us in a real bind. We were six weeks from opening with no possibilities of sharks for the exhibit. I again called a friend at Sea World in Florida, who said he too had heard the rumors but couldn't recommend anyone else to catch brown sharks for us. He offered to help us. If we would come down they would put together a crew to catch lemon sharks in the lagoon of their Florida Keys shark research station. He also said that they had shark shipping boxes and would help us arrange to truck our sharks to Omaha. We had no choice but to grab his offer and be thankful. I told him we didn't want bull sharks because they got too big and had an aggressive reputation. Our exhibit was relatively small, only 20,000 gallons on display in an hourglass configuration with 36,000 gallons in the whole system. Putting divers in with bull sharks would not be wise.

With the water in the exhibit conditioned and ready, our head aquarist and I flew to Miami two weeks before opening, arriving at the airport at midnight. By the time we had collected our gear, rented a car and found a motel it was 2 a.m. After checking in we realized that we had not had anything to eat, so we asked the desk clerk if there was any place nearby to grab a bite. He said that the only place close was just across the parking lot, and it happened to be the Miami Playboy club. I explained our situation to the maître d', and for the first and only time in either of our lives we went into a Playboy club. I had a nice steak, but all our aquarist wanted was a hot dog and some ice cream.

The next morning we drove to the research station to meet the Sea World crew. They had a long net that would be pulled out across half of the shallow lagoon, and then with all of us lined up reasonably close together, our bare toes looped through the bottom of the net and holding the top of the net at shoulder height, we would slowly walk forward to trap whatever was in that end of the lagoon and shove it up close to the shore. When a lemon shark of the right size charged into the net, someone would grab it by the tail and maneuver it into a large long hoop net to be transported to shore and placed in a shark transport box. The plan worked well. The only excitement occurred when a small sawfish tangled in our net. Thankfully nobody's ankles got lacerated. And we decided that since it would fit in a shark box, a sawfish in the exhibit would look good.

We had nearly filled our seven boxes when a large bull shark charged and rammed the net into a bag between my knees. He was thrashing about back and forth with his head—and more importantly his teeth—just behind my knees. My arms weren't long enough to grab him by the dorsal fin and push him back clear of my legs. This was my first encounter with sharks, and I was seriously afraid of becoming a soprano. Just then, one of the Sea World guys grabbed his tail and jerked him free. Naturally, the folks from Florida thought it was damn funny and not at all unusual if you work with sharks. I didn't quite see it that way. We caught our last lemon shark, helped load the truck and made sure all of the animals were doing well and drove to the airport. Our six lemon sharks and one sawfish arrived in good shape and we were able to open on time.

DDVP

Our shark story has a short companion story, which I'll share with you now. Around that time, it became apparent that all of our animals were heavily infested with a monogenetic (meaning no intermediate host was needed to reproduce and complete their life cycle) fluke, which was therefore difficult to control. Our colleagues at Sea World said that the shallow water lagoon was heavily infested, and all of the animals that came out of it had flukes. We decided that since most sharks don't tolerate copper our best bet was DDVP (Dichlorovos or Vapona), an organic phosphate insecticide.

We calculated a dosage based on the tank volume and watched as the flukes stood up at right angles to the skin and then dropped off. All of the lemon sharks did well, but unfortunately the poor sawfish had so many flukes that it looked like it was wearing a fur coat. It swam slowly through the water with blood seeping from each of the wounds where a fluke had fallen off, leaving a faint pink trail in its wake. It simply bled to death, and there was nothing we could do about it.

Strangely, while the organic phosphate had a short half-life, we noticed that for the next two weeks whenever a housefly would attempt to fly over the tank it would never make it across. It would drop dead on the top of the water. Each morning the tank would be covered with dead flies. After further investigation we found that DDVP broke down into secondary, tertiary and quaternary compounds, all of which were obviously still toxic to insects. At least we had been smart enough not to put any divers into the exhibit until we had progressively changed out substantial amounts of the water. We never found out if our shark supplier ever reentered the country.

We later learned through experimentation that lemon sharks will tolerate low levels of copper, which made it easy to prevent them from re-infecting.

A FLYING TIGER SHARK

More than eight years after our shark acquisition, we decided to build a 1.3 million-gallon, full-fledged marine aquarium. We did our homework and found a new shark supplier who, after a thorough background check, proved to have a clean record. We made arrangements for him to hold and quarantine our animals and treat them for parasites multiple times before shipment to Omaha. When it was time to bring the animals in we shipped polyethylene shark boxes, designed and rotary molded in Lincoln, Nebraska, to the Florida Keys. We flew down with a crew to supervise loading and transport. We had chartered a Flying Tigers DC-8 to fly the sharks from Key West to Omaha.

In addition to the brown sharks we had requested, our supplier had caught a small tiger shark, and since the animal had acclimated well and was feeding, we agreed to buy him. Equipping a transport box to keep animals that must swim constantly to maintain a constant flow of oxygenated water over their gills for survival is no small task. It required two circulation pumps per box, powered by heavy automotive batteries. One of the pumps was situated in front of the shark's mouth. We had a considerable number of spare batteries and spare pumps, just in case. We also had a number of oxygen bottles to keep the oxygen content of the water in the boxes high during transport.

The animals had been starved for three days prior to transport so their G.I. tracks would be empty. We caught the animals, transferred them to the transport boxes and trucked them to the Key West airport without incident. Using a forklift, we loaded them into the DC-8 and then topped off their water, three quarters of the way up the side of the boxes. We had enzymes, precipitating agents (just in case) and fine nets to skim the protein and foam that accumulated on the top of the water.

I told the pilot that we needed to take off with a long runway roll and a flat rotation to keep the plane as close to horizontal as possible. He seemed offended that I would deem to instruct him on how to fly his airplane, but his attitude changed when I explained that the shark boxes were full of saltwater and too much rotation during takeoff would put gallons of saltwater in the belly of his airplane which would be bad for the aluminum and wiring of the plane. He executed a long takeoff roll and climbed out with the airplane as level as possible. At two-thirds of the way to Omaha, everything was going smoothly. Then the young tiger shark vomited, fouling up his water supply. This was a surprise, especially considering it hadn't eaten in three days. We had a little reserve water on board but not enough. When we landed in Omaha we had spare water waiting for us, and we rushed him down on the apron and did a partial dump and fill, then rushed him to the zoo. He was the first one into the new exhibit but refused to swim.

For the next eight hours our aquarists took turns swimming him to keep water flowing over his gills until he finally revived. All of the brown sharks acclimated to the new 850,000-gallon system with minimal problems. For the next five years the Tiger shark was our most interesting shark. Most sharks have a black, dead, expressionless eye. The Tiger shark had a live eye with a lot of expression in it, and he seemed very curious. He liked watching divers in the water, and he'd even tilt sideways to see better. For the divers, this was a sometimes-unnerving experience, even though the never expressed any aggressive behavior.

Even a well-behaved Tiger shark—with a mouth as wide as your body—cannot be described as friendly.

A GRAND TOUR OF EUROPE

In December 1968 I had a subtotal gastrectomy to solve some of my ulcer problems. Two months later, in February 1969, I went to Europe to bring back a shipment of rare antelope from Bremen, Germany. Franz Van Den Brink had a USDA-approved quarantine station in a very large barge moored out in the River Bremen. I went first to Soest, Holland, where Franz had his headquarters and then on to see some of the European zoos. I had never been to Europe before, and the plan was to see as many European zoos as possible in about two weeks.

AMSTERDAM, ROTTERDAM AND ANTWERP

After touring Van Den Brink's large animal compound in Soest, Holland, and seeing an incredible number of exotic species, Franz's brother-in-law took me to see the Amsterdam Zoo one day and the Rotterdam Zoo the next, two large, extensive, well-run zoos. Then I borrowed Franz's Mercedes and drove to Antwerp, Belgium, to see the zoo there. Antwerp was a small zoo completely surrounded by the city and located next to the central train station. It had a very exotic collection of animals, many of which I had never seen, such as okapi, red river hogs, Congo buffalo and Eastern lowland gorillas, which were then billed as mountain gorillas. On the way back to Soest I got lost and ultimately picked up a young couple hitchhiking. In return, they gave me instructions to get back on the right track. I stopped at a small café with only seven tables where they spoke only Flemish. I tried to explain that I wanted something typically Belgian, and they managed to communicate "pork," so I nodded. Shortly afterward I was served Chinese sweet-and-sour pork. As I was finishing, the owner, who spoke English, came in and asked me how my meal was. I told him it was good, but I was a little curious how I ended up with Chinese sweet-and-sour pork in a Belgian Café. He asked the waitress, and her reply was, "That's what all the English eat."

Driving in Europe, particularly Germany, was great since there were no speed limits and Franz told me there were no limits on how fast I could drive his car. Only two cars passed me: one was another Mercedes and the other was a V-8 Maserati which zoomed past me like I was standing still even though I was doing 120 miles-per-hour. While in Europe I was also able to connect with two classmates, Jean Luther and Louie Birch, who were in the U.S. Air Force at Frankfurt.

FRANKFURT

The Frankfurt Zoo was small and totally surrounded by the city, but it housed a large collection and many species I had never seen. At one point the assistant director showed me their brand-new quarantine building, a dedicated facility that most zoos lacked. The folks in Frankfurt were rightfully quite proud of it. Unfortunately, the moment we came through the second set of doors into the building, there was a zoo keeper stretched out across the hall on a thick layer of coffee bean sacks, sound sleep. European zoos in those days were very proper and rigidly bureaucratic operations, and I thought for a moment he was going to have apoplexy or commit murder. He then straightened up, got his face under control and we very quietly stepped over the keeper, walking down the hall to inspect the various quarantine areas. The keeper was still sleeping when we came back out, so we quietly stepped over him again and left the building. I always wondered what happened to that keeper after I left the zoo.

From Frankfurt I flew to Zürich and then Basel, Switzerland, where things went awry. The airline lost my luggage, so for the rest of my stay in Europe my luggage was two days behind me. Thankfully I was carrying my camera bag and my medical bag and a change of clothes. That meant I had to do laundry every night, but that beat not having any clothes. I visited the zoos in Munich, Frankfurt (for the second time), West Berlin and finally East Berlin before going on to Bremen, where my clothes finally caught up with me.

THE BERLIN ZOOS

The great thing about traveling in Europe was a room in a small hotel cost just four or five dollars a night and included breakfast. One exception to that was in Schweizerhof, next to the zoo in West Berlin. That is where the president of West Germany stayed and cost me a whole $14 per night with breakfast included. The West Berlin Zoo was the largest in Europe in terms of animals and exhibits. It had been virtually destroyed in the bombing during World War II, and by then had become very modern with an extensive collection of animals.

On the train into East Berlin to see that zoo, I started to feel that I had gotten lost. It was an interesting ride since West Berlin was a very well-maintained modern city, but immediately across the border East Berlin still showed all the signs and destruction left over from World War II. Every train car had a guard with a submachine gun. The guards wouldn't talk, but I could tell by reading their eyes that they understood what I was saying. After asking a guard where the zoo stop was, I started to think I had missed my stop. A young housewife with a string bag of groceries caught my eye. She held up three fingers, looked up at the map above the windows of the train car and again held up three fingers. She never said a word, but I took the hint. I got off three stops later and said to the first man I met on the street, "Tierpark." He pointed, and I walked to the zoo.

The folks at the zoo were relieved to see me. The staff at the West Berlin Zoo had wired them three days before to tell them I would be coming, but they had only received it 20 minutes beforehand. Since I hadn't shown up they assumed I was lost. The East Berlin Tierpark was huge and had extraordinarily large pens for hoofed animals. It also had the largest cat exhibit in Europe but was obviously on short rations for money. The whole European zoo scene was eye opening for a country boy like me who had previously only visited Canada and

Mexico. I recall marveling at the size of their hospital and the fact that there was hardly any equipment inside. They also had perhaps the most extensive collection of rare hoof stock in Europe, including a herd of Russian Saiga antelope. They also had a very large collection of heroic, greater-than-life-sized animal bronzes, which had apparently come from Kaiser Wilhelm's Imperial Garden.

ACROSS THE NORTH ATLANTIC IN MARCH

Van Den Brink's quarantine barge was anchored in the River Bremen where it would be impossible for any domestic hoof stock to expose the exotic hoofed animals to disease and vice versa. It was large and had antelope pens down below in the hold and a small house for the keeper and his family up on the deck. Together we examined the 43 animals that were to go to Omaha. There were sable antelope, scimitar horned oryx, saiga antelope, chamois goat antelope and addax. We discussed their feeding and care and the arrangements for transferring them and all their feed and supplies to the ship that would take us across the Atlantic to Pier 19 New York.

The next day they craned the crated animals aboard and placed them in the hold, immediately forward of the superstructure. The ship was a 95-meter long Norwegian freighter. The superstructure was completely aft. USDA regulations stipulated that once the hoofed stock was loaded, the ship had to sail directly to the US without any stops. Once the crated animals were stowed below, cranes lifted a large metal hatch cover in place, leaving only a 20" x 20" man hatch on the deck to descend through to care for the animals. Small freighters like this frequently have passenger cabins so they can pick up extra income. Ours even had a stewardess on board to take care of the captain, his officers and the passengers. I was the only passenger on this particular trip, and I stowed my clothes, camera gear and medical bag in my cabin. We went down the River Bremen, and the next morning we came out onto the open ocean. I felt a little queasy but by noon had decided that if that's all there was to being seasick it was a piece of cake. Franz had recommended I ask the captain for a seaman I could hire to help take care of the animals in his spare time. Luckily, I had three days to train him before the first major storm hit. I soon found out that the queasiness of that first day had little to do with being seasick. For the next three-and-a-half days that old cliché "You have to get better to die" became my reality. The captain was afraid I would cave in and go to bed, leaving him responsible for the animals. He stressed that I should not take any medication. He also told me to sit at the breakfast table every morning, then go down into the hold for four hours to supervise the animal care until noon, come up to sit at the table for lunch, go back down in the hold for another four hrs. and then finally come up to sit at the dinner table before going to bed. He said that if I did that I would get over being seasick and be cured for life. He said that if I took seasick pills or just went to bed I would be seasick for the whole voyage. He was the captain, so I did as he said, particularly since all of the animals were insured with Lloyds of London. In today's market they would have been worth approximately $3 million. I didn't want to be responsible for anyone dying of neglect.

I spent the four-hour shifts sitting on a hay bale giving instructions to the sailor in between bouts of dry heaves, which came every hour on the hour. I sat at the table three times daily and drank hot tea and ate a few crackers. The ship was small and low and the waves roared over the deck so that many times the only part of the ship visible above water was the superstructure at the aft end. The captain had reduced speed to less than three knots, just enough to steer it, to keep from driving under and going straight to the bottom. The only way to get into the animal hold was to go down to the lower deck of the superstructure, crack the door open and wait for the wave to hit and then recede. The two of us would then pop out of the door and dog it behind us. Then we ran to the middle of the deck in front of the cabins, jerked open the small hatch, climbed part way down the ladder and pulled the hatch cover shut and dogged it down. All this before the next wave rolled over the deck! After four hours we climbed up the ladder, waited for the hiss as the wave receded and then repeated the procedure in reverse. On the morning of the fourth day I got up, went to the breakfast table and was hungry. We had two more major storms on the crossing but I was not seasick again, just ravenously hungry. I ate things like blood pudding and codfish soup for breakfast that I would have never thought about touching before. I'm quite sure the captain was worried about the animals and was rather lenient about the amount of the sailor's time I monopolized. The last storm was so bad that even some of the hoofed animals got seasick. One male saiga, a small antelope from the steppes of Russia, had ataxia and torticollis so bad that he would just curl rigidly up in a ball. We could not uncurl him until we learned to hold his head still and level with what would be the horizon. After several minutes, he would then slowly uncurl and stand up. This procedure had to be done multiple times each day. Happily, the bosun and some of the crew volunteered to take over the night duty so I could at least get some sleep.

We stopped briefly beside a cod-fishing trawler on the Grand Banks where the captain traded whiskey and beer for fresh codfish. The whole crew fell out and processed the fish while they were still flopping and put them in the freezer. The captain explained that when he was at home in Norway he didn't eat codfish because it was rancid and hadn't been frozen quickly enough. I had never enjoyed codfish before, but we had codfish (in some form) three times a day and it was delicious. The captain turned out to be not just a good seaman but also a good trader. He bought beer and whiskey in ports where there were no taxes, and it was cheap to trade for cheese, fish and other foodstuffs all over the world. He ran a well-fed ship.

It took us 17 days to cross, and before the ship crossed the 12-mile mark offshore, the USDA required us to clean out all of the used bedding and manure and scrub the crate floors with disinfectant. This is no easy task in the hold of a ship at sea. I asked the captain if I could hire the bosun and some of the crew to help, and he agreed. I asked what a fair price would be and he suggested paying them with cases of beer for their shore leave in the Norwegian Seaman's Hotel. That day I had just about every seaman not on duty down in the hold. We used a long-handled scraper to pull all of the bedding and manure out into the aisle between crates. This worked well, even considering we had to scrape around antelope feet in each crate. Then we scrubbed and disinfected the floors with a long-handled brush. We placed the bedding and manure in heavy plastic bags with holes cut in them, then loaded the bags up with bricks and threw them overboard. Everything went well until a large male sable antelope got his horns under the door and propelled it over the tops of the crates. When I got out of danger I looked around and the walls and overhead beams were festooned with nervous sailors like ornaments on a Christmas tree. We got the door of the crate back in its tracks and ultimately managed to herd the sable back into his crate. After three major storms, I was grateful to see the Statue of Liberty. The next morning in port I paid the seaman who had helped me, but he wouldn't take as much money as I wanted to give him. I paid the crew with 10 cases of beer and 10 bottles of whiskey that I bought from the captain. I was amazed at the low price. After breakfast all of the crew left the ship except the captain, the bosun and a few others. The longshoremen came on board and the Captain locked himself in his cabin. He hated longshoremen and refused to come out of his cabin as long as they were on board his ship. I thought this strange until later on that day. At noon I went into the dining room and saw a meal all laid out with a cloth over it. I thought this was rather considerate, and I sat down to eat. The stewardess came in and gasped before snatching the food out of my hands. I was eating the captain's lunch! The galley was closed, and there was no other food on board.

When the longshoremen got to the hold where the animals were, again things went to hell in a handbasket. They were handling the crates with spindly legged antelope inside like bales of cotton, tipping them up on end and handling them very rough. I could hear hoofs and horns hitting the sides of the crate in panicked chaos. I started waving my arms and tried to tell them to hoist the crates out level. But, it seemed, none of the longshoremen spoke anything but Italian. I was sure we would have broken legs and dead animals, so I grabbed my camera and started documenting how they were handling the animals for Lloyd's of London. Suddenly three longshoremen charged at me and were ready to throw me overboard when the bosun and three crewmembers came to my rescue. With the bosun shouting at them and the crew guarding me I continued to take pictures. Then, suddenly, the longshoremen remembered they could speak English and started handling the animals properly. I now knew why the captain hated longshoremen.

CHIPPY OVERBAUGH

We loaded the animals on three trucks brought to the dock by Chippy Overbaugh. Chippy's real name was Harry, and he was internationally respected as the best animal hauler in the business. If you had Chippy hauling your animals, Lloyd's of London would give you a special insurance rate. I found out the hard way that Chippy had a wicked sense of humor. We transported the animals to the USDA quarantine station in Clifton, New Jersey, with a short stop at a bar and grill so I could get a sandwich. I had missed lunch and was starved.

Almost totally through body language alone, Harry convinced me that he must be, at the very least, a bishop in the Mormon Church, and I was forcing him against his will into a place that would put his soul in mortal danger. Never before or since has anyone put one over on me that convincingly. I later learned that Chippy had frequented many hundreds of bars, but I wolfed my sandwich and got us out of there before his soul could be ruined. The nickname "Chippy" was apparently because he enjoyed the company of ladies of the night on his travels. Safe to say, he was not your average Mormon bishop.

After settling the animals into the USDA quarantine station, Chippy dropped me off at a bus stop where I could catch a bus to the Newark airport. The day's adventures were not quite over. It was dark and I had 45 minutes to kill until my bus, so I decided to walk across the street to a White Castle hamburger joint. I ordered a cup of coffee and a piece of banana cream pie. I caught my bus and made my flight, which was scheduled to make one stop in Pittsburgh before Chicago. By the time we got to Pittsburgh they tried to take me off the plane because of violent food poisoning. Somehow, I convinced the stewardesses that if I was going to die I would hang on and do it in Omaha.

TRANSPORTING ANIMALS

One thing I learned quickly working with exotic animals is that the only thing totally predictable, is unpredictability. Murphy's Law generally reigns supreme. Early on in Omaha a large albino Burmese python was shipped to us. When we went to the airport to pick it up we found that it was a coiled up frozen block of ice. In those days airliners had a pressurized heated cargo compartment and frequently an unpressurized unheated cargo compartment, and the snake had been mistakenly put in the wrong compartment. You learn to never assume anyone knows what they're doing and always address potential problems and contingencies in advance and in detail or, more than likely, they'll happen and bite you in the rear.

Another zoo had an incident where a leopard (Panthera pardus) had gotten loose in the cargo compartment of an airliner and a ban on shipping leopards was issued. We had a snow leopard to ship. You should never lie to reporters or airlines, but they have to ask the right questions. We shipped an Ounce (Uncia uncia). An absolutely true declaration.

GORILLAS FROM KENNEDY IN MAY 1969

Like the aoudad going to Canada and the flamingos coming to Omaha, transporting animals can almost always be counted on to provide unexpected adventures. In May 1969 I went to New York because we had a shipment of seven lowland gorillas coming in from the Cameroons in equatorial West Africa.

They were coming on a Pan Am flight that arrived at Kennedy at 3 a.m. After a good dinner I was dropped off at the Pan Am freight terminal to wait for the flight. The plane arrived on time and they unloaded our gorillas: two babies, four adult females and an adolescent male. Things then went horribly wrong. There was a lot of arm waving and shouting, and whole freight crew walked off, leaving seven gorillas sitting on the ramp in a cold drizzle. The plan had been that we would get them inside into a warm bay and then wait with them for a truck that was scheduled to come at seven the next morning to take them to the New York USDA/APHIS Animal and Plant Health Inspection Services facility near the airport. The next day the USDA/APHIS agents would inspect their crates and clear them for shipment to Omaha.

I followed everyone into the building to see what was going on but nobody would talk to me. I was doing some shouting of my own when a little Italian guy came up to me and said, "That's not going to do any good because the union steward has called a grievance." I told him my gorillas sitting in the cold rain were not used to this kind of weather and would probably get pneumonia if we didn't get them inside to warmth. He said nobody was going to help me because they were having a grievance meeting. There was also a meeting scheduled for the next shift. I was starting to panic when he said he liked animals and although he wasn't supposed to he'd help me load them if I brought a truck out on the ramp. I asked where I could possibly find a truck at 3:30 in the morning and he said, "Just walk down that road over there until you find one with keys in it, start it up and drive it out on the ramp."

The first covered truck I found that had keys in it was blue and white and had "U.S. MAIL" printed on the side. I drove it out on the ramp, and my new friend and I loaded seven gorillas into it. He was little and I was skinny, but we managed to do it. Then he gave me instructions to get to the USDA/APHIS facility which luckily was close and right on the edge of the airport. When I got to the APHIS building, there was a light on and I could see somebody moving inside. I backed the truck up to the overhead door, got out and opened the rear door and then backed it up close to the building. When the overhead door opened it would have been hard to get a good look at the outside of the truck. Then I knocked on the door and window until somebody answered. I explained that I needed to unload the gorillas and get them in where it was warm. We unloaded the truck, and I asked if there was a couch I could sleep on. I put my suitcase and medical bag inside the building. We closed the overhead door, and I went around outside and drove off. I drove the truck back, took my undershirt off and wiped everything, hopefully, clean of fingerprints and then walked back in the rain. In the morning I got up, found a shower, bummed some breakfast and waited for the APHIS inspectors. Thankfully, nobody had noticed what kind of truck I had been driving overnight.

The crates that housed the gorillas presented a problem. For one thing, there was no operable door. They were made of 2x2 dark hardwood frames screwed to ¾ inch plywood floors and tops and covered with heavy ½ inch square screen wire. To make matters worse the floors of the cages were covered with a two-inch layer of all kinds of exotic fruit and vegetables mixed with gorilla feces. Unless we could clean and sanitize the cages, APHIS would never pass them. When the inspectors arrived, I outlined the only plan I could think of that wouldn't get us stranded in New York for several days. Luckily, they bought my plan. We took the babies out of their cages and put them in a shower room. The four adult females and the adolescent male seemed very intimidated by being in a strange place surrounded by strange people. They sat in the middle of their cages hugging themselves. We unscrewed the top of each cage, and with six of us holding it in place, gently turned the cage over onto its side and then onto its top. We assumed the gorillas would cooperate by walking onto the side and then onto the top as we rotated the cage. One by one, all five gorillas cooperated better that we could possibly have imagined. As we rotated each cage all of the accumulated fruit and feces on the bottom rained down on the gorillas and onto the now upside down top. With six people holding on to the cage we picked it up about three inches off the top and walked the gorillas over to a bare patch of floor on top of the drain. We cleaned off the debris with a soap-dispensing hose nozzle and then hosed down the gorillas. A wild gorilla covered with soap suds, looking like he had just stepped out of a bubble bath, was a sight to behold. Amazingly, the gorillas didn't fight back or try to escape. When the inspectors were satisfied that we had gotten all of the fruit and seeds washed off we applied a generous quantity of fresh sawdust to the cage tops and then simply reversed the procedure. The APHIS inspectors signed the paperwork, and then all I had to do was wait for a United Airlines 737 cargo plane to Chicago where a truck from Omaha would meet us.

Our truck came at 5 p.m., so I got to the airport early to strap the gorillas' cages onto pallets and cover them with tarps so they'd stay quiet. The freight handlers used a cargo lift to place each pallet in the space directly behind the cockpit. This way I could ride in the jump seat and still keep an eye on the gorillas. When the pilot and co-pilot arrived, they wanted to see the gorillas. Since the pilot was technically the captain of the ship, I had no choice but to untie one of the tarps and show him.

He looked at the gorillas and said, "Those look like awfully flimsy crates. Are you sure they are strong enough to hold the gorillas?"

Admittedly, I had the same thought myself but didn't want to get stranded in New York. I said, "That's exactly the type of crate every gorilla I have ever transported has been in." He looked somewhat dubious but said okay. I just failed to tell him that these were the very first gorillas I had ever transported or that I had a CO_2 dart pistol in my belt and five loaded phencyclidine darts in the inside pocket of my jacket. I was careful to keep the jacket buttoned. The ride to Omaha, thank goodness, was uneventful.

SLEEPING WITH A GORILLA

On August 27, 1969, Benoit, one of our two female gorillas, gave birth to a male. Being an inexperienced mother, she took the baby to the top of the enclosure and either dropped him or the baby lost its grip on her fur. The result was massive head trauma, and despite our best efforts the baby died 12 hours later.

Thus, we were apprehensive when we determined that Bridget, our other female, was pregnant. Both females had been brought into the U.S. when they were fairly young and were used to humans. We didn't know her due date and decided that we would start a training program to further condition Bridget to being handled and to teach her proper neonatal behavior. Our training program to get both females to allow us to do almost anything with them was successful, but when we tried to condition Bridget to properly hold a ragdoll or a replica of a gorilla baby she refused to cooperate.

We decided that when she got close to giving birth we would simply keep somebody with her around the clock so that we would not have a repeat disaster. We took down all of the climbing apparatus in her exhibit and a group of four or five of us took turns being in with her all the time. Jerry Stones, Jackie Stones, Johnny Martinez and I—along with a number of other volunteers—did most of the watching. During the daytime someone could sit outside the exhibit and watch through the glass, but at night we were afraid of dozing off and would spend our time in the exhibit. We set up a television set outside the glass for both the keepers and the gorillas to watch. From 8 p.m. until 8 a.m. somebody would stay in the exhibit reading or sleeping. If one of us fell asleep we assumed the labor process would wake us. Jerry Stones took the vast majority of these graveyard shifts.

Bridget was very cooperative with this whole process and actually came to depend upon and want the company of her keepers. However, there were a few drawbacks. For one, her lack of sanitary habits. If one of us brought our lunch or had anything to eat or drink, she wanted part of it. Then there were what Jerry Stones called "the munchies." If you were stretched out on your sleeping bag and happened to doze off you are almost guaranteed to wake up around 2 a.m. when Bridget got the munchies. She would gather up a double handful of monkey biscuits and come join you. She liked to lean with one elbow in the middle of your chest and crunch the monkey biscuits. Having a gorilla elbow poking your midsection was guaranteed to wake you up, not to mention that she was not a delicate eater. And she had a tendency to break wind while she was eating, which did little for morale.

After nearly two months of nonstop attention, we unfortunately missed the birth. On the evening of March 1, 1970, a 32-year-old female orang named Tia went into labor, her first pregnancy. Due to her age, the tissues of the birth canal had very little elasticity left in them. After a much longer labor than normal, the baby's head crowned. Then labor stopped, and Tia gave up. It was obvious that we would have to intercede, and so with the help of the small crew on the gorilla watch I immobilized Tia, did an episiotomy and delivered Tye, a healthy female. Tye later came home with Marie and I because her mother refused to have anything to do with her when she recovered from the immobilizing agent. Despite our best attempts to introduce the baby, Tia refused to even touch her.

While we were helping deliver the orang baby Bridget delivered a female gorilla baby all on her own with no problems. You can imagine our surprise when the first person to visit the gorilla building rushed down and said Bridget had a baby and was doing just fine.

She was very cooperative in allowing us to examine the baby, to tie the umbilical cord and cut it loose from the placenta. She was supporting the baby properly, and so we simply sat and watched for the rest of the night. The only problem that arose came when it was time to nurse. Bridget's nipples were very tender, and while she'd allow us to check for milk production she wouldn't allow the baby to nurse. Every time that baby would latch onto a nipple she would pull the baby's head away. We solved the problem using a technique that would likely be frowned upon today. We put our hands under her hand and pushed the baby up to her breast, and when she tried to push the baby's mouth away from the nipple we would bang a short piece of broomstick on the floor and threaten to hit her with

Tia, pictured, wanted nothing to do with her baby Tye after the assisted delivery.

PHOTO COURTESY OF THE DURHAM MUSEUM.

it. This distracted her and allowed the baby to nurse. We did this every few hours for three days or so, until her tenderness subsided. From then on, she allowed the baby to nurse freely and was a wonderful gorilla mother. By the way, we never had to actually hit her with the broom stick. I wonder if this would work with human mothers who are neglectful?

Sadly, the final outcome was not good. At 90 days of age, while being carried in the outside exhibit, the baby was observed to reach down and pick up some fresh gorilla dung and put it into her mouth. We didn't think too much about this because it's normal behavior, but by the next morning the baby was very lethargic and looked dehydrated and had bloody diarrhea. We separated her from Bridget, and she was in very bad condition. Despite fluids, IV antibiotics and oxygen she only lived a few hours. It was an acute E. coli necrotizing enterocolitis and, despite being raised on her mother's milk, she apparently did not have the antibodies to fight it off.

AN ELEPHANT SITTING DOWN IN A TRAILER

After I became director we once had a very rambunctious young adult male African elephant who had been boarding at the Omaha Zoo until the boarding bill got to be worth more than the elephant, at which point the dealer gave him to us. We sold him to another zoo, which sent a truck and trailer to get him. This animal was somewhat pugnacious, and since we had never intended to keep him we had not put in a great deal of time training him. He was the same animal that, in a disagreement with our adult bull, was pushed off into the moat, suffering a mid-shaft fracture of the radius, and had earlier lost the tip of his trunk to this same old bull.

Both the fracture and trunk healed without complications or impairment.

Shortly after leaving the zoo the driver stopped because the elephant was lurching around in the trailer. When he went back to look, the elephant's hind legs had slipped forward, and he was sitting on his rump like a dog begging for a treat. He couldn't seem to regain his feet so the driver came back to the zoo. It was a narrow trailer, just wide enough for the elephant, and given the fact that he seemed more intent on fighting with anyone who tried to help him than cooperating we weren't sure how to get him on his feet short of calling in a crane. We finally solved the problem by threading a two-inch soft nylon rope into a figure-eight sling with a loop around each upper hind leg, meeting in the middle of his back over his pelvis. We then drove the trailer under a large oak tree branch, snugged the rope tight to the branch and then drove forward, lifting him back onto his feet. Then we shoveled in a foot of dirt to make sure he had good footing for the rest of the trip. We were not unhappy to see an elephant so intent on getting into trouble leave.

FLAMINGOS FROM BERMUDA AND A CESSNA

Omaha had a group of small Chilean flamingos, and we wanted to add the larger, brighter Caribbean or Cuban flamingos. The aquarium in Flats, Bermuda, had, for a number of years, been raising Cuban flamingos. We made arrangements to buy 18 and fought our way through the permits procedure with the federal government. After finally receiving the permits, with stern directions to make sure that the permits were attached to each of the crates that the birds would be shipped in, we made arrangements to ship the birds from Flats on British Airways to Nassau, Bahamas, and then on Bahama Air to Miami, where they would have to be quarantined.

We had been warned not to leave our birds overnight at the airport in Nassau because animals had a way of disappearing there. I was worried that if a mix-up occurred we wouldn't know about it and couldn't address it until it was too late. The flamingos were going to be quarantined in a facility owned and run by a fellow named Matt Block. We had never dealt with him before, but it seemed logical to ask him to fly to Nassau, take charge of making sure that the birds got transferred and ride with them back to Miami. He agreed.

On a Sunday at noon I got a frantic call from Matt saying we had a problem. The Bahama Air flight was canceled and he needed us to wire him $1,000 immediately. I did as instructed. Only later did I learn that his solution to the problem was to rent a single-engine Cessna. He then took all of the flamingos (who were on a diet that included ground shrimp) out of their crates and put them loose inside the Cessna and flew to Miami. He had very conveniently left all of the crates with the permits attached on the airport apron in Nassau. On landing he didn't check in with customs or the Department of Agriculture but taxied directly across the airport to where he had his station wagon parked. He unloaded the flamingos into his wagon and drove to his quarantine station.

The phone started ringing immediately with calls from U.S. Customs agents, Department of Agriculture agents, APHIS quarantine agents and U.S. Fish and Wildlife agents. We had broken almost every rule and law possible, most of them felonies. The last and angriest of all the calls came from the owners of the Cessna who said that they were going to have the whole inside of the airplane steam cleaned and would send us the bill, and if the smell and stains didn't come out of the carpet and seats we would have to pay to replace them. Luckily the fishy smell came out, and we only had to pay for the steam cleaning.

I had a classmate who worked for the Department of Agriculture. He interceded and assured them that I was an honest zoo director and would never knowingly do anything illegal like this. They could have confiscated the flamingos and euthanized them or sent them back to Bermuda, but they only slapped our hands and told us we would be very wise not to do business with Matt. Forty-five days later we had 18 new Cuban flamingos in the zoo. If you consider flying and navigating a single-engine airplane over the ocean with 18 tall flamingos loose in that small cabin, climbing and pooping all over the seats, he was obviously unflappable and a pretty good pilot. And since none of us ended up in jail, I'll give him credit for being a decisive problem solver.

OSCAR, A GORILLA FROM POLAND

Frank Thompson, a friend and former zoo director in Bradenton, Florida, who was representing the Jackson, Mississippi, Zoo contacted me. They wanted to build a gorilla exhibit. There was a male gorilla named Oscar available at the zoo in Wroclaw, Poland, and I agreed that Omaha would do the importation and hold him until they had raised the money and built their gorilla exhibit. They would, of course, pay all expenses.

In late Sept 1983 I flew to London and connected with Frank's broker, Lettie Van Tol, a Dutch animal dealer living in England. She was Franz Van den Brink's sister and, I had been told, very religious and proper. I knew I would have to watch my language. Being Dutch, she also spoke many languages.

To get to Wroclaw (formerly Breslau, Germany) we had to clear immigration and customs in Warsaw. In those days that was an interesting experience. I remember being in a thin-walled cubicle with a Polish customs agent counting my money after having to turn out my pockets and give him my wallet. He went through my suitcase and medical bag with a fine-tooth comb. The sounds coming from Lettie's cubicle left little doubt that she was being strip-searched. They ultimately found nothing illegal and cleared us.

Since we had a four-hour layover we grabbed a taxi and asked our driver to give us a windshield tour of Warsaw, particularly the old quarter. Then we boarded our flight to Wroclaw where were picked up by the zoo director. Despite Lettie's knowledge of languages, she did not speak Polish, which was the only language spoken by the zoo director and his staff. The hospitality was great, but for the next three days we had to communicate totally by sign language. They indicated that a government interpreter was on the way, but no one ever showed up. After seeing the zoo and some of the city we started preparations for transporting Oscar. They had constructed a strong, heavy crate, and their plan was to get a couple of heavy rope nooses on him and pull him into the crate by brute force. I indicated that was not the way I wanted to do it and would rather immobilize him with drugs (phencyclidine). It turns out they had never successfully immobilized a great ape. The crate was chained to one of the doors in his enclosure, and I used a CO-2-powered dart pistol to inject him. He went down smoothly but then had another problem. With no experience with immobilization, the staff refused to believe he was no longer dangerous. They wouldn't even open the other door so that I could go in his cage and roll him onto his side. He was laying on his back, and if he vomited he could have aspirated. No amount of arm waving, pleadings or sign language would solve the problem. I had to grit my teeth while they used poles to fish two ropes onto his wrists and drag the unconscious gorilla into the crate. He regained consciousness without incident, and we left him in the crate overnight so that he would be fully recovered for the journey next day.

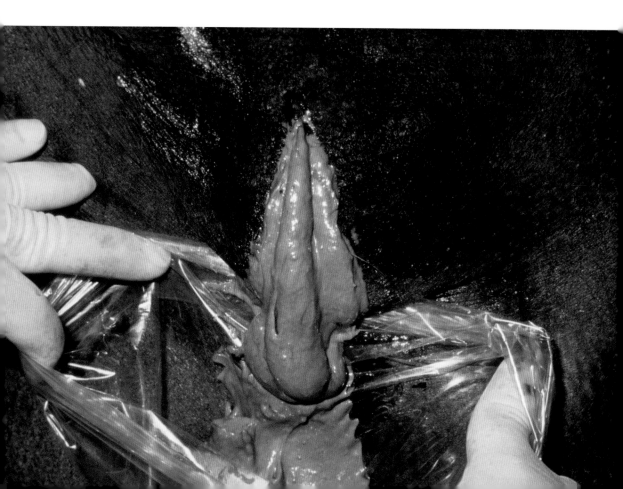

The next morning a large Volvo covered truck arrived early and we loaded him into the back without incident. With the truck already loaded and everyone standing around to say goodbye the long-awaited interpreter finally arrived and the zoo director began speaking to her very earnestly. She came over and said the zoo director wanted me to know that I should not worry, that the leprosy Oscar had been exposed to through the female gorillas had been cured. This sent us immediately over to take a close look, and sure enough two females had badly deformed, scarred fingers. The possibility of introducing a gorilla who could potentially have leprosy would scare the hell out of any zoo man. I was really being between a rock and a hard spot and did not know what to do. Finally, the zoo staff produced a published clinical report, written in Polish. With the help of the

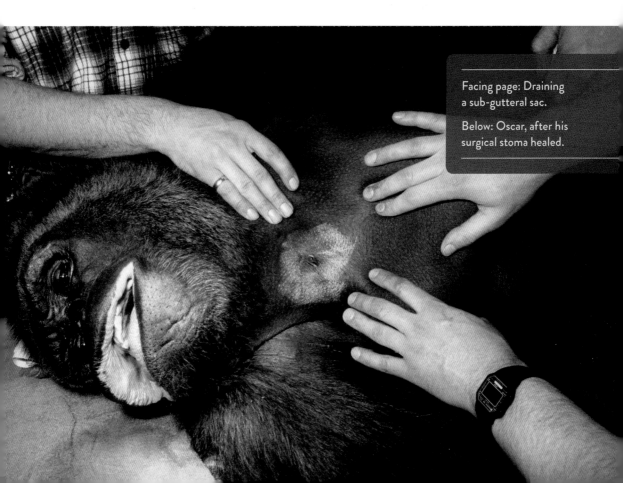

Facing page: Draining a sub-gutteral sac.

Below: Oscar, after his surgical stoma healed.

interpreter we determined that the report said that the condition in the females had been completely cured with streptomycin. To the best of my knowledge leprosy could not be cured using streptomycin alone, plus leprosy is not easily transmissible and since there was no mention of Hansens disease or Mycrobacterium leprae I could only assume that in this case the term "leprosy" was a translation problem from Polish to English. I took a deep breath and decided to go ahead with transporting Oscar. Happily, after many years in the U.S., Oscar never developed leprosy.

Even though the truck had a large cab with plenty of room for Lettie and I, at the last moment someone decided that the director's wife should drive us in a small Russian car, following behind the truck, to the East German border. The truck driver spoke English, and I told him in no uncertain terms that I wanted him to make sure we were behind him at all times. Then through the interpreter I told the director's wife that we wanted to stay close behind and in sight of the truck at all times. This plan worked until the first steep hill when the Volvo accelerated and left our feeble little car in the dust. The zoo director's wife kept saying "border crossing" so I assumed we would catch up there. Four hours later we arrived at the designated crossing and the truck was not there. The border guard explained that even if it was, they did not allow animals to cross at that gate. For the next four hours we went from border crossing to border crossing looking for the truck and a place where they would let animals across. Finally, we found the right border crossing but no truck. An hour later he showed up, explaining that the price of diesel had been too high in Wroclaw and he had gone on a hunt for a cheaper supply. We said goodbye to the zoo director's wife and started the process of crossing into East Germany. The Polish side was easy, but we hit a stone wall on the East German side. Lettie spoke German fluently but to no avail, and so for another four hours we tried unsuccessfully to get across. Finally, two Dutch trucks pulled up and when the Dutch drivers got out Lettie asked them for help. They immediately asked me if I had $180 in American $20 bills. I gave them the money, they went over to the booth and came back five minutes later with our permit. They said the only way to get across the border was to bribe the guards. For anticorruption reasons there were always three guards in each booth, so it cost $60 per guard.

We saddled up and headed for Berlin. I was worried that we would have a problem with the East German guards at the Berlin crossing but it only took 10 minutes. But difficulties arose again when we presented our permits to the West German border guards. We thought we had given ourselves a safe time cushion to get to Berlin, but between the truck getting lost and searching for the right crossing we were now down to the wire.

At Check Point Bravo the West German side was manned by two men, a young-looking guy and an older redhead who was obviously not thrilled with being subordinate to the young guy. Lettie heard the redhead tell the young guy that the gorilla was obviously being smuggled illegally and if he let it across he would be in big trouble. This discussion went on and on, and on and every time I tried to get into the conversation they simply ignored me. Lettie said they apparently didn't speak any English. Even with all our paperwork in order she didn't seem to have enough clout to convince them that we were not smuggling the animal. It was obvious the young guy was being buffaloed by the redhead. Out of desperation I went out to the truck to get our U.S. import permits to show them that if we were doing anything illegal we would be in big trouble when we tried to get into the United States. Happily, Lettie was not in the room or I would have had to watch my tongue. I put the permits on the counter, and out of frustration I said more to myself than to the young guy that it was one hell of a note that he was letting that g******** red headed c***s****** bastard buffalo him. It was immediately apparent that both of them understood English. I was angry and I let them know it in as profane a way as I could muster having mostly to do with the red heads sexual proclivities and ancestry. The redhead charged at me over the counter, the young guy grabbed him by the belt. It was obvious that they spoke English perfectly. I even picked up a chair to hit him with if he made it across the counter. The young guy was hanging on to his colleague for dear life when Lettie came from using the restroom. The young guy finally got the redhead under control. I asked Lettie to explain to them that if we missed our airplane we would have three days in their town before the next flight, and if they thought I was angry now they should just wait until I saw their bosses in the morning in the company of the American Consul. Ten minutes later we were in the truck behind a police escort complete with red lights and sirens all the way to the Lufthansa cargo terminal of the airport. We unloaded, and the truck driver took Lettie to the passenger terminal.

On our climb out of Berlin in a 727 cargo plane over East Germany the pilot said, "Damn, look at that climb indicator."

I said, "We're doing pretty good?"

And he said, "Hell no! We're loaded too heavy, and if we lose an engine we're going down in East Germany." We got to Frankfurt and offloaded into one of the best airport animal holding facilities in the world to wait for our connection with the Flying Tiger 747 flight to Boston. I cleaned and fed Oscar and put fresh bedding in his crate. In addition to great animal facilities they had great people facilities, so I had a room where I could sleep, get a shower and shave, change clothes and then get something to eat. I was well rested by the time we loaded Oscar into the nose directly under the cockpit of the Flying Tiger 747 freighter. We strapped his crate to the deck so it couldn't move. While the rest of the airplane was for freight, the bubble right behind the cockpit was a nice passenger area with seats, a galley and three bunk beds. There were only a few other passengers, one of whom was a stewardess deadheading back to Boston. I took the left front seat at the top of the stairs leading down into the nose with my medical bag strapped into the seat next to me, just in case. Oscar was behaving great. The spaces between the bars on his crate were wide enough for a human hand to get through, so before we took off I gave everybody instructions that he was dangerous, prone to biting and no one was to go down into the nose without me accompanying them. I took everyone down and let them watch me feed Oscar carrots, celery and apple slices.

It was a long flight, and after eating some of the passengers went to bed. I was reading and had dozed off when I heard Oscar screaming. Someone else was screaming, and the whole front end of the airplane was shaking violently. The pilot was shouting profanities and telling me to get down there and do something to stop it. When I went down the steps the stewardess was back against the bulkhead in a neck to ankle, long white nightgown. Oscar was screaming and violently shaking the bars of his crate, which shook the whole front end of the airplane side to side. Once he saw me, everything was all right. She had apparently snuck past me, gone down the stairs and found Oscar asleep. I'm not sure if gorillas understand or believe in ghosts but when he woke up he saw her in her long white nightgown, he jumped up, hit his head and started screaming and shaking the bars. The stewardess went backwards into a bulkhead so hard that she cut the back of her head and her back on the frame. We went back up the stairs, tended to her cuts and the rest of the flight was uneventful. In Omaha we had to perform sub guttural sac surgery on Oscar.

FLYING A BABY ORANG TO JACKSONVILLE, FLORIDA

In May 1978, we had agreed to donate a young male orang who had been born in Omaha to the zoo in Jacksonville, Florida. The orang was still a baby on a bottle, and it wouldn't be safe to load him into a crate and air freight him. Our solution was quite simple, although it wouldn't work in our modern world of airport security.

I bought a first-class airplane ticket and loaded the baby in a soft airline carry-on bag full of extra disposable diapers, bottles and a plastic bag full of wet wash rags.

Then I boarded the plane with the bag zipped up until we were in the air.

When we were safely off the ground I unzipped the bag, the baby's head popped out, and I asked a stewardess if I could get a bottle warmed up. For the rest of the flight it seemed that nobody in the airplane could hardly get a drink because all of the stewardesses were upfront taking care of the baby orang. This made for a fun trip, save a dubious look I got from a female passenger who spotted me changing the orang's diaper in the Atlanta airport. We used this technique a number of times until the world changed.

WALTER & TIMU

Transporting another ape baby was even more interesting. Timu, the world's first test tube (IV) gorilla, was born at the Cincinnati Zoo. This was the result of a collaborative project between the reproductive physiologists and veterinarians from that zoo and the Omaha Zoo. Rosy, her mother, was at Cincinnati. We transported frozen semen from Mo, an Omaha male, to their lab to work collaboratively. The decision was made to transport the baby to Omaha for hand raising; however, the baby was too young and valuable for a commercial flight. Walter Scott, our board chairman, volunteered his jet, and a number of us flew

to Cincinnati. On the trip back to Omaha, Walter was reclining in his seat with the baby fast asleep on his chest and stomach. It soon became very obvious that she had filled her diaper.

I offered to change the diaper, but Walter said, "No problem, don't bother her. All little babies smell like that." Then he promptly fell asleep himself. It was a 14-passenger jet but still just a bit small for those of us who were awake and could still smell.

CASEY AND ULIE IN A CESSNA

One of my most interesting gorilla transport stories took place in 1968 when we made a deal with the Como Zoo in St. Paul, Minnesota, to borrow "Casey," a 576-pound male gorilla, on a breeding loan. To put it mildly, he was more than a little obese, and we couldn't find a transport crate for an animal that size which would fit in any airliner to Omaha. On top of that, the airline wasn't anxious to transport him.

We considered driving him from St. Paul to Omaha by truck, but even then, we didn't have a suitable crate. The problem was solved when a board member from the Como Zoo volunteered an airplane. It was a twin-engine six-passenger Cessna 310, which, of course, was not big enough for a crate. Ulie Seal came up with a plan to strip everything from the plane except the pilot's seat. Casey would be immobilized with phencyclidine, they would load him into the airplane, strap him onto a stretcher and keep him immobilized during the flight. Everyone agreed to the plan, even the pilot. The plan went off without a hitch with Ulie riding beside Casey, monitoring his respiration and heart rate. In addition to his medical bag, in one shirt pocket he had extra syringes full of phencyclidine and ace promazine, which he used periodically during the flight to Omaha. In his other shirt pocket were two large syringes each with a more than lethal dose of succinylcholine, just in case. A 576-pound gorilla, even if just a happy drunk staggering around in the back of a small plane, would not be good.

Casey the gorilla.

PHOTO COURTESY OF THE *OMAHA WORLD-HERALD.*

When they landed in Omaha we had to take Casey off of the stretcher in order to get him out of the airplane and into a van for transport to the zoo. This went down as one of the few animal transports with absolutely no surprises, and I'm sure the pilot was happy about that.

CASEY AND THE FOOTBALL GAME

Dealing with the press is always tricky. You want them on your side, but you never know when someone will take something out of context or misinterpret something you said. Sometimes these are innocent mistakes, and other times they're deliberate. You need to be very explicit and keep your sentences short and to the point.

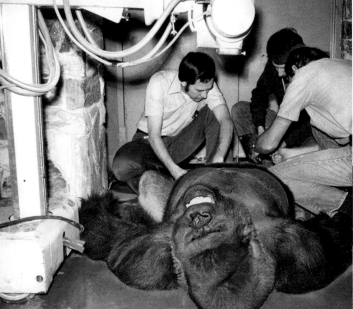

Dr. Ulysses S. "Ulie" Seal, pictured above, and Casey during an exam.

Casey, the large male gorilla on breeding loan from the Como Zoo, was being examined during our routine medical check for TB and blood collection, when he began wake up from the anesthetic, sat up in the exhibit and leaned against the wall. His exam was complete at this point, and he was under the influence of sernylan, which has a slow recovery time. Animals rarely exhibit any aggression in cases like this, so we weren't overly concerned. A young photographer from the *Omaha World-Herald* was there that day, recording the procedures, and our head ape keeper sat down beside Casey and asked the photographer to take their picture. After the head keeper, other keepers took their turns posing with the gorilla. The head keeper returned with some Nebraska Cornhuskers football apparel, including a Big Red Nebraska hat, which he put on Casey's head, and a pennant, which he placed in one of Casey's hands. He put a Nebraska beer stein in his other hand.

I had been watching what was going on, and it made me a little uncomfortable. I never wanted to depict our animals in a disrespectful or cartoonish manner, so I told the photographer he could take the photo for the head keeper, but I absolutely did not want it appearing in the *Omaha World-Herald*. He assured me it wouldn't.

What I failed to explain "explicitly" to the photographer was that I didn't want that photo to appear in any newspaper or publication anywhere in the world, ever. Sometime later when Nebraska went up to Minnesota to play a football game (Nebraska lost 13-12), you can guess what photo appeared on the front page of the St. Paul newspaper. There was Casey, their famous gorilla, appearing drunk and leaning against a wall, decked out in Nebraska Cornhuskers paraphernalia. The fallout was fierce. A member of the state legislature angrily demanded that the Como Zoo recall its breeding loan under which Casey came to Omaha in the first place. The incident caused a chuckle among Nebraska fans, but it was a lesson to never assume anything with the press, be succinct and always be prepared for the worst.

CASEY AT THE BAT AND OTHER STORIES

Casey had been named after "Casey at the Bat," the hero of the 1888 baseball poem by Ernest Thayer. The first year he was in Omaha somebody from the press dreamed up having Casey hold a baseball for the opening of Omaha's College World Series.

We went along because it's hard to turn down three TV stations and your daily newspaper. On the appointed day, with all the press lined up cameras at the ready, one of us threw Casey a baseball. He picked it up, looked at it and then side-armed it back to us. Everybody thought that was great, but then we did an incredibly stupid thing. We threw him a baseball bat. He picked it up and side-armed it back with incredible force, knocking over a TV camera tripod, the cameraman and causing everyone else to dive to the ground. Luckily no one was hurt and no cameras were broken, but if anything will scare the daylights out of you, a baseball bat whirling at 100 miles an hour will do it.

Casey, like his baseball namesake, was a thrower, and we learned to be very careful not to give him any ammunition. An incident occurred when three teenage boys were throwing rocks into Casey's exhibit, not directly at him but nearby. A retired mailman from Council Bluffs who was a regular visitor to the zoo saw this going on and shouted at the boys to stop. Casey picked up a four-pound rock and, recognizing the mailman, side-armed it into the man's head, knocking him unconscious. When I got there, he had a star-shaped three-cornered wound clear to the bone in his forehead. He said he was all right, but I insisted on putting him in my Jeep and taking him to the emergency room where they sewed him up. Luckily, he was a zoo fan, and Casey was one of his favorites so he didn't sue us.

One winter a couple of young male green monkeys slipped through the mesh and entered Casey's exhibit. He caught both of them. He was walking around the exhibit on his hind legs while we marveled how gently he seemed to be holding them, one in each hand, fingers around their necks, when he

Casey with Johnny Martinez, John Gedrose, and John Jereki.

calmly walked over to the water bowl and drowned them. So much for Disney's togetherness theory.

Casey was not a bad guy, just a dominant male gorilla. Another winter morning when Mike July and Johnny Martinez were making early morning rounds, they came into the gorilla house kitchen for a cup of coffee and started talking to John Jarecki about the day's activities. John had apparently had a full night of partying and the conversation broke his train of thought. When they finished they helped themselves to another cup of coffee while watching John go back about his business. He walked over to the barred door into the front exhibit, and with Casey sitting directly on the other side of the door watching him, unlocked and threw both bolts on the door. As he started to open the door he looked up and there was Casey. He tried to slam the door back shut and throw a bolt but Casey held out one finger and stopped the door from closing. John shouted and ran. He and Mike went out one door while Johnny Martinez ran for the other door.

We had always questioned whether you could, if you were loud enough and aggressive enough, bluff a male gorilla. Johnny had been a boxer and had a lot of grit so he opened the back aisle door and shouted as loud and aggressively as he could, "Casey get your ass back in there!" Casey charged instantly. A steel safety bannister slowed him down so Johnny was able to outrun him down the back hallway. I came down with the capture equipment, but we didn't have to use it. Both Bridget and Benoit had come out into the kitchen and gathered up as much fruit as they could carry and gone back into the exhibit. Casey had picked up Jarecki's goose down parka and had gone back in the exhibit. The rest of us snuck into the kitchen and quickly bolted the exhibit door while watching the girls eat their fruit. Casey tore apart John's parka and ate the goose down, causing three days of very firm stools.

ESCAPES

We had a fair number of escapes, particularly during the early years when we had a green crew and young animals that were handled a bit too casually. Usually escapes were simply the result of keeper error or the mechanical failures of locks and doors. Most of our escapees were young gorillas or young orangs who were not a real danger to anyone but were prone to climbing trees from which it was difficult to get them down. As our collection grew, it became necessary to tighten our management procedures and training. However, most animal escapes still occurred as a result of keeper error. Here are a few I remember.

MICKEY THE CHIMP

Mickey was a 140-pound male chimpanzee that Willy Kubler from the Ringling Circus had given Omaha. He got out past a keeper, came across the zoo and took refuge in the old public restrooms at one end of the pavilion office building. Jerry Stones and I had developed a close relationship with Mickey, so instead of getting the dart gun I went into the restroom hallway intending to just take him by the hand and lead him back. Mickey was screaming and wasn't having any of it. He was standing up with his arms crossed in front of his face. At close range, a screaming male chimp with his hair standing on end looks bigger than a 500-pound gorilla. I had a hickory post mall handle but the low ceiling prevented an overhead swat so I reversed and came up from underneath, hitting him on the side of the face below his left eye. He immediately reverted to subordinate behavior and decided he wanted to be friends. With Jerry and I holding him by each hand, we walked down the hill and across the zoo back into his exhibit. Behind us were 10 or so keepers, trailing us just in case. All the way back to the exhibit, Mickey screamed and challenged them as if he was protecting Jerry and me.

AMUR LEOPARD LOOSE

Another escape I remember extremely well involved a large adult male Amur leopard. Again, human error was the culprit. A supervisor lost track of what he was doing and opened a sliding door into an outside cage with the leopard standing right there watching him. The leopard charged out, and the supervisor was able to shut and lock the door before the female also came out. An Amur leopard on the loose in a zoo with visitors is a very serious thing. We grabbed our capture equipment and charged up to the maintenance area where he was. We stationed one keeper with a double barrel 12-gauge between the leopard and the public area of the zoo with instructions to shoot to kill if he came that way and another keeper with a sawed-off double 12-gauge immediately to my right. I had told the keeper beside me not to fire until he heard me say the word, "Shoot." I elected to use an emergency succinylcholine dry powder dart. These are fast acting but have a short effective down time. As the leopard was coming toward us on the north side of the maintenance building I put the first dart into his left shoulder at about 30 yards. He whirled and ran away, turning left around the back of the building, so we shifted to the south side of the building as he came around and headed toward us. I was chambering another dart as he came on full tilt.

My shot was successful, and the leopard immediately skidded to a stop, turned and ran. Shortly thereafter he was ataxic and then down. We measured the distance from where we were standing to the end of his skid mark and it was 12 feet. The keeper protecting my rump could almost have touched him with the shotgun barrel. Luckily everybody kept their cool, and the leopard was back in the cage before he regained the ability to move, a moment that came quickly, even with two doses of the drug.

A WOLVERINE IN NEBRASKA

While most of our early escaped animals never actually made it outside of the grounds of the Henry Doorly Zoo, we did have a small number who made it beyond our boundary fence. Most were birds such as peacocks and flamingos whose flight feathers grew out and they flew off.

One external escape was more notable. We had received a pair of wolverines from Al Oeming in Edmonton, Canada. We were exhibiting them in one of our modified hyena grottoes. One morning a year or so after their arrival, a fight broke out, and the male wolverine killed the female. We decided it made little sense to have a single animal in the exhibit, so we moved the male to an old leopard cage in an older part of the zoo. He only stayed one night, and the next morning we found a hole in the chain link of the cage.

We searched the zoo grounds but found nothing, and after a week we assumed we'd never see him again. Of course, we worried that if word got out that a wolverine had been introduced into Nebraska the zoo would get blamed for every dead calf carcass that coyotes had chewed on for a 100-mile radius. After six months, when we had finally begun to relax, a call came from the head of the Nebraska Humane Society. He asked what the probability was that there could be a wolverine in Nebraska. When I asked him why, he was evasive. I told him that while anything was possible, especially since we were located on the Missouri River, it was highly improbable. He hung up and then called back four hours later. This time his voice was a couple of octaves higher. He explained that a farmer had called up, and when he went out to see the animal, the wolverine, locked up in the farmer's garage, had nearly eaten him alive and then escaped. If he had just told us the situation we would have responded and recaptured the animal.

It was another six months before we heard of our wolverine again. This time two nurses from St. Joseph's Hospital came in and said they had been hiking in Fontenelle Forest when a big brown animal had blocked the trail. Rather than run off, the animal had stomped its front feet. We gave them a Peterson's Field Guide of North American mammals and watched while they thumbed through it. When they got to the page with the Wolverine both of them gasped, pointed and said, "That's him." Thankfully, that was the last time we heard anything about our wolverine. But from that point on we answered every call when someone reported a large brown animal in their yard. Thankfully, they all turned out to be groundhogs.

PACHYDERM MOAT

One morning on rounds I drove up to the new Pachyderm Hill, and there was Paj, our big male elephant, standing in the flower bed. When we had designed Pachyderm Hill we had set the moat width at eight feet, but at one point it was a little less than seven feet due to an old piece of concrete foundation. Paj found that spot and stepped across. I stopped my Jeep and shouted, "Paj what are you doing?" He looked like a kid caught with his hand in the cookie jar and stepped back across the moat. We hotwired that section from then on.

On another occasion a male white rhino jumped down into the moat. We built a ramp and tried to herd him out, but he was stubborn and wouldn't budge.

Jerry Stones' green sweater is visible on the front of this stubborn rhino.

PHOTO COURTESY OF THE *OMAHA WORLD-HERALD.*

We tried coaxing him with grain, fruit and water but nothing worked. Finally, Jerry Stones remembered that this rhino had taken a great dislike to an old green sweater Jerry used to wear. Jerry got his sweater, went down into the moat and slapped the rhino in the face with it. He got an immediate charge and outran the rhino up the ramp across the yard and into the building. White rhinos are generally very docile animals, and this pair was so easygoing that two of our keepers used to Roman ride them around the enclosure with a foot on each rhino's back.

SNOWED IN

One January we had a heavy blizzard moving our way, and we advised our staff to finish their work in advance so they could get home before the storm hit. We kept a 10-man snow crew at the zoo so they could make rounds of the buildings and animals quarters to inspect furnaces and so forth. Our only piece of snow equipment in those days was a snow plow attachment for the front of my Jeep. I drove it home to make sure Marie and the kids were situated, and just as the storm hit decided to make a quick run back to the zoo to make sure everything was in place there. As I backed out of the drive, a neighbor asked me where I was going. I explained, and he asked to ride along since we would only be gone an hour. So off we went.

Everything was fine at the zoo. Bernie and I should have left immediately because the storm was building rapidly and visibility had deteriorated to near zero. Just as we were about to leave our dietitian decided to make a run for it, but his old car stalled in the middle of the zoo gate. The snow was coming down so fast and the wind was blowing so hard that before we could do anything his car was covered in a snowdrift. We were stuck, thus increasing the size of the snow crew from 10 to 12. We made walking rounds, kept the furnaces burning, pulled hay, grain and food to the animals on a makeshift sled and kept everything going for the next three days. In those days because we worked prisoners at the zoo for six hours a day, we also bought dented cans of soup in bulk. The prisoners hated tomato soup and wouldn't eat it, which meant that we had plenty of leftover tomato soup on hand. But that was about it. For three days we ate week-old bread, boiled eggs, apples and tomato soup three times a day. One member of our crew broiled himself a horsemeat steak, but the rest of us passed. The animals all survived, and so did we. When the city snowplows finally hammered their way into the zoo I took Bernie home. We both agreed that the next time I was making a quick run to the zoo, he would just stay home.

A few years later we found ourselves snowed in at the zoo again. By then we had a three-person snowmobile and sled and were much better equipped and provisioned to survive the four-day storm. That time we elected to fight the storm, so we took a hammer to the padlock of the city maintenance shop, which then was located in the park. We borrowed the city's big V plow to stay ahead of the snow. We were doing fine until the engine stalled in the service gate. By the time we got it started, the snow had drifted around the plow, trapping it. Five days later, the city's maintenance staff asked if we knew where their snowplow was. We pointed to the service gate where the plow's exhaust pipe was barely poking out of a nine-foot drift. They were not happy.

A DIFFERENT KIND OF RARE ANTHROPOID APE

At a 1971 zoo conference in L.A. there was a two legged creature that none of us had heard of called a "Docent." A Latin word meaning "teacher guide." We had no education department so this seemed a good solution. We started with six Junior League ladies. We devoted most of the year to developing a curriculum and a program plan. The second year we put an ad in the paper and had over 60 serious applicants. We started 17 weeks of training classes with me being the primary lecturer. There was a lady in the front row who was just eating me alive with questions. At a coffee break I decided I better find out who this was. Jean Bressler was a professor and head of the English department at UNO who was so well organized that she had time to be a docent. I went back to the front and told everyone to listen very close, because next year they would have to do the training themselves. I would just be a guest lecturer but would appoint a docent coordinator who would run things. At the next coffee break Jean agreed to accept the unpaid position but only on her strict terms. There would be an exam at each weekly class with a 70 percent minimum score, a take home exam every week with a 90 percent minimum score and everyone had to volunteer a minimum of four hours a week or you were out. I was afraid everyone would immediately quit, but Jean was adamant. The alternative was to keep teaching classes forever. The only qualifications for being a docent would be the ability to absorb knowledge and then transmit it accurately back to students and visitors. AMAZINGLY NO ONE LEFT OR EVEN TRIED TO ESCAPE, and 250-300 docents became an incredible educational asset to the zoo with a high degree of esprit de corps. Some would become "Monkey Moms" to take care of baby animals in the zoo nursery and many traveled the world with us on safaris. Like our staff, many docents have served for 30-40 years or more.

PUPPIES AND THE MOTEL FIRE

In the fall of 1979, Marie, our two girls, their two schnauzer puppies and I attended the Nebraska Veterinary Medical Association annual conference in Grand Island. I had been an active member of the NVMA since coming to Nebraska and that year was being awarded the Veterinarian of the Year award. Unfortunately, the award ceremony never happened.

We had arrived at the Holiday Inn in Grand Island early the evening before, and after registration and check in I visited with a number of Omaha and Nebraska veterinarians. A group of us decided to go to supper at a popular restaurant. It was so popular, it was past nine o'clock before we actually sat down to eat. Arriving back at the motel, Marie said it was time for the girls to be in bed so we went to our room. My plan was to get everybody tucked in and then go back to the hospitality suite and visit. Luckily there was a Cousteau movie about whales on the TV, and I got interested. About midnight Marie smelled smoke, and when I went to the door the smell was stronger. Remembering a TV special on hotel fires I checked the door handle to make sure it wasn't hot and then cracked the door open an inch. Dense black, oily smoke rolled in through the crack so I slammed the door shut, wet some towels and packed them along the bottom of the door and began filling the bathtub with water. We tried to call the front desk but there was no answer. I didn't know how we were going to get out of the room. We were on the third floor, and it appeared the hallways was full of black smoke. Looking out through the window we could see people gathering outside. I decided to break a window and make a bed sheet rope. Breaking the big picture window turned out to be a problem because it was tempered glass. I hit it repeatedly with a chair as hard as I could but it wouldn't break. I stopped to catch my breath and realized I was hitting it in the middle, and the chair was simply bouncing back. I grabbed the chair by 2 legs and aimed the tip of a third leg at the bottom right-hand corner of the window. I hit it as hard as I could, and the window shattered into a million small pieces. We tore strips of bed sheets from the two beds and made a rope just like in the movies.

Heather and Heidi refused to leave until their puppies were safe, so I called out to some of the vets on the ground to catch them as I dropped them from the window. Country veterinarians are pretty steady in a crisis, and they caught both puppies and put them on top of my Jeep for safekeeping. I put a double layer of blankets over the windowsill to cover the glass and lowered both girls, one at a time, out the window and into waiting hands below. I tied the bed sheet rope around Marie and lowered her out the window to the vets below. In order to climb down the rope myself I had to tie one end of it to a bed leg across the room, which made it too short to reach the ground. The vets below rolled up a 55-gallon barrel and with one of them standing on the barrel, I climbed down the rope and the vet guided my feet into cracks in the brickwork until I could stand on the barrel. By this time there were a substantial number of veterinarians gathered outside the motel, but we could still see people unable to get out of their rooms on the second and third floors. Some of the rooms were full of smoke, and it was obvious that some of the guests had opened their doors wide without thinking. We could see people pounding on their windows just as I had but the tempered glass windows wouldn't break. I had an old 22-caliber Stevens Favorite rifle in my Jeep Wagoner that I used for predator control around the zoo. I grabbed it and starting shooting out each window where I saw rooms full of smoke. By cracking the tempered glass at the top right-hand corner, it shattered into a million small pieces without endangering anyone. With the windows broken out the rooms ventilated, but there was still no way to get people out of their rooms. A couple vets came back with a long ladder they had borrowed off of the side of a barn from a nearby farm. With everybody cooperating and working together we got everyone out of all the rooms and on the ground. The Grand Island volunteer fire department had responded to the call but long before they got to our side of the motel the Nebraska veterinarians had organized and gotten everyone out safely.

The fire turned out to be confined to the bottom floor of the other wing where a musician had been smoking in bed. Unfortunately, the motel staff had committed two grave errors. First, they had put wedges under all of the fire doors in the corridors to hold them open because it made housekeeping easier. Second, they had been having problems with drunks pulling fire alarms, so they had installed a switch behind the desk for nights when there were a lot of problems. On this night the fire alarm circuit had been shut off, and when all of the oily black smoke from the fire billowed into the hallway it filled the corridors of all three floors in both wings of the motel.

Luckily no one died, but two of our veterinary colleagues had burns, one of them serious. We took the girls to a pancake house for some coffee and hot chocolate and then found another motel for rest of the night. The next morning, we were able to get into our room and retrieve all of our smoky clothing and belongings.

We learned that the Holiday Inn Corporation, while not the best at fire safety, had a legal department full of expertise in hotel fires.

DR. ULYSSES S. SEAL

Dr. Ulysses S. Seal arguably had a greater positive impact on the science and practice of zoo management, exotic animal husbandry and species conservation than any other individual in the collective memory of those who practice these disciplines. And he wasn't a zoo person, at least not in the classic sense.

Ulie was a biochemist, hematologist, and conservation biologist. His involvement in conservation began as a scientist and professor at the University of Minnesota and as head of the laboratories at the Veterans Administration Hospital in Minneapolis. He had a wide range of wildlife interests beyond humans. He was involved in collaborative research programs which became decades-long projects working on wolves with Dave Mech, white-tail deer with Ed Plotka, bears in Minnesota and Wisconsin and working with the Como Zoo in St. Paul, Minnesota and the Minnesota State Zoo in Apple Valley.

My second contact and the broader zoo community's first contact with Ulie came at a zoo veterinarians conference in East Lansing, Michigan, in 1969 where he presented papers on the pineal gland in wolves and thyroid function in white tail deer. Later that same evening at an informal gathering of 25 plus zoo vets we were having a few drinks and passing around lab reports for comment or advice. We were lamenting the fact that no one really knew what was statistically normal for many blood values in exotic animals. A stranger with a mop of hair, and now with a full beard and a booming voice stepped out from the back of the crowd. The first thing that we heard Ulie say was, "It looks to me that what the zoo world needs is a physiological norms database for each species." Talk about making an entrance.

Clint Gray from the National Zoo, in his usual tactful manner, replied, "Hell, don't you think we know that!" Everyone readily agreed on the need, but it was a huge task given the range of species spread across North America. No one zoo had the resources.

Ulie introduced himself as a professor at the University of Minnesota and head of the laboratories at the Veterans Hospital in Minneapolis.

He then promptly volunteered to do all of the lab work at the VA Labs, pro bono, if the zoo vets would all work together to collect a broad representative set of blood samples. Many in that room were unquestionably thinking, "Wow, what

Here I am with a rare Dibatag antelope in 1967.

an incredible resource!" Only later did we realize that Ulie was probably thinking, "Wow, what an incredible resource!"

After he left, someone asked, "Do you think he's for real?" Clint Gray said, "And who in the hell invited him anyway?"

Even at that early stage, Ulie's intensity and innate credibility came through so strongly that within two weeks of the meeting he was in Omaha and we drew blood from nearly every animal in the collection, including 16 adult cheetahs that we hand grabbed. Clint Gray shortly invited Ulie to the National Zoo. Thus began a round of zoo excursions for Ulie, myself and others to collect blood for the project. After collecting, receiving and processing more than 5,000 blood samples from many different institutions, Ulie came to the 1972 Zoo Veterinarians Conference in Houston having been able to establish statistically normal blood values for 12 species. We all thought we had died and gone to heaven. As soon as the excitement and backslapping died down, Ulie dropped the first bombshell of what would become a three decades long series of bombshells and innovative ideas. He said, "You know that all of this is really worthless unless you have a database to tie it to individual animals." Then he volunteered to see if such a thing was possible. From this, the SEAMAK ZOOGAD system was born, a computerized database in the days when very few North American zoos even had computers.

No sooner was this system up and running on a mainframe at the University of Minnesota when Ulie dropped the next bombshell. "To be truly useful, what the zoo world needs is a computerized species inventory system which could cover all individuals of all species in all institutions everywhere in the world instead of just a U.S.-based census and clinical database," he said. Thus, was born, ISIS (The International Species Inventory System, now renamed "Species 360" for obvious reasons), which has led more than 1,060 zoos all over the world down the path toward having a single standardized database to communicate with each other. After 43 years it included 62 million records on 10 million animals of

22,000 species. This has now been greatly expanded to include medical records, husbandry, behavior, genetic information and more.

During this time Ulie became actively involved in a broad range of research and reproductive programs with many institutions around the country. Also during this time, the zoo world began to realize that, in addition to being a scientist, leader and mentor in the fields of medicine, reproduction, management and conservation, Ulie had also become one of the all-time great volunteers and collaborators in support of individual zoo institutions worldwide. He had a unique ability to grasp a subject thoroughly, yet you never felt that he was talking down to you. As a driven workaholic, the number of hours and effort that Ulie put into helping solve problems for the zoo world were huge and led more than a few people to wonder what he hoped to get out of it all. The answer, of course, was nothing, at least monetarily speaking. For Ulie, the payback was simply good science that answered questions, solved problems and benefitted animals, zoos and conservation. Ulie's fiercely held independence to do science, be innovative and think out of the box hinged on his refusal to accept any personal remuneration for his efforts.

Ulie developed a reputation for enthusiastically going anywhere to help solve a problem or answer a question, all for just a plane ride, somewhere to sleep and a good meal. He was frequently accompanied on these marathons by his life partner, Maryalice, who was also one of the world's ultimate volunteers. If you couldn't afford the plane ticket, he'd find the money elsewhere or pay for the tickets himself. These efforts were more often than not collaborative, involving multiple disciplines and institutions. And so grew a network of individuals, scientists, zoo professionals and biologists who began to work together, to collaborate and communicate.

What also grew was an industry-wide trust in Ulie's out-of-the-box and over-the-horizon ideas and suggestions. His contributions were good for zoos and conservation, even if we often didn't fully understand where each one was leading. A growing group of individuals and institutions evolved to support research and conservation worldwide. The result has been that individuals and institutions who likely would never have worked together on a collaborative project, did so.

If Ulie was the father of ISIS (Species 360), then Nate Flesness was certainly the mother. Nate came onboard in 1979 and served as executive director until 2009. During that time Nate wrote code, did programing, became a successful grant writer to support database development and generally did whatever was necessary to make the system work for its user zoos. Plus, he helped keep the organization afloat financially.

When in 1979 Ulie was asked by Peter Scott to become chairman of the newly formed Captive Breeding Specialists Group of the IUCN he agreed to take early retirement from the VA and serve pro bono. Unfortunately, there was no money for an operating budget. Under the gentle arm twisting from Katharine Roberts, director of the Minnesota State Zoo, 10 U.S. zoo directors got together and each pledged $10,000 per year for 10 years. The evolution of CBSG under Ulie's iconic leadership was the ultimate example of what can be done with innovative, out of the box thinking, active collaboration and a hell of a lot of determination. When Ulie was asked to become chair of CBSG, it's likely some folks in IUCN probably thought, "Boy, what a great resource he could be for conservation in zoos!" And all the while, Ulie was probably thinking, "Boy, what a great resource the CBSG platform could be to change the way we do conservation worldwide."

Under Ulie, CBSG evolved from the Captive Breeding Specialists Group to the Conservation Breeding Specialists Group and now has become The Conservation Planning Specialists Group, complete with a large group of active supporters and regional resource centers in India, southeast Asia, Mexico, Meso America, South America, Southern Africa, Brazil, Austral-Asia, Japan, Indonesia, North America and Europe. The result has been an ever expanding and rebounding ripple of collaboration that has now spread worldwide, leading individuals and institutions to work together to commit manpower and resources to projects which may or may not have immediate benefit to their individual institutions but have advanced the cause of insitu and exsitu conservation and population management worldwide.

In addition to working with Ulie on conservation projects in Russia, Laos and Vietnam it was my good fortune to work together on zoo master planning projects in Thailand, Saigon, Rome, Budapest and Seoul and on CBSG programs all over the world. Ulie was an inveterate fence jumper, and it was impossible to keep him out of territories which others had already staked out. This sometimes made life interesting.

In 34 years of working with

PHOTO COURTESY OF THE OMAHA WORLD HERALD

Drawing blood with Ulie Seal from a Jentinks Duiker; below with "Mombasa," a user-friendly cheetah in 1969.

Ulie we only had words once. It was when he mortgaged his house to support a conservation project we didn't have money for. We solved that problem, reimbursed Ulie and established a balanced budget policy.

Through his innovative leadership, mentoring and gentle coercion, Ulie has changed all of us in the way we think, manage zoos and support conservation. This change is in all likelihood irreversible, and the Ulysses S. Seal ripple effect will likely go on forever. Ulie was one of the most intelligent and scientifically knowledgeable people I have ever known, and he was a friend. Another friend, Dr. Ed Plotka, and I were honored to give his eulogy.

NEW ORLEANS

In late 1970, Ulie Seal and I were asked by Phil Ogilvie, the director of the Minneapolis State Zoo, who was doing some consulting work for the New Orleans Zoo, to assemble a medical team to evaluate the health of all of the animals in the Audubon Zoo in New Orleans. The Audubon Zoo today is one of the top zoos in the country and is professionally run, but this was not always so. Since we were just beginning to develop our physiological norms database for blood values, it seemed like an opportunity to collect blood samples from all the animals in the entire zoo. Plus, they were willing to pay for our work and expenses.

Ulie and his wife Maryalice put together a team of laboratory technicians from Minnesota, and I put together a small team of two husky zookeepers, John Jarecki and Marty Stumbaugh, from Omaha. In February 1971 the Minneapolis team boarded a Braniff airliner to Omaha where they met us and continued on to New Orleans. We had nearly two feet of snow on the ground when we left Omaha, so when we arrived in New Orleans and it was 72 degrees, we thought we had died and gone to heaven. We went to the zoo, offloaded our gear and inspected the facilities just before dark. Then we retreated to our hotel. The next morning, we got up at five, ate breakfast and went to the zoo. Thus began perhaps the most intense four days of activity and work I can remember.

We logged 18-hour days while chemically immobilizing or hand grabbing 384 animals. We tested for tuberculosis, took blood samples, hair samples, fecal samples, skin biopsies and radiographed their long bones and chests where applicable. To this day, no one has ever immobilized that many animals in such a short period of time.

In collaboration with Tulane University Medical School we had arranged for an x-ray machine and a team of staff and students to take and evaluate radiographs on designated animals. All of the blood samples, hair samples, fecal samples and skin biopsies would be processed and evaluated by the Minneapolis Veterans Hospital team.

Ulie and I pooled our consulting money for film and a cameraman to record everything on 16 mm film. Unfortunately, our cameraman had an illness

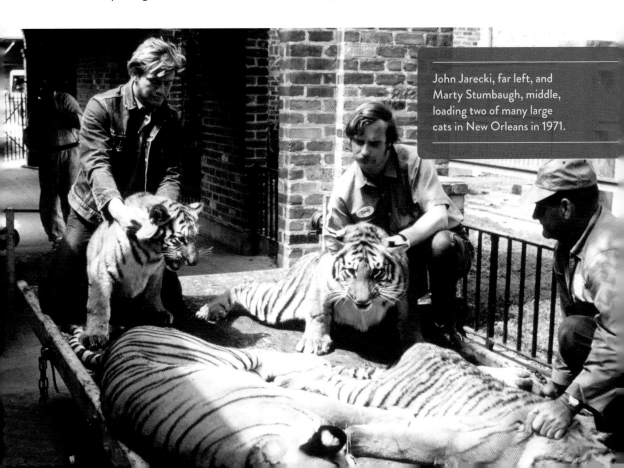

John Jarecki, far left, and Marty Stumbaugh, middle, loading two of many large cats in New Orleans in 1971.

in the family at the last minute, so we had to substitute one of Dr. Seal's graduate students. Despite no actual cinematography experience, he turned out to be very steady with the camera and took directions well. For four days I had both a stethoscope and a light meter around my neck and gave instructions to our new cameraman in between working on animals. The result was nearly an hour of edited film that shows—among other things—whole wagonloads of big cats and bears, all immobilized and being transported and processed at the same time.

Don Bridgewater, assistant director at the new Apple Valley Zoo outside Minneapolis, had come along to handle all of our liaison work and had made a couple of preparatory visits to New Orleans prior to February. Before leaving for New Orleans, we were under the impression that our invitation came from the Audubon Zoo and the City of New Orleans. As it turned out it was not the city but a nonprofit organization investigating graft and corruption in New Orleans Parish that had arranged for this zoo evaluation and was paying all of our expenses. Shortly after takeoff we learned otherwise when Don said, "Now about that bomb threat, we really don't think they are going to do it." Apparently, the city officials and zoo staff were actually quite opposed to our coming, but it was too late to turn back.

The New Orleans Zoo at that time did not have any professional staff and was managed by a nephew of the current mayor. Some of their keepers had been there for some time and others were fresh off the street. There were no veterinary staff, curators, dietitians or anyone with formal biological training.

During our walk around that first evening it seemed the condition of the exhibits and facilities was not as bad as had been represented. This opinion would change dramatically the next day. What was apparent was that their favorite color was battleship gray, since most of the exhibits and enclosures and even the floor and walls of the large room we had been assigned were freshly painted gray. The next day as we began setting up the lab space to process blood and hair samples and biopsies, the paint, which had been acquired surplus from a shipyard, began to flake up. By noon all of the traffic areas in the room were covered with ground-up paint chips, which likely were heavy in lead, copper and other substances to inhibit marine growth on ships. It turned out that in the week before our arrival just about everything in the zoo had been painted. The staff had not done any preparatory work, so that whatever was on floors and walls, be it left over food or animal feces, simply got painted. When we opened the first cages the next day there were gray lumps on the floors that turned out to be painted-over feces and food. Many of the animals' feet were gray; the painters had painted with the animals still in their cages. The padlocks were rusted shut and couldn't be opened, so for four days we kept the zoo staff busy buying new padlocks. By the time we had worked our way through all of the exhibits and enclosures in the zoo, most of that battleship gray paint had turned to flakes and dust. We never found out if it was lead based.

The zoo had a sizable collection of bears and a large collection of cats. We went down the line and darted all of them, one after another, and loaded them onto large farm wagons to be pulled by a tractor to a central lawn area outside of our temporary lab. We laid them out side-by-side on the grass, sometimes as many as 20 or more animals at a time, and processed them.

Each team had specific duties while Ulie and I did the darting, drew blood and kept track of the level of anesthesia. Since we were using sernylan as our chief immobilizing agent we didn't have to worry about animals coming up suddenly or being aggressive when they did. Nor did we have to worry as much about regurgitation and aspiration as we might have with other anesthetic agents. We had asked that all the animals be held off food for a minimum of 24 to 48 hours to avoid such problems. As it turned out, our instructions hadn't always been followed, but more on that later. With so many animals immobilized at once it was inevitable that some of them would begin to metabolize the drugs before we finished our procedures. Whenever somebody shouted that a tiger or lion had gotten up, one of us would go over, grab it by the tail and administer another dose of sernylan. At a casual glance I'm sure this all looked pretty chaotic, but it was actually more like the controlled chaos you might see on the deck of an aircraft carrier where everyone had a specific job and got it done quite efficiently. As I said, never before or since have this many exotic animals been immobilized and sampled in such a short period of time.

While immobilizing a female tigress and her four cubs, each of which weighed between 50 and 60 pounds, we witnessed another of nature's countless phenomena. Our plan was to immobilize the mother and then net and hand grab the cubs. I put a dart in her, and she went down smoothly, but as she became ataxic amazingly all four cubs attacked her with a vengeance. There was no question they were seriously intent on killing and eating her. This was the first time that I realized that predatory behavior is hardwired. Even though she was the cubs' own mother, once she was unable to defend herself she became a prey species. We rushed in and pulled the cubs off—not without difficulty—and carried her out to the wagon. We ultimately put them back together but only after she was fully recovered from the phencyclidine. By then she was again the boss.

There were other surprises. We only lost one animal under anesthesia, a female hippo. We had asked that all animals be fasted for 24 hours and the hippos, elephants and large ruminants be starved out for 48 hours before they were scheduled to be immobilized. Unfortunately, some members of the hippo staff disagreed and just before we started had given them all they could eat. The grain immediately swelled up with water in their stomachs, and when we administered what should have been a light sedating dose of M99 and the female went down, her stomach and abdominal contents pushed up and compressed her lungs. Her respiration was severely compromised. She sat with her mouth open, head up, trying hard to get air into her lungs to no avail. Despite immediately administering the reversing agent for M99 in a tongue vein (and a rather heroic attempt at resuscitation) the animal died of anoxia very quickly. Late that night when we did a postmortem examination the stomach was so large and heavy that two strong men could barely lift it out of the abdominal cavity. Given the relatively small lung capacity, short rib cage and large abdominal content of a hippo it was little wonder that her lungs were compressed to the point that she could not exchange oxygen. Additionally, this animal had more than five gallons of vile-smelling brown fluid in her uterus which later cultured out a cosmopolitan population of bacteria.

From that point on we asked very pointed questions of the keepers just before we immobilized each animal.

We had another interesting surprise just before dark at the end of a very long day when Ulie broke my concentration with a question. We were about to immobilize a small herd of Tule elk, and I had just loaded a succinylcholine dart when Ulie interrupted me. We talked for a moment, and then I went back to immobilize the animal, loading a second dart into the gun barrel behind the first one. When I squeezed off the shot I remember thinking, "Gee, that's the first time I ever felt a CO-2 dart gun kick." I watched in wonder as a red yarn tailpiece and a yellow yarn tailpiece slowly separated as they traveled downrange to strike the animal in the rump about 6 inches apart. Both darts fired and injected identical doses of succinylcholine into the animal. Luckily this is a drug that is very effective on cervids, who happily have a wide dosage tolerance. It's a short-acting skeletal muscle paralytic agent that is quickly metabolized. Ulie and I were totally astonished at what had just happened, yet it was the smoothest immobilization that I had ever made on an elk. The animal stayed in sternal decumbency and never exhibited the slightest bit of distress or anoxia. Murphy's Law still ruled.

Late one night we decided to get a blood sample from a large male (six-foot, 190-pound), double-wattled cassowary. In those days we had no good immobilizing agents for birds, so I decided to throw a large lariat loop on the floor and when he stepped into it with both feet, snap it up around his legs and pull him up against the mesh enclosure. The surprise came when he jerked one leg up just as we yanked the loop tight. When the keepers pulled his left foot up against the mesh he kicked with his right foot, breaking a 2 x 4 into my midsection and knocking the wind out of me. We grabbed his legs and found out that cassowaries have sharp scales, almost like a big wood rasp for taking the skin off of your fingers. Ultimately, we got our blood sample from the jugular vein. We went for the jugular because we could not find a vein in the cassowary's rudimentary wings. We have continued bleeding birds from the jugular to this day.

While we were immobilizing animals and doing our medical evaluations, Ralph Waterhouse was digging up animal records so that we could at least have some data such as names and ages for our database. In the process he inadvertently uncovered some financial information. It turned out there were two chunks of zoo money, one for $60,000 and one for $25,000 that were going directly from the zoo to the mayor's office. Mr. Brown, who was head of the nonprofit investigating New Orleans Parish, was not surprised but very interested. It also turned out that the main diet for almost any animal that would eat it was day-old French bread collected from the French Quarter restaurants in New Orleans. So much for good nutrition.

Even though it was not our primary mission, we always quietly took credit for the fact that our report and some of the other things we inadvertently uncovered kicked off the scandal that ultimately led the New Orleans Zoo to hire a professional director and redirected it toward becoming the first class zoo it is today.

As an interesting aside, each morning Don went to the café early and ordered our breakfast so it would be on the table when we came down. Then he'd go out and give three guys $10 apiece to go into the garage to drive our cars down and idle them at the curb. Still, he said, no one really thought the bomb threat was serious.

On the last night before the Minneapolis group went home we were intending to grab a quick dinner at the little café across the street from our hotel, but Mr. Brown wanted to take us out for a real New Orleans meal. We tried to tell him that it wouldn't work because it was already very late and we were covered in mud and manure. By the time we could get back to the hotel, shower and change clothes, it would be midnight. "No problem," he said, since his wife's family owned Delmonico's and he had reserved a private upstairs dining room.

So, we went to the restaurant, trouped upstairs, had a few drinks and a fabulous dinner. Everybody was happy and frankly somewhat amazed that we had been able to accomplish as much as we had in four days. Then as we started down the stairs to leave the restaurant, John Jarecki, an Omaha keeper who was a very muscular, physically fit, farm boy suddenly got charley horses in the calves of both legs. He had spent most of the last 4 days squatting on his heels or lifting. It was a runaway as he fought to keep his feet, charging down the stairs and out into the main dining room on his toes. He tipped forward and grabbed a small table with both hands in a death grip, his toes were pointed rigidly out behind him. John made unintelligible, agonizing sounds in front of a well-dressed older couple as he gripped their table like he was doing pushups. Maryalice Seal, who was an RN, recognized the problem immediately and told me to massage one of his calves while she massaged the other.

As we did that, I watched as the little old man and the little old lady, quietly pushed their chairs back, folded their hands in their laps and watched us without uttering a word. We must have been a sight. Maryalice and I finally got the spasms in his calves massaged out and stood him up. I apologized to the couple for disturbing their dinner and explained that he had spent the majority of the last four days lifting and carrying animals and squatting on his heels. They looked at me but never said a single word as we left the restaurant and returned to our hotel.

After Ulie Seal and the Minneapolis team left, we stayed on for an extra day to read the intradermal TB tests on the great apes and some of the hoofstock. We had a rental car all loaded with our gear but were slow in starting for the airport. Thus, we got caught in traffic. I was afraid we would miss our plane. We roared up in front of the Braniff terminal, piled all of our gear helter-skelter on top of the scales and told the agent to simply get it to Omaha as soon as they could. We also told him to notify the car agency that their car was parked at the curb. We grabbed the dart guns and poll syringes and ran for the airplane. We had to go down a flight of stairs, and at the bottom was a small kiosk where a man was supposed to be guarding against hijackers. When he saw the three of us charging down the stairs with rifles, he thought we were hijackers, completely lost it and ran. Happily, no one shot us and the rest of the airport and airline staff were somewhat amused. They let us get on the airplane carrying the two 50 caliber dart rifles and a bundle of poll syringes. Things probably wouldn't turn out that well in today's world.

RUSSIA IN THE WINTER

During the first week of December 1978, Dr. Ulysses S. Seal and I, accompanied by a researcher from the Bureau of Land Management, visited Russia. We had been invited to be part of a scientific exchange program on the chemical immobilization of wild animals. We considered it an honor to be chosen. However, Ulie and I had an ulterior motive. The Moscow Zoo had a number of rare animals that existed almost nowhere else, and we were still in the process of expanding the physiological norms database for exotic animal blood values. This was before perestroika and glasnost, so we went through Washington, D.C., for a State Department briefing on the way there. Ulie was then a professor at the University of Minnesota and head of the V.A. laboratories in Minneapolis.

Ulie was generally acknowledged as the father of conservation biology for the zoo world in the United States and had immobilized a large number of zoo animals to draw blood. Milton was working on reducing the impact of wild horses on government land in the west by capturing them. I was invited because I also had immobilized a large number of exotic animals. I had also invented and was manufacturing and selling three pieces of equipment for long-range chemical immobilization. The first was an aluminum-pole syringe with two-foot sections that could be screwed together to make six, eight, 10, 12 or 16-foot-long poles. The second was a 50-caliber dart rifle powered by a heavy 22-caliber blank cartridge. The gun had a metering valve that allowed for adjustment of the muzzle velocity from 150 feet-per-second up to 1100 feet-per-second. It could be used as close as six feet or as far out as 85 yards. Unlike CO-2-powered guns, which were useless when cold, our Zoolu Arms Guns worked at any temperature. The third piece of equipment was a red plastic finned tailpiece for the Palmer dart, which greatly enhanced its accuracy and range.

A representative from the State Department briefed us on things to do, things to avoid and generally how to stay out of trouble. We had previously given them a list of all of the drugs, equipment and materials we were bringing to Russia. They had telexed it to their Russian counterparts and also to the Moscow office of the Department of Forestry, which was analogous to the U.S. Department of the Interior.

That night we went out to dinner so Ulie and I could get to know Milton. We ordered a bottle of wine, and Milton, a Mormon, explained that he didn't strictly follow the precepts of his church, so he had a glass with us. The next morning, we flew to London to transfer to British Air for the flight to Moscow. In London we were offloaded down a rollup stair and led through a door. We then walked up a set of stairs and down a long hall to a security checkpoint where our carry-on luggage could be searched. Here our problems began. Ulie and I had both been worried about the drugs in our medical bags freezing in the cold, so we bought Johnny Warmers, used by hunters to warm their hands in the winter, to put in our medical bags and pockets when we were in field. They work by flamelessly combusting lighter fluid to produce heat with a catalytic converter. We had stocked up on lighter fluid in Omaha and Minneapolis, but both of us panicked a bit in Washington and decided to buy more. Between us we had well over a gallon of highly flammable lighter fluid in our carry-on luggage when we hit the security checkpoint. The British security agents took a very dim view. We knew they meant business because we had just watched them take a German guy behind a screen in the hall and strip search him. Regardless, I argued strongly because I was unsure if we could find lighter fluid in Russia, and without it our drugs would surely freeze. I noticed Ulie was quietly giving me the sign to shut up. Having worked together for a long time, I followed his signal, but I was still uneasy about it. We got on the airplane, and once we were airborne Ulie told me that he had two pint-sized cans of Johnny Warmer fluid in the toes of his felt lined boots that the search had missed.

Our next adventure began the moment we landed in Moscow. As we got off the plane, before we even got to customs, we were met by a large Russian delegation that included Alexander Nikolaevsky, the official interpreter for the Ministry of Agriculture; V. V. Krinintsky, the vice minister of the department of forestry; Dr. Razmahnin, deputy director of their Central Laboratory; Dr. Vassely N. Popanov and Dr. Michael M. Tchizov, two senior scientists of their Central Laboratory and others. Dr. Seal was the leader of our U.S. scientific team, and Dr. Razmahnin was the leader of the Russian scientific team. We were surprised at the size of the delegation, but it turned out that they had neglected to read the State Department's telex until we were already in the air from London. Only then did they realize that I was bringing three rifles and a pistol—all dart guns but nevertheless prohibited—and we were also bringing a large supply of phencyclidine (angel dust) and M99 (etorphine), a narcotic 6,000 times more potent than morphine. Both were prohibited. The biggest surprise seemed to be when they realized we were carrying small radio-tracking transmitters that would fit on our darts and a radio receiver and directional antenna. They surrounded us and told us that under no circumstances were we to open our suitcases or show their customs agents any drugs or equipment or we would never be allowed out of the airport and we would be sent immediately back to the U.S. They told us to get out one bottle of M99 and if we had any drugs, then they literally herded us through Russian customs without any inspection whatsoever. They rounded up a small bus to handle our luggage, and we went to the Hotel Russia where Dr. Vladimir Spitsin, the director of the Moscow Zoo, joined us.

For the rest of the night our Russian colleagues told us to not do anything that would get us in trouble because the authorities would just send us back home, but their necks were on the line. They would be in trouble because they had vouched for us. They were fascinated by my dart guns, but what troubled them most was the radio dart transmitter and the receiver. After supper they insisted that we show them how they worked, so we spent an hour or so tracking a Russian man carrying a transmitter up and down the hallways of the very large Hotel Russia. Then the Russians told us they wanted our transmitter checked out by their equivalent of our FAA to make sure that they would not interfere with aviation. We gave them the dart transmitter, the receiver and the antenna. They then said they had no other concerns, and when we opened another suitcase and showed them 11 more dart transmitters and a second receiver and antenna set they just laughed. We assumed they simply wanted to reverse engineer our equipment.

Vladimir Spitsin, the fairly new Moscow zoo director, quietly pulled me aside and said, "You're a zoo director and a veterinarian so you should understand my concern. You have sent a list of animals at the Moscow zoo that you want to draw blood from, and my boss has given his permission so I really have no say in this matter. I am very worried because we have never successfully immobilized any of these species. How am I going to explain all of these dead animals to the public?"

I assured him that I understood his concerns, but we were pretty damn good at what we did and would work very hard to not kill any of his animals. Later we learned that the whole trip had been blessed from higher up and was under our complete control, we just didn't know it at the time. I suggested that Vladimir should make a list of all of the animals that had medical problems or that he wanted examined, and we would immobilize those for them. He was relieved and agreed.

Early the next morning we loaded everyone and our equipment aboard a train and headed south for a 27-hour ride to Krasnodar, near the Black Sea. We were supposed to stop and work in a large conservation breeding reserve in Voronezh, but there was a problem with the natural gas supply and they said all of the water and sewers were frozen. On the train, a pretty young girl with lots of makeup came into the compartment Ulie and I were sharing and sat down. She didn't appear to speak English, and we thought it unusual since she was virtually the first woman with any kind of makeup on that we had seen in Russia. We were in a first-class compartment with two permanent narrow lower bunks separated by a foot of space. There were two upper bunks that could be folded down. We were working on paperwork when Dr. Razmahnin and Irina, our interpreter, came in to check on us. There was an immediate discussion between them and the girl which got loud and angry, and Dr. Razmahnin literally shoved her out of the compartment with his hands. We were puzzled until he said, "KGB." He was past retirement age, and as head of their central laboratory, I think he did pretty much as he wanted. He explained through Irina that he was a Cossack, and traditional Cossack hospitality demanded that we be treated with respect. We were the first Americans that he had ever met, and he was very curious, as he put it, "to measure what the Russian newspaper propaganda said against what we said."

When I went to use the restroom at the end of the car, it, like all train restrooms, was quite small, but what surprised me was that everything was totally covered with a white fluid that had been applied with a brush. I went back to the compartment to see if I could find a newspaper to make a seat cover and was told that nobody in their right mind sat on the seat. You stood on it with your feet and squatted. It was an interesting experience to look down and see the snow on the tracks whizzing by below as the cold air rushed up through the toilet.

KRASNODAR

We arrived at Krasnodar late in the morning, checked in with the local police, took a quick tour of the town and went to what they called the hunters lodge. It was a large, two-story masonry mansion that had belonged to a wealthy German farmer before World War II. It was now used primarily to entertain members of the Politburo who came to hunt red deer. After lunch I asked if there was a place where I could sight-in two of my rifles since they had only come off of my workbench immediately before leaving for Russia. This set up an interesting turn of events with an impromptu shooting match with the Russians. It was probably somewhat unfair since both of their systems were inherently less accurate. Once I had sighted-in my rifles and the match began, we progressively increased the range. After 40 yards the Russians declined to shoot, but I progressively pushed

Ulie Seal, left, during our 1978 trip to Krasnodar, Russia.

Four different, unique Russian capture gun darts.

the range out to 80 yards. As a result, I automatically drew their best hunter the following day. He had an uncanny tracking ability, and if you put a dart into a red deer and there was even the slightest track through other deer tracks in the woods, he could follow it. Fortunately for me he was quite a bit older, shorter and wore layers of heavy wool clothing and heavy rubber boots. Even so he nearly walked me into the ground despite the fact that I had much longer legs, was wearing lightweight goose down clothing and lightweight insulated boots.

While we were using phencyclidine and M99, the Russians were using succinylcholine, a skeletal muscle paralytic that we had mostly abandoned 20 years before. They did not have a syringe dart like ours and instead mixed their paralytic into a paste with glucose and a pharmaceutical gum and smeared it into annular grooves on the penetrating stylets of their darts or around their brass bullets. The number of grooves they filled determined the size of the dosage. Their method was less precise from the standpoint of controlling dosage, and the paste could deteriorate or fall out, thus altering the amount injected into the animal. It had one advantage however, in that succinylcholine acts as a meat tenderizer when used to euthanize an animal. We had some difficulty convincing them that phencyclidine was not readily destroyed or metabolized in an animal, and a red deer that we had immobilized with it could not be taken back to camp and eaten. A red deer steak laced with phencyclidine (angel dust) coupled with the amount of vodka, wine and brandy consumed at each meal could have knocked everybody unconscious. They solved the problem by sending a hunter out with a rifle, and we still had red deer steaks that night.

The former "farmhouse" was spacious, leading me to conclude it must have been palatial before the war. I shared a room with Dr. Michael Tchizov, the chief wildlife veterinarian for the Ministry of Forestry. Previously Michael had worked at the Moscow Zoo and now spent a considerable amount of his time working with Vassely Popanov on the Kamchatka Peninsula. Michael had most of his field equipment and supplies in a pouched belt around his waist. He pulled out a large capped vial full of white powder marked "M99," and in it was enough M99 to kill half of Moscow. He said that they hadn't been able to keep it from precipitating out of solution, a problem the U.S. had solved years before. Vassely was their chief inventor and responsible for the development of two interesting types of darts which they used in a standard rifle and a shotgun. They were studying elk (what we call moose) and had even wintered over on the Kamchatka peninsula in a dugout on two occasions—not something I would be eager to do. On the second morning I woke early and looked out the window. It had gotten progressively colder and had snowed overnight. The Russians had a small four-wheel-drive van for our transportation, and it drove up under the window. The driver opened the engine cover and took blankets off of the engine and radiator. After the van had idled for a few minutes he went into the basement and came out with a rubber inner tube full of steaming hot water, which he poured into the radiator. The inner tube was cut in half and clamped shut at one end between two wooden sticks bolted together. I found out later that they had no antifreeze, so standard operating procedure was to get the engine hot, pour hot water from the boiler in and never let it stop running until they drained the water out of it at night. Later that day we experienced what happens when an engine dies and won't start. First, our driver got out and cranked, and then two men from the vehicle behind us got out and cranked until they were exhausted. When the van wouldn't start after they had cranked repeatedly, they drained the water out and transferred us to the second vehicle. That explained why there was always a second vehicle behind us. It wasn't KGB.

On occasion, Dr. Razmahnin wanted to talk to us about U.S. politics, particularly the mass cyanide poisoning that had taken place at Jonestown, Guyana, not long before our visit to Russia. Our interpreter Irina, who wore a mink coat and hat, even when we were in the field, informed us that those kinds of discussions were absolutely forbidden and shouldn't be happening. She was the chief interpreter for the Minister of Forestry and therefore carried some clout, but, as she said, "Dr. Razmahnin has said that I will interpret and therefore I will interpret but I wash my hands of all responsibility."

When Ulie and I were isolated with Irina and Dr. Razmahnin in the van out in the woods (both of them warned that we could not have a candid conversation in the lodge because there were microphones) she relaxed, and we had hours of question and answer. Razmahnin was interested in how our government worked and our individual chains of command. He seemed amazed at the extent of our freedom of speech and freedom of action; for instance, he was amazed that I answered to a small board of directors but not to any governmental entity. The fact that Dr. Seal, as head of the V.A. laboratories in Minneapolis and as a university professor, was not also rigidly supervised also surprised him. The discussions were wide-ranging since he and his colleagues were all well aware that what they heard and read in their press was not entirely true. Still, they had no way of judging just how biased the propaganda was. On the subject of the Jonestown massacre, both Ulie and I were having difficulty explaining how a single charismatic preacher like Jim Jones could have perpetrated a mass suicide like that without government involvement. Then I had a flash of insight and compared Jones to Rasputin, the charismatic Russian holy man who had helped bring down the Czar. That seemed to answer his question.

Dr. Razmahnin was very proud of being a Cossack and of Cossack culture.

We decided that he had been born 100 years too late and would have been more at home on a horse with a sword in his hand. He had vivid memories of WWII and extraordinarily strong opinions about Germans. He explained a lot of their culture and the Cossack requirement for hospitality, which extends even to an enemy, as long as he is on your property. On that subject, the hospitality of the hunters and local people was overwhelming, above and beyond what you experience even in the southern United States. We came away with warm feelings for all of the local people. The Russians had a rigid sense of rank and hierarchy, determined primarily by your expertise. This determined where you sat in the van and where you sat at the table. Luckily, Ulie and I were in the front and near the head of the table. The very head of the table was for the political types who joined us at meals.

At supper each night we found out that the propaganda about Russians and their vodka drinking wasn't propaganda at all. They drank with a vengeance, striving for that click point just before you fall over unconscious. They not only encouraged us to drink with the same vengeance but insisted upon it by always keeping our glasses full. Or they'd hold up a thumb and forefinger spread wide beside the glass and say "man" and then pinch the thumb and forefinger together and say "woman," thereby indicating that anyone who didn't tip it back and let a full glass slide down in one gulp was not a man. There was vodka before dinner, wine during dinner, in between vodka toasts and brandy and more vodka after dinner. Ulie and I also learned that some Russians are not physiologically capable of this kind of drinking. Vassely Popanov was one, but since he could not refuse to drink an equal amount when someone of higher rank proposed a toast, he would periodically go outside, stick his finger down his throat and vomit. These dinners were not a happy time for him, but he was helpless to do anything about it. Ulie and I learned our lesson that first night and paced ourselves from then on, despite being labeled "women."

The rest of our stay went well, and we didn't kill any animals. On the last night before boarding a train back to Moscow, they threw a big banquet. We had been told of the Russian custom of exchanging gifts on such occasions and came prepared. I had brought pocket knives, Boy Scout flint and steel fire starters plus souvenirs and t-shirts from the Omaha Zoo. Ulie had brought books and souvenirs from the Apple Valley Zoo. However, we still made a big mistake that night. Someone had told us, erroneously I think, that Russians appreciated good scotch. It was a very long banquet, and after carefully pacing ourselves through wine, brandy and bottomless vodka, after we exchanged gifts Ulie presented the head hunter with a quart bottle of Johnny Walker Black label. This old man, who had never even seen an American or heard of somebody capturing a red deer instead of shooting it with a rifle, teared up, threw the bottle cap back over his shoulder and insisted that we pass the bottle around, each of us drinking directly out of it until it was empty. So much for pacing yourself. Luckily, we were already packed.

We went to the train that night in three vehicles: one with people, one with luggage and a spare, just in case. Ulie and I staggered on board. Milton, who should have stuck to being a teetotaling Mormon and had complained about Ulie's snoring, was carried on board and placed in an empty compartment. I think Ulie and I were unconscious 10 seconds after our heads hit the pillow. At daylight the next morning we woke up to someone knocking on our door. There was Milton, looking like death warmed over. It appeared that the train had stopped somewhere during the night, and a large Russian woman was occupying the bunk next to his. When she woke up and found out he was still half drunk and hung over, she grabbed him by the collar and belt and physically threw him out into the aisle. We later found out through the interpreter that she did not like drunks. Milton asked if he could come in with us, and we said there was no room but he said he could lay sideways between our bunks. I was worried he might die right there. Needless to say, that was a long day for Milton, whose Mormon upbringing had not equipped him to drink with the Russians.

MOSCOW

In Moscow we returned to the Hotel Russia. The next day we headed for the zoo. Vladimir Spitsin met us and gave me a list of all the animals they wanted to have immobilized, starting with an adult male Asian elephant. We went to the elephant house to look at him. At 28 years old, standing 10-feet, six-and-a-half inches tall, he was the largest Asian male I had ever seen. He had broken off both tusks just outside the gum line, and the right one had been abscessed since 1964 (14 years). It apparently gave him a lot of pain, and he was very aggressive. The staff had welded steel spikes all over the inside of his pen to keep him from tearing his way out. We agreed to immobilize him with M99. They had arranged for two oral surgeons to perform a root canal on him. The surgeons turned out to be two little ladies in mink hats, which they wore all the way through the four-and-a-half-hour procedure. I should note here that, as you might guess, elephant houses, at their best, smell strongly. This one had been built in 1864, and the concrete floors were like sponges. It was winter, and there was very little fresh air. The smell was rank. That smell gets into your clothes, hair and fingernails and doesn't come out. I am sure those two ladies were unwelcome at home until they had their coats and hats dry cleaned. The Russians were nervous because they had only tried to immobilize an elephant once. They had given him chloral hydrate (as in a Mickey Finn) and vodka in

Ulie Seal and the elephant in the Moscow Zoo.

sweet tea. He went down but never got up. We darted the elephant with M99 and acepromazine, and he went down sternal in about 10 minutes. With help from the staff we pushed him onto his left side. The zoo wanted to x-ray the tusk and had brought in a large portable unit from a hospital and a team of human radiologists. They positioned a large cassette partially in his mouth and under the tusk and we hid behind a wall while someone pushed the button. It was like an old movie where when they execute someone in the electric chair; the lights in the building dimmed. Because of his massive size the exposure time was long, and after running the cassette to the hospital for development they said it was underexposed and would have to be shot again. They repeated this four more times before they gave up on the x-ray. The ladies started on the root canal, which must have seemed extraordinarily large by human standards, while Ulie and I monitored and supplemented the elephant's anesthesia level.

Midway through the four-and-a-half-hour procedure our interpreter said it was time for us to go back to the hotel to shower and change so we could attend the Bolshoi Ballet. On our arrival they had asked us if there was anything we wanted to do when we came back to Moscow, and I had said, "The Moscow Circus." Ulie had said, "The Bolshoi Ballet." We told them that the ballet would have to be canceled since we couldn't leave the elephant while he was down. We had to supplement him multiple times during the procedure. There were copious amounts of blood and foul-smelling pus to deal with, and they soon reached the maximum depth of their instruments. There was a lot of discussion, and two people left while everyone else took a coffee break. In about 20 minutes they returned carrying two pot handles, each about four feet long. They said that they had come from a restaurant with a big stove. It most have been a large flat-topped wood burner to make use of a pot with those handles. They had wooden handles on one end and the steel rod flattened and bent almost 90 degrees at the other end with two rivet holes. They had just ripped them off the pots. They worked great, and our surgeons finally burrowed down to the end of the canal at the ethmoid plate and scraped everything clean. We measured the canal and it was 31 inches from the gum line to the end. The problem then was to stop the bleeding. Ulie and I took over and asked them to find us a bed sheet, from which we tore into long strips. We tied them together, soaked them in iodine and packed the canal tight with a broom stick. We left a short strip of sheet hanging out the end so the elephant could remove it himself. We then administered M 50-50, the reversing agent, and in approximately four minutes the elephant began to stir. Within six or seven minutes he was on his sternum. From there it was just a few minutes until he was standing and steady. We told everyone that we needed to watch him for about an hour to make sure he didn't experience re-narcotization.

The Russians solved the ballet problem by suggesting that we wash our hands and faces while we waited. They also said we could wipe the blood and gore off our field boots in the snow outside the building. We had already been in the building for more than four hours, and the elephant smell had permeated our clothing and our hair. We told them we'd just forget about the ballet, but the Russians were insistent and wouldn't hear of it. We sat in the second box back from the stage one level up from the audience, orchestra pit and main floor. There were eight seats in the box occupied by four Russian ladies in ermine and mink, we three Americans—who smelled so bad we could hardly stand to be next to each other—and Irina, our interpreter, who hadn't been in the elephant house but wore her mink coat. I felt sorry for the Russian ladies in our box. As the elephant smell drifted down onto the main floor I could see people directly under our box sniffing and then ultimately looking up toward our box and pointing and whispering. This behavior spread like a slow-motion ripple throughout the whole Bolshoi audience. I'm sure that night instead of talking about ugly Americans, they were talking about smelly Americans. It was my first real ballet, and they performed Giselle, which was marvelous. Until then I hadn't realized that ballet stars are incredible athletes. At intermission we had plenty of elbow room around us. I'm not sure we improved relations between Russia and the United States that night.

Over the next two days Ulie and I immobilized chimpanzees, gorillas and a whole series of Moscow Zoo animals with medical issues that needed attention. True to our promise to Vladimir Spitsin, we did not kill any animals. We had brought a large supply of disposables, including syringes and needles. Over the years I had developed a habit that was almost an unconscious reflex. Whenever I finished using a disposable syringe and needle I would bend the needle over with my thumb and crack the hub off of the plastic syringe with my thumb, rendering it completely unusable, before throwing it away. After working on an animal, I looked up as I unconsciously preformed this little ritual, and three Russians flinched. It occurred to me that when we had toured their veterinary facilities we had seen very little medical equipment and no disposables of any kind. They had glass syringes that were so old the calibration

Our trip to the Moscow Zoo was a lesson in the political climate of Russia.

numbers were no longer visible. I also realized that we had not been introduced to any of their veterinary staff, other than Dr. Michael Tchizov. Our interpreter told me the three Russians were zoo veterinarians. The next time I finished with a syringe I simply slid the cover back on the needle and pitched it into a corner. It hardly hit the ground before it was scooped up. That was a real eye-opener.

At the end of our stay we gave the Russians all of our disposables, antibiotics and supplies. They obviously needed them much more than we did.

We also got to see the Moscow Circus and a modern ballet in the Kremlin. It didn't compare to the Bolshoi, but we smelled much better this time around.

PUSHCHINO

From Moscow we went to Pushchino, a town on the Oka River close to Prioksko-Terrasnyi, the UNESCO biome number seven where the northern taiga, the southern taiga and the steppes all meet. We were there to exchange immobilization techniques on European bison, red deer and introduced eld's deer. Additionally, they had a few American bison and American elk, a larger version of the red deer. In addition to Dr. Razmahnin, Michael Tchizov and Vassely Popanove, we had a new interpreter. We also added a new field biologist to our group, Dr. Komorove, who had invented an immobilizing bullet. More on that later.

On our second working day in the field a number of high-ranking guests came from Moscow to watch us work. Some of these observers made sense to me, such as the Russian minister of forestry. However, others were something of a mystery, including the minister of culture, until I learned that the zoo fell under his purview. But there were a number of other high-ranking Muscovites. The preserve was run by a 72-year-old scientist and his wife, who had devoted a good part of their lives to preserving European bison.

The weather had turned progressively colder during our stay in Russia, by then dipping to -27 to -28 degrees Fahrenheit. On the first day we had immobilized an old female American bison and a red deer. Our new Russian colleague shot an eld's deer buck in the right rear. The bullet was a 22-caliber long rifle hollow point shell with the hollow point cavity greatly enlarged so that it could be packed full of succinylcholine paste. The Russians said it was useful for immobilizing large muscled animals like red deer or moose, which the Russians referred to as elk. It was primarily a dumdum bullet that, when fired into the heavy rump of a moose, expanded and literally exploded in the muscle, creating a very large cavity. There would have been no possibility of retrieving the lead bullet fragments. The eld's deer buck obviously didn't have enough muscle mass, and the bullet appeared to have hit an artery. We tracked a heavy blood trail until we found him. Dr. Komorove packed the wound with gauze before we left, and I figured he would end up on our dinner table. At dark (4:00 p.m.) we went back to Pushchino for dinner. We were dropped off at a restaurant while they took the van to be drained and put inside. They apologized for not having good fresh fish, but they did have a far eastern preserved fish. It turned out to be smoked salmon and was delicious.

On the walk back to our little three-story guest hotel we passed a long line of people that stretched from a small building out to the sidewalk and down the block. We learned this was the only bookstore that handled foreign books, and a new shipment of western books had just come in. The store was full so they could only let customers in as someone else left. They asked if we would like to see inside, so they took us to the head of the line and into the store, obviously explaining along the way that we were visiting Americans. We were not interested in the side with Western books but gravitated toward the side were the Russian books and maps were. It was virtually empty. We had brought with us a supply of accurate Rand McNally maps of Russia. The Russian field biologists had been very interested in our maps and had indicated they would like to have them since they said the maps that the average Russian was allowed to have were inaccurate, particularly with the location of bridges, rivers, and dams, which had been deliberately moved. We decided it would be interesting to compare our maps with the ones for sale, so we bought several.

When we got back to the hotel room I realized I had left my briefcase in the bookstore. I was panicked because it had my passport, my Russian money, and $1,400 in U.S. currency. As I ran out the door the interpreter caught me and asked what was the matter. I told him, and he said not to worry because it would be where I left it or with the cashier. I wasn't buying this, but he held onto my arm and told me that Pushchino was a closed city because of their large polytechnic institute. My money and passport would be safe, he insisted; in Moscow, however, it might be a different story. "Here, no one could explain having it," he told me, "and there would be no place to spend it."

He was right. We walked back to the bookstore, and my briefcase was exactly where I had left it.

Later on that night, after a bit of vodka, Dr. Komorove was lamenting that the West was not paying him proper respect for his bullet. It was more accurate and much cheaper to make than any of the syringe darts that we were using. Additionally, succinylcholine was much cheaper to use than phencyclidine or M99. Plus, he was feeling blue because of a recent motorcycle accident that had killed his wife. He had been the driver.

Dr. Komorove was right about his bullet, but we didn't want to tell him the real reason we hadn't adopted his invention. Western medicine would consider his bullet—and the damage it would inflict—totally inhumane. I tried to deflect the conversation by telling a funny story I had heard from an Omaha friend who was from the Ukraine, he taught folk dancing and played the violin. Komorove stiffly got up and informed me that he was from the Ukraine, taught folk dancing and played the violin. Then he left the room.

The following day we performed for the big shots from Moscow and everything went well. One exception came when I overshot a bison and injected a tree. I joked that it was a perfect immobilization since the tree had not moved since I shot it. At about 1:00 p.m. the Russians said they were very impressed with our equipment, drugs and techniques and the fact that none of the animals that we had immobilized during the trip had died. Now it was time to go to the table and have "several drops of liquid," which was code for a substantial amount of vodka. Ulie and I were not ready for another serious drinking bout, so I explained that we had one more technique to show everyone. It was now 27 degrees below zero, and they really had no choice but to acquiesce. I looked around and chose a good-looking bison bull standing in a corral and asked through our interpreter if that animal would be suitable for an experiment. He spoke to the vice minister of forestry who nodded his head and told me the animal was okay. The mistake I made was in not asking the old scientist who was in charge of the preserve. What we didn't know was that the bull was the most valuable European bison in Russia. He was about three years old and had been discovered in a forest in Poland and had as yet not bred any cows. Once the vice minister of forestry had nodded yes, no one could say anything. For the next three hours we simply played with the animal to keep from going to the table and drinking. The head of the preserve and his wife rung their hands and bit their lips. First, we gave the bison a cocktail that was just strong enough to produce a standing immobilization, so we could walk around him, look in his mouth and take his temperature. Later, we put him completely down on the ground to pass more time before finally reversing the drugs and getting him back on his feet. We insisted that everybody wait until we knew that he would stay on his feet and not re-narcotize.

About 4:00pm as dark approached we packed up our equipment and went to a lodge where they had food waiting for us. There were a few toasts and speeches in which the Russians from Moscow heaped praise and flattery on us. Then our meal was served. After eating there were a few more toasts and speeches. The Russians asked us if we could immobilize a Russian wild boar because they had never successfully done so.

It was a not-so-subtle challenge that couldn't be refused.

In those days pigs were difficult to immobilize, but since we had had a good 16-day run and had not killed any animals we were feeling fairly bulletproof. We accepted the challenge, assuming it would be something to tackle the next day. The Russians had a different schedule in mind. They explained that the pigs only came out at night, and they had some tree stands for observations which would be perfect to shoot from. They paired us with three unfortunate Russian field biologists, who had to have known the score, and took us out into the woods at 6 p.m., destined for three isolated tree stands. They dropped some grain on the ground below the tree stands and left us there until midnight. I was paired with Michael Tchizov, and the plan was that if we heard a noise below he would spotlight the boar and I would quickly pull a warm dart from my inside pocket, load the dart gun and shoot. It was pitch dark, extremely cold and we didn't see or hear anything. Finally, they returned to pick us up at midnight. Michael and I had discussed walking back but had no idea where we were. The party was in full roar like a disco on a Saturday night, but now with a lot more vodka. We warmed up by the fire with a drink in our hands. Gleefully, the Russians told us they didn't think anyone who wore funny clothes that rustled and made noise—like Dr. Simmons—or who stomped his feet as much as Dr. Tchizov would ever see a Russian boar. There were, of course, no Russian boars. They had simply been getting even with us for making the Russian bigwigs from Moscow stand around stomping their feet in the snow for three hours while we played. It was a Russian snipe hunt. They were laughing too hard at what they had done for us to hold a grudge. I always felt sorry for what we had inadvertently done to poor Michael Tchizov and Vassely. We found the head of the preserve and made sure his bison bull was all right, by way of atonement.

The last day at Pushchino we went into the field for a couple of hours, then back to the hotel. We had pre-packed the night before and planned to grab our bags, load up, go to the restaurant for lunch and drive back to Moscow. Our rooms were on the third floor. Ulie and I propped the door of the elevator open with a bag and dragged all of our luggage and equipment into the elevator. Just as we were finishing loading, a young Russian woman got into the elevator with us. The elevator floor was completely full of luggage and equipment with just enough room between bags for our feet. Just as she pushed the button for two I leaned over to push the button for one. I overbalanced and accidentally stuck my thumb in the middle of her left breast before skidding off and pushing number one. She immediately began screaming at me in Russian and waving her finger at me. I could just see big red headlines across the front page of the Omaha World-Herald: "ZOO DIRECTOR SEXUALLY ASSAULTS RUSSIAN WOMAN IN ELEVATOR." She continued screaming in Russian and waving her finger, but the elevator didn't move. After pushing all the buttons several times—including the alarm—we decided that it was stuck. It was hot in the elevator shaft, so 90 minutes later when the hotel finally got it running and got us out, we had stripped off our outer parkas, our goose down under parkas, unzipped our insulated overalls and were still melting. The minute the elevator opened on the first floor she jumped out, grabbed our interpreter and started screaming in Russian and waving her finger at me again. As my mind wandered, picturing what a Russian jail looked like, I explained to our interpreter that it was an accident and I had just overbalanced. I had no intention of sticking my thumb in a soft part of her chest. The interpreter told me not to worry, and I asked him what she had said.

He told me that she said, "Tell him that you never push two buttons at once, the elevator doesn't like it!"

The rest of the trip back to the U.S. was anti-climactic. We did some shopping in Moscow that night and gave the Moscow Zoo all of our disposable equipment and supplies. As I've mentioned, they needed it far more than we did. The Russians wanted to buy my guns and darts but could only pay for them with rubles, which were totally worthless outside Russia, so I declined.

Some of the friendships we made, particularly with Vladimir Spitsin and the zoo staff, have endured to this day. The trip also began a long-standing relationship with the Moscow Zoo. Six years later I was to return with a male sea lion for their newly revamped sea lion exhibit, and multiple times Spitsin either brought or sent Russian architects, designers, engineers and biologists to Omaha to discuss designs. The most immediate spinoff was that we periodically became suppliers for vaccines and antibiotics that were simply not available in Russia. The quickest and most reliable way to get a 25-pound box of tetracycline powder to Moscow to treat an outbreak of psittacosis in their parrot collection was in a State Department diplomatic pouch. On two occasions Vladimir brought his wife, Svetlana, to Omaha, including for our 50th wedding anniversary. I ultimately took Marie to visit in Moscow and St. Petersburg.

VIETNAM

In January 1988 Ulie Seal, as chairman of CBSG, helped put together a conference in Hanoi to examine the status of the kouprey, also known as the Cambodian gray ox. The range of the kouprey was thought to be primarily in Cambodia with seasonal migrations into Thailand, Laos and Vietnam. The kouprey, an endangered member of the wild cattle family, was thought to number just a few hundred individuals or less. Stakeholders and wild cattle experts from Vietnam, Cambodia, Laos, Thailand, Malaysia, UK, Switzerland, Germany and the U.S. were invited to attend. I was invited because of my CBSG membership and because I was the SSP coordinator for gaur in North America, another endangered species of wild cattle that, along with the bantang, was found in the same range as the kouprey. Both the gaur and the bantang had much larger populations and much larger ranges than the kouprey.

Most of us assembled first in Bangkok, Thailand, and then went on to Hanoi as a group. Getting into Vietnam in 1988 was by invitation only. I had managed to acquire two sets of U.S. government high-resolution maps covering the areas in Cambodia, Laos, Thailand and Vietnam where we thought the kouprey might be. In one set, individual trees could be seen. They were, needless to say, of much higher resolution and scale than any of the biologists from the range countries had ever seen. The conference was convened at the University of Hanoi.

Each of the range country experts were asked to bring any published or anecdotal data on population size and range for all three species of wild cattle.

We first reviewed all the historical data for wild cattle and plotted their former ranges on the map, and then each of the field biologists from each country plotted what they knew of the current population sizes, geographical ranges and seasonal migrations of the animals in their territories. After three days we had a pretty good idea of the status in the four countries, and it was not good. We agreed to conduct dry season and wet season surveys between Cambodia and Vietnam and to survey hunters and villages along the southern border that Laos shares with Cambodia. I agreed (or was drafted) to serve as the coordinator for the kouprey project and to raise the necessary funds. A consensus was reached that we needed to bring a group of kouprey into captivity as a safety net for the population. And we agreed to build a holding station west of Ban Ma Tuot, Vietnam, close to the Cambodian border. We planned to send a U.S. team in with the necessary hardware and tools and to help supervise construction.

This was my first experience working in Southeast Asia with such a diverse group of players. It was eye-opening and valuable for future endeavors. For one thing, I observed the intensity of the college students we met before and during the conference. We had brought with us database software that they didn't have. We provided them a small demonstration of its capabilities on the first afternoon of the conference, and when we came back the next morning those same students were still there and had the software completely mastered and the databases we wanted set up and working. They shared the same work ethic that we observed in the farm fields and rice paddies as we toured Hanoi and some of the hill country.

When we toured a 13th century Buddhist monastery there was a surprise, a tile mosaic on a wall that portrayed a standard orange tiger and a white tiger. Some of us then went to the Hanoi Zoo, which at that time was in very sad shape. There we saw Chrotogale or Owston's palm civets, animals that virtually no westerner had seen in many years. A German colleague and I photographed them, perhaps for the very first time since there were no actual photographs in any of the old natural history books.

BILLABONG NIGHT

On the flight to Hanoi I had met a member of the Australian Embassy staff who invited me to come to the Billabong bar the coming Thursday night. The Australians put on a get together for all of the expatriates every Thursday night where everyone brought a bottle and food and had a really great party in a building behind their embassy. We were staying in an old French hotel, and I got directions and walked to the embassy where I experienced typical Australian hospitality. About 2 a.m., while having had a very good time, I decided I should get back to the hotel since we had a meeting the next morning. The hotel was much farther away than I wanted to walk, so, I hailed a cyclo-rickshaw, which seemed to be on the streets at all hours of the day and night. As best I could I told him the hotel I wanted to go to and everything seemed to be going well until we got to the lake. There he turned left instead of right. I stopped him and pointed to the right, but he was adamant that we needed to go left. I was equally adamant that we needed to go right. After I started to get out he reluctantly turned right, and I ultimately recognized my hotel, tapped him on the shoulder and pointed. He peddled up in front of the door I got out, held out some money in my hand and he carefully counted out what he needed. It was much less than I was prepared to pay.

There I had another problem: it was late and everything was locked up. It took some considerable pounding on the front door before someone opened it, and then I had to show them my hundred-year-old room key before they let me in. I learned the next day that the cyclo driver had mistaken me for a Russian. For years Russians had been the only Caucasians in Hanoi, and the big Russian hotel was to the left. Perhaps if I had had just a little bit better time at the Billabong Bar I could've tried my sign language in Russian.

DENGUE FEVER

On the way out, we stopped in Thailand to see Bangkok and visit some wildlife preserves. While there I picked up some mosquito bites, which led to a case of dengue fever. By the time my plane landed in the U.S. I knew why they called this "bone break fever" and was simply too ill to continue. Since there was no real effective treatment I holed up in the airport hotel for three days until the chills and fever abated enough to continue on to Omaha and a visit to a doctor.

VIETNAM, LAOS AND CAMBODIA

We would ultimately continue our pursuit of the kouprey in this part of the world for years. We arranged for a dry season survey along the Vietnamese/Cambodian border west of Ban Ma Thuot. The survey did not reveal any clear evidence of kouprey. Locals and the Vietnamese field biologists told us that they migrated into the area from Cambodia but only in the wet season. On the assurance of our Vietnamese colleagues that we were in the right spot for the kouprey, we arranged to have a wild cattle holding station built west of Ban Ma Thuot. After designing a building with indoor and outdoor corrals, Bruce Reed from the St. Louis Zoo and Jim Dolan from the San Diego Zoo volunteered to carry over a large shipment of hardware and tools as luggage to facilitate the construction. There was an ample supply of large, dark tropical hardwood timbers available. Any of these would have done justice to a fine dining room table. But hardware and fasteners were almost nonexistent and extraordinarily expensive to import. Good labor and Vietnamese carpenters were not hard to find, and the station was completed in a short period of time at a bargain price. The American dollar went a lot farther in those days than it does today. I remember well my first visit to the station and was in awe of the size and quality of the timbers used. It was similar to the heavy timber frame construction that you would expect in a 17th or 18th-century American barn. Ultimately, we decided to do a wet season survey along the border before mounting a capture operation.

BANGKOK, HANOI, VIENTIANE, KUALA LUMPUR, KOTA KINABALU, SABA

In January 1989 we went back to Hanoi for additional kouprey work. Afterwards, Simon Stewart from the the IUCN and I went on to Vientiane, Laos and then back to Bangkok.

In Vientiane we stayed in the Swedish Embassy guest house, having been advised that being seen going in and out of the U.S. Embassy would be counterproductive. With the help of a Canadian biologist working for the Swedes we made contact with the army general in charge of all wildlife activities in Laos to ask permission to conduct a wildlife survey among the hunters and villages in Southern Laos along the Cambodian border.

The survey covered a large number of species and was designed so the hunters being questioned couldn't tell that we were primarily interested in kouprey and wild cattle. They had a reputation for telling people whatever they thought you wanted to hear if there was money at stake. We were greeted cordially by the general, and after the usual hospitalities he informed us that getting permits to work in southern Laos would be no problem. It would even be possible to hunt Kouprey, Gaur or Bantang he told us. The Lao hunters, he explained, were skillful and routinely ranged far south into Cambodia hunting on elephant back. For a fee he would be happy to facilitate anything we wanted to do. However, the rub came when we asked what it would cost to do our survey work in the south. He had an answer: $10,000 in U.S. cash plus two new Toyota Land Cruisers. Since there was a 100 percent tax on all imported vehicles this was a very big tab for a survey.

We pleaded extreme poverty and politely said goodbye to the general. As a fallback we decided to work through the biologist at the Swedish Embassy. Perhaps we could try to bootleg a few surveys into southern Laos just to see if we were on the right track. Then we could come back and negotiate. We agreed to buy the Lao Wildlife Department a cheap, used Russian jeep on the premise that no one of any consequence would want to drive one and therefore wouldn't take it away from them.

After Vientiane, we went through Bangkok to Kuala Lumpur and then up to see the zoo in Melaka and talk with Mohamed Kahn about gaur, seladang and bantang. The Melaka Zoo had the largest collection of seladang, a Malaysian form of gaur. From there we went back to Kuala Lumpur to see the Kuala Lumpur Zoo. Then I went on to Kota Kinabalu in Sabah Malaysian Borneo. In Saba I met with Patrick Andowe to talk about bantang and proboscis monkeys. I returned home through Singapore, Taiwan, Honolulu and Los Angeles.

1990 FIELD SURVEY AND SHOOTING

After returning to Omaha we made arrangements to do a wet season survey in late summer and early fall of 1990. The British ex-pate who, along with his biologist wife we had hired to do the survey, ended up with an acute bile duct obstruction while in China and had to be flown back to England. Luckily, we were able to contract another British field biologist named Roger Cox. Roger had been doing fieldwork in a rebel-held area of Mindoro Island in the Philippines. He was very capable and politically savvy.

When Roger got to Ban Ma Thuot he found out the Vietnamese were insisting that an army squad accompany the survey team. This was unusual, and when Roger pressed them they admitted that there was still unrest and fighting in the high lands along the Cambodian border west of Ban Me Thuot. In view of what ultimately happened we were very lucky to have a biologist as experienced and politically savvy as Roger. He made what can only be described as an informed decision to go ahead.

The team primarily included Roger, a Vietnamese field biologist named Ha Den Duc, some Vietnamese students, camp support, five elephants and their Hmong drivers and the army squad commanded by a Vietnamese regular army captain. Two days in they had barely started the survey when they met a group of armed, uniformed rebels speaking with North Vietnamese accents on the trail near the Cambodian border. Under ordinary circumstances (and without the army squad along) they would have gotten down off of the elephants, started a fire, brewed some tea, cooked some food and asked them if they had seen any wild cattle. The team would have gained some insight into the wildlife of the area, and everyone would have been satisfied and happy. However, the army captain immediately challenged the rebels and demanded they throw down their rifles or else. Gun fire opened from all sides.

In the melee that followed three people on the team were shot, including Duc, who was hit five times. The army captain sustained the worst injuries, with AK-47 wounds to his stomach and back. Two elephants were hit and stampeded into the forest. The team jumped off the elephants and hid in the tall grass until they were sure the rebels were gone. That ended the survey. The captain and Duc had to be evacuated by elephant to a hospital. Despite being hit five times, Duc was probably the luckiest man alive. He had been hit in the neck twice, once front to back and once crosswise, neither of which hit any veins or arteries. His were primarily skin and flesh wounds. An AK-47 round had pierced the skin of his chest between two ribs on one side, traveling all the way across his chest under the sternum and out the other side without getting into the pleural cavity or causing any major damage. His wristwatch had also been hit. We were lucky no one died.

This made it necessary to go in and find out exactly what had happened. Simon Stewart and I met in Bangkok with the intent to go on to Vietnam through Hanoi and then on to Ban Ma Thuot, but the Vietnamese Embassy, knowing the reason for our visit, refused to give us visas. Without visas Air France and Thai Air refused to sell us tickets, so we went to Hang Kong Air, the Vietnamese airline, and each of us slipped the ticket agent an extra $100. He was happy to sell us tickets to Saigon. This was better than going to Hanoi anyway, since once we were there a Vietnamese biologist helped us get visas and a permit to go to Ban

Ma Thuot. The only downside was that we had to fly in an old Russian jet held together with bailing wire.

In Saigon we hired a driver and drove north on Highway 1 along a beautiful coastline. We turned northwest and drove to Ban Ma Thuot where we stayed in an old French colonial mansion. There we united with Duc, Roger Cox and the rest of the team. We decided that we should discontinue the project until some future date when the fighting was over and the area was safe. We paid the team, and after another look at our palatial wild cattle station, which now probably has people living in it, we headed east to Da Nang to catch a plane for Hanoi.

One aside on Ban Ma Thuot: on the way there we stopped for lunch at a little seaside restaurant before turning west to Ban Ma Thuot. Siting in a little pagoda out over the water, the waitress—through our driver—asked if we liked octopus. We said yes and watched as she waved to a fisherman who proceeded to pole out into the bay in a round, tarred, canvas boat similar to an Irish Coracle and pulled up clay pots that contained small octopi. The stir-fried octopus and vegetables were very good.

No sooner had we arrived in Da Nang when a major typhoon hit. We were staying in another old French hotel where half of the roof leaked like a sieve. Our rooms were happily on the second floor of the "good" side, but the stone stairs coming from the third floor down to the lobby were like a waterfall. Guests had to take their shoes off to get to breakfast. For three days the wind roared, and the rain came down in torrents. I can still vividly picture looking out the lobby window and seeing a Vietnamese cyclo-driver pedaling against the wind and rain with a huge block of ice on the flatbed of his three-wheeler. I remember wondering if he would have any ice left by the time he arrived where he was going.

We met two other guests in the hotel: an Australian aquaculture specialist who was trying to help the Vietnamese with their king prawn production and a British engineer from a BP oil platform off the coast. They had evacuated the platform ahead of the typhoon. They suggested leaving the hotel for supper and said they knew of a great Vietnamese restaurant where the locals went. It was still raining sheets, but we were ready to get out of the hotel and put our raincoats on. They hailed cyclo-rickshaws, gave our drivers directions and headed for the restaurant. We made arrangements for the drivers to have dinner so they would wait to take us back to the hotel. We were the only non-Vietnamese in the restaurant, but they seemed to know the Mama San owner well. They recommended the salt-and-pepper crab, which we all ordered, and then the Brit produced two bottles of Bulgarian red wine. We opened the first bottle, and it was the worst wine I've ever tasted. The second bottle was equally bad so we decided to switch to the local beer. We ate delicious salt-and-pepper crab, drank beer, ate more salt-and-pepper crab, drank more beer and talked. It was such a great night that I offered to pay for dinner. Much to my surprise, the whole tab came to $11 U.S. Our cyclo-drivers took us back to the hotel, and late the next day we caught a plane to Hanoi.

HANOI

In Hanoi, Simon and I decided to take a walk late one night after supper. The city seemed to be laid out in multiple circles with streets radiating out from the hub of each circle. There were no streetlights, nor were there any tall buildings to help find our bearings. We finally had to admit that we were lost. At midnight there was still a lot of activity on the streets. People were outside cooking, and kids were running around. Sometimes the kids would shout and throw rocks. I had been advised to always carry a small American flag on a stick; if you had a bad reaction you just pulled out the flag and said, "Me Me," and they would know you were an American. The kids' negative reactions were because they thought we were Russians. The flag brought out a friendly reaction every time, even though we had bombed the hell out of Hanoi and the Russians had supported them during the war.

If you are lost and in the center of a wheel almost any spoke you choose to follow will probably get you further lost. I had a small compass tied to my jacket, and we decided that since no one seemed to speak English the only way home was to plot a course of an expanding spiral until we saw a recognizable landmark. We walked in this ever-larger spiral until we recognized our hotel and could get some sleep. The next day we discussed the situation with Vietnamese colleagues at the university and then went on to Vientiane, Laos.

This time we were told we could bypass the general, and we were issued permits to conduct the survey among the villagers and hunters on the Lao-Cambodian border. One Saturday morning I decided to go alone to the morning market. There was almost anything imaginable for sale, including endangered animal skins, bones and pickled parts. There were many display cases full of gold jewelry and coins with goldsmiths at work behind the counters. There were native apothecary shops where you could find a herbal or animal cure for almost

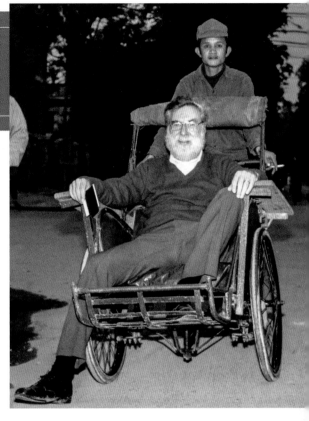

Facing page: Here I am during my 1989 visit to the Hanoi University Museum in Vietnam.

Right: Ulie Seal catches a lift around Hanoi in this cyclo-rickshaw.

anything, including a long case with what appeared to be many large and small pieces of rhino horn. When I asked what they were the folks in the shop produced a book with a picture of a Javan rhino, which at that time was considered to be the rarest of all rhino species and is now considered to be extinct. A little farther along in the case was a small rhino horn still attached to a circular, bloody scrap of skin. I had been taking pictures of the market, and before anybody realized what I was doing I photographed all of the rhino horns in the case and then went back to tell Simon and our Canadian colleague what I had seen. We ate lunch and then went back to the market, but there was not a single piece of rhino horn to be found.

THAILAND

As a result of our conservation efforts for kouprey our reputations—and those of CBSG—had grown. Thus, CBSG was invited by the Thai Zoo Association to help produce master plans for five zoos in Thailand. Ulie Seal and a small group of us from various disciplines made a number of trips to consult and advise in their master planning. This allowed us to see a lot of Thailand and meet a wide range of people, some of whom are still good friends. As a result, we brought a substantial number of individuals and groups from Thai zoos and Vietnam to Omaha for specialized training in veterinary medicine and other disciplines. Both the Omaha Zoo and the National Zoo in Washington, D.C. sent veterinary personnel to Thailand to assist training an even wider group of Thai veterinarians and zoo personnel.

One Sunday I hired an English-speaking Thai taxi driver for the day and went to the Sunday morning market in Bangkok. I had heard about it but had never been there. It was huge, and there were stalls and vendors selling any conceivable type of merchandise that you could imagine. There is an area in the market primarily devoted to domestic animals and exotic animals. I had the taxi driver spread the word that I was a wealthy American zoo director building a brand-new zoo in the United States and was looking for animals to stock it.

We walked from stall to stall in the market looking at the animals. The Thais were very savvy about what was legal and illegal, so most of the animals on display were legal. A common scenario that played out many times during our four or five-hour stay at the market went like this: You would be looking at a cage full of birds or an aquarium full of fish and somebody would tug on your sleeve. When you turned around there would be a Thai with a big shopping bag, and inside would be a baby Douc Languor, a rare and endangered falcon or some other rare and endangered (and unexpected) species. By the time we left I was convinced that if I had said I wanted 10 baby mountain gorillas and was willing to make a down payment, I could have returned a month later and they would have been there in the market. I saw more endangered species in shopping bags that day than you see in some zoos.

SAIGON

In addition to our master planning activities in Thailand, Ulie and I were invited to do the same thing for the Saigon Zoo. We spent five days there, and it was interesting. The Saigon Zoo was in a pretty old park with original ornate enclosures obviously patterned after the old Paris Zoo. Due to the war and economics it was badly in need of modern upgrades. Unfortunately, some of their personnel were involved in the Bear Bile Trade. Surprisingly, they had an off-site breeding facility for Golden Cats and Clouded Leopards that nobody had heard of. I haven't been back, so I don't know if our suggestions were ultimately followed, but there were some highlights to the visit. The botanical collection was quite extensive. In addition to an orchid house there was a bonsai house with hundreds of small ornate bonsai trees and a horticulturist who said that many generations of his family had worked in that house. He said some of the trees were as much as 300 years old.

Another noteworthy aside was their endangered species carousel. We have an endangered species carousel in Omaha, as do many U.S. zoos, but theirs was different because the animals on it were real animals that had been taxidermied and stuffed. There were tigers and leopards and clouded leopards and sloth bears and black bears and sun bears and ostriches and zebras and lions, etc. Many of them looked quite shopworn, but the children were having as much fun as kids do in our zoos here.

I visited the Saturday morning animal market in Saigon by myself, halfway expecting to see the same things I had seen in Bangkok, and instead I found that almost everything there was destined to be eaten. And most of it was shipped to China. There were all kinds of turtles, including sea turtles and very large freshwater soft-shelled turtles. There were pangolins and monkeys and baby bears and tens of thousands of geckos and anoles. Most amazingly there were large crates made out of heavy storm screen wire and lined with window screen that were completely filled with hundreds of live snakes, venomous and nonvenomous. I wondered how the snakes and anoles in the middle of those crates could possibly breathe and stay alive. They were likely all being shipped to China or were destined for local consumption as food.

OMAHA MEDICAL FACILITIES

In the beginning our medical facilities in Omaha consisted of a brown leather panda bag with some surgical instruments, one bottle of penicillin and some cockroaches. There was no hospital or even a room suitable for a small clinic and surgery.

While I still had all my surgical instruments and packs from school, it was obvious we needed help. I contacted Dr. Bill Hamsa, a member of the board who was an orthopedic surgeon, for help, and he introduced me to a number of physicians and pathologists at Clarkson Hospital and the University of Nebraska Medical Center. The response was overwhelmingly positive, and while this didn't yield any immediate new facilities at the zoo we had a lot of eager volunteers to help wherever possible. One such volunteer was Dr. Miles Foster, head of pathology at Clarkson Hospital, who had a large horse facility west of town. He volunteered to do all of the zoo's clinical lab work and histopathology for free. A huge gift.

Another volunteer pathologist was Dr. John Fitzgibbons from Bergan Mercy Hospital, who as an amateur herpetologist, had a keen interest in snakebite injuries in humans and in the pathology and diseases of great apes.

Dr. Nate Atkins, head of radiology at Clarkson, volunteered to x-ray any animal we could bring into the hospital garage. We had contacted Dr. Otto Rath, a highly recommended pediatrician for our son, and he volunteered to be the zoo's pediatrician for great apes. Doctors Rumboltz and Jernstrum volunteered OBGYN support. Dr. Rusty Crossman, a human ophthalmologist, adopted us.

We also made contact with veterinary practitioners in Omaha and members such as Dr. Jim Harless, Dr. Bob Perry, Dr. Lowell Smally, Dr. Al Erickson and Dr. Randy Roberts. And there were others who volunteered expertise and facilities as needed.

Without such an overwhelmingly positive response from the community we could not have met the medical needs of the collection in those early days.

It was a number of years before we could actually afford a hospital and a nursery, so we improvised. Most treatments were done in the animal's facilities, and surgeries were either done in the old WPA monkey house we had converted into a diet kitchen or on the counter in front of our secretary. Smaller animals that needed continued care or treatment frequently ended up in the library or in the men's restroom shower.

M99

I recall when we got our first vial of M99, an experimental narcotic that was approximately 6,000 times more potent than morphine. Our first shipment arrived in a bottle as a dry powder. In talking with the pharmaceutical company, we learned that the drug had some interesting properties, including that the amount of powder that you could hardly see on the head of a pin would kill you. Secondly, it could be absorbed through the sclera of your eye or the mucosa of your lips. And third, it had an electrostatic charge so that small grains of it would hop like a flea and stick to anything that attracted it with an opposite charge.

There was enough M99 in that initial shipment to immobilize everything in our collection many times over, but our problem was how to accurately weigh it into aliquots that could be put into separate vials for reconstitution into an injectable liquid. We also had a problem settling on what to use to dissolve it with since it had a tendency to precipitate out. Without an accurate scale, I talked to Dr. Miles Foster, head of the Clarkson pathology department, about borrowing one. He suggested instead that we use the scale he had in his office. On the day that we weighed it out, he and I first drew up several syringes full of Naline, an antidote for narcotics, and put on surgical gowns, masks, goggles and gloves. We closed the door to his office, and with his staff peeking through the window proceeded to weigh up the M99 into usable aliquots and put it into vials. We had a number of damp disposable sponges ready to absorb anything that electrostatically hopped to the glass enclosure of the scale. Their warning of the electrostatic

charge turned out to be all too true, and we needed to use some of the sponges. Ultimately, we weighed everything out and sealed it in individual vials. I was pleased when the next batch arrived already weighed up, in solution and in vials.

The potency of M99 was such that even for large animals such as elephants and rhinos only a small dose was needed. For some species like great apes, its potency was so great that it was virtually impossible to titrate a dose small enough to be safe. We tried to work out a dosage using a 140-lb male chimp named Mickey, but just a total dose of 0.1 mg was still stopping all respiration. Each time we would have to resuscitate him until we gave the antidote M55. We finally abandoned the effort.

PRACTICING ZOO MEDICINE

Practicing medicine on exotic and zoo animals in those early days was not nearly as advanced as it is today. While there was a huge knowledge base for human medicine and even for most domestic animal species, there was virtually no knowledge base for exotic animal diseases or even simple things such as blood, urine and other physiological parameters.

We did a lot of extrapolation, meaning if you are dealing with a primate, whether it was a small monkey or an orang or guerrilla, you assumed that the physiological norms would

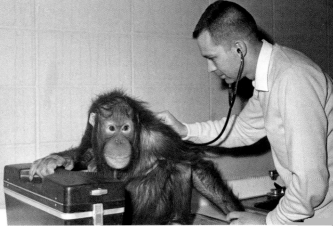

Facing page: A jaguar cub with broken legs and a prong horn antelope with an articulated splint.

Right: Conducting an orang exam in 1969.

PHOTO COURTESY OF THE DURHAM MUSEUM.

be comparable to those of a human. If you are dealing with a zebra or a Somali wild ass then the comparison was to domestic horses. Rhinos, hippos, tapirs and elephants, while distantly related to the horse, can be unique. If you were dealing with a giraffe or antelope species or, for that matter, any ruminant including deer and elk, you assumed that the values would be similar to a domestic cow. An exception of course is that a long legged and long-necked animal like a giraffe has a much more complicated circulatory and blood pressure regulation system than a milk cow.

PHOTO COURTESY OF THE *OMAHA WORLD-HERALD.*

Johnny Martinez and I are pictured here with a polar bear.

For the most part this worked, but not always. Since each family of exotics and each species can have idiosyncrasies that are unique, problems arise. Lions and tigers are not necessarily directly comparable to a domestic cat. Among the bird species there can be substantial differences to domestic chickens. Then there were those species such as spotted hyenas, sloths, anteaters, snakes and other reptiles for whom the depth of our ignorance was, at that time, profound.

POLAR BEAR WITH A BROKEN LEG

When we first came to Omaha our collection included four baby polar bears that weighed about 20 pounds each. The male and two of the females ultimately produced a number of offspring that we sent to other U.S. zoos and to Europe. By the 1970s these active bears were grown up, and on one occasion a female got shoved off into the moat. She struck the bottom of the moat hard and suffered a mid-shaft fracture of the femur. Since we still did not have a hospital or x-ray equipment, after she was immobilized we loaded her into the back of my little Jeep universal and drove her to Immanuel Hospital to get a radiograph. We then drove to Clarkson Hospital where we carried her into the new postmortem, and there Dr. Bill Hamsa, his father and his partner put in a K nail and a compression plate. We had many spectators in a small space, and another urban legend was born. The bear healed but had a limp.

ALBUQUERQUE POLAR BEAR

One day my secretary called and said, "Dr. Stringer (a classmate of mine) from Albuquerque is on the phone, and it's an emergency." I picked up the phone and Bruce said, "Quick, I don't have time to talk. What's the dosage for succinyl-choline in a polar bear?"

I gave him the information he wanted, and he hung up. Two hours later he called back and said Albuquerque had a torrential rainstorm, and since everything is flat with little drainage their dry polar bear moat had filled full of water and their two polar bears were swimming in the moat. Two keepers in a pickup were driving back and forth in front of the bears with one of them firing a shotgun into the water in front of any bear who got close to the public edge of the moat. The immobilizations were a success. The paralyzed polar bears amazingly did not drown in the moat or regain mobility before they could be put back in their dens. Nobody was eaten, and the exercise was a success. Bruce bought me a Jack Daniels at the next zoo vet conference.

A SPLINT FOR AN ELEPHANT

A problem occurred when a partly grown young bull elephant lost a shoving match and got pushed off in the moat by our big male. We built a ramp, and he hobbled out on three legs, having suffered a mid-shaft fracture of the radius and ulna. The opposing ends of the bones seemed to be in apposition but with a noticeable angular deviation to the leg. An elephant can stand well and actually move about slowly on three legs, but a traditional cast that would stand the water and pressure was going to be a big problem. We decided that a steel clamshell splint, the two halves of which could be bolted together allowing for a small amount of padding, would be the only thing that was elephant proof.

This elephant was not terribly user-friendly, yet he allowed us to measure the injured leg and the other front leg for a pattern. We took our patterns to a local sheet metal specialty shop, and about three hours later had two stainless steel half cylinders with flanges down each side. The plan was to put a small amount of dense padding around the leg and then bolt the two clamshells together by their flanges. But by time we got to back to the elephant house the leg had swollen to nearly twice its size because the animal would no longer put pressure on the pad of the foot, which is essential for an elephant to push blood and lymph up out of the leg. With elephant leg skin being as thick and relatively non-elastic as it is, Mother Nature had splinted the leg quite effectively on her own. He continued to hobble on three legs during his convalescence and healed without complications or problems. Being young, active and still growing, by the time we sold him the leg showed no deviation or difference from the other legs. This same male was feeling in the channel of a door frame with the tip of his trunk when the big male slammed the door shut, cutting off the tip of his trunk. We surgically reshaped the tip to give him two fingers, but he couldn't use the trunk to feed himself or drink. We had to hand feed him by placing food in his mouth for months. Being hand fed and drinking out of a hose civilized him considerably. He healed completely, regained the use of his trunk fingers and could pick up a peanut.

NECK SPLINT FOR A CAMEL

Once in Columbus and later in Omaha we had female dromedary camels who were knocked down by amorous males who kushed on their necks, tearing the lateral cervical ligaments on one side between two vertebrae. The angle of deviation of the neck was approximately 30 degrees, and it was a wonder that we didn't have paralysis due to spinal cord damage.

The lateral vertebral ligaments on the opposite side and the dorsal and ventral ligaments seemed to be intact. In both cases we designed a lightweight, full-length padded clamshell splint out of plywood, wooden spars and padding that could be bolted together to correct the

Mike July, watering a camel wearing a Thomas splint we made.

alignment in the neck. The vet school in Ohio had been hesitant to attempt a surgical fixation with stainless steel plates bolted to the lateral vertebral bodies due to the extreme forces involved. We had reservations about whether we could get enough reattachment and healing in the ligaments to stabilize the neck by simple splinting, but the alternative was to euthanize the animal. Even though the splint was kept as light as possible it was still too heavy for the camel to easily raise her neck, so in both cases we attached a light nylon rope with a counterweight through a pulley high enough overhead that it gave her the ability to stand up and lay down and move around. In the beginning both animals would voluntarily rest their chins on strategically placed stacks of hay bales to relieve the strain. Both camels recovered with slightly observable

PHOTO COURTESY OF THE *OMAHA WORLD-HERALD.*

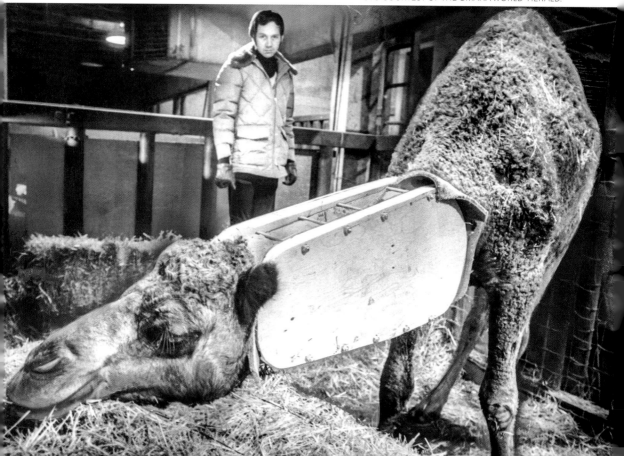

deviations in their necks and lived long enough (approximately four-and-a-half years each) to reproduce calves. Unfortunately, the healed ligament attachments broke down with resultant spinal cord damage and death. A more aggressive surgical approach using the large animal stainless steel plates and screws that are available today would probably have extended their lives.

ROOT CANALS

Large carnivores such as lions, tigers and bears have a problem that severely limits their ability to survive in the wild and in captivity can cause

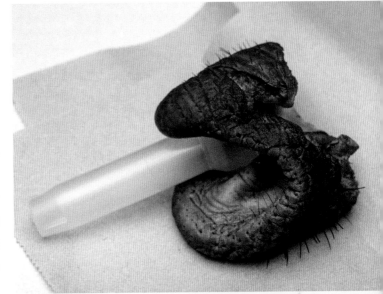

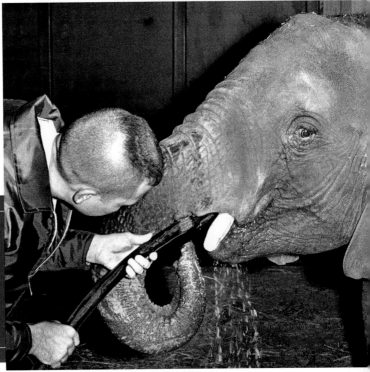

Facing page: We fashioned a splint for this camel with torn neck ligaments.

Right: A severed tip of elephant trunk is extremely painful for the elephant. Here I am watering that same elephant.

PHOTO COURTESY OF THE *OMAHA WORLD-HERALD.*

A Stanley crane with a fiberglass peg leg.

ongoing pain and problems. The problem is they can break a canine tooth. Big cats in particular tend to be right or left-handed and in captivity tend to use one side over the other to attack hard objects such as bars, doors or water bowls.

In the early days of zoo keeping these problems were mostly ignored because no one had the skills to deal with them. But as with Stinky the jaguar in Columbus, we decided to address the problem. Our first patient was an Amur leopard with a broken upper right canine. Since I had an appointment as an adjunct professor at the Creighton School of Dentistry we had the contacts to enlist Dr. Charlie Meyer and Dr. Newt Kelly, who were on the clinical faculty, as co-conspirators. We immobilized the leopard, put him into a small lightweight cage and then put that cage into a wooden crate with a big equipment label on it. We carried the "equipment" crate past the guard at the medical arts building and onto the elevator to take it up to Charlie and Newt's offices. We took the Leopard out, strapped him into a dental chair and watched as the two of them did a root canal procedure. All of this was executed undercover. Subsequently we were able to bring animals into the main dental school laboratory and do them in front of students. Over the years there were leopards, small bears other big cats and even apes and primates. Eventually Charlie and Newt taught us the procedures, and for many years we have done these procedures right in the zoo hospital surgery ourselves. And we've since passed these skills and technologies along to many students and interns.

A PEG LEG FOR STANLEY

Early on in Omaha we had a Stanley, or Blue crane, from South Africa. She made the mistake of opening his wings in a strong windstorm. The wind blew her into a fence and broke her lower leg about one third of the way distal to the joint. The damage was such that the blood supply and innervation to the distal part of the leg were destroyed, so amputation was the only option.

We first smoothed the bone and formed a pad over the stump and closed the skin. After bandaging the stump, we found that Stanley could still stand, but of course could not walk without lowering herself down so that the stump of the bad leg could touch the floor. To solve the problem, we slipped a lightweight plastic tube over the stump and taped it in place below the joint. We added a ball of tape over the end for traction. After the stump had healed completely and stabilized we wanted to make a more permanent prosthesis, but finding a lightweight tube of exactly the right diameter and length was going to be difficult. Then I remembered that they made 12-foot long telescoping fiberglass fishing poles with 3-foot long tapered sections that collapse into themselves. When telescoped out, they formed rigid stable joints.

Finding the right size section for a prosthetic leg was as simple as paying $10 for a pole, taking it apart and measuring the diameters of the stump and the different sections of the poll until we had a match. We first made a female cast of Stanley's stump and then from that made a male duplicate of the stump in wax so that we

Similar to the stanley crane, this flamingo was fixed with a peg leg.

PHOTO COURTESY OF THE *OMAHA WORLD-HERALD.*

could carefully add enough diameter for the padding that would go around and over the end of the stump. Over this male duplicate we laid up a fiberglass socket using materials from a glass bedding kit for rifle stocks, which cost us $12. This socket exactly conformed to the shape of Stanley's stump and padding. We then mated that fiberglass socket to the chosen piece of fishing pole, and after curing and fitting it on Stanley's leg we trimmed it to the exact length of her good leg. A lightweight rubber tip finished the process.

Stanley used this prosthesis and a couple of subsequent ones for more than 25 years. She could even wade in the aviary pool with no problem. An unexpected consequence was that with all the human interaction Stanley had during this process, she became imprinted on humans. When it came time to mate, she was not interested in other cranes. We had to revert to artificial insemination.

After we published a case report the veterinary school at the University of California, Davis, which had a similar patient in a California zoo, contacted us. We told them everything they wanted to know above and beyond our publication, and they proceeded ahead with one small twist. They involved bio-engineers and materials experts in the project so that by the time they had a functional leg on the California bird the bill was $3,000. Our cost had been a total of $24 plus our time. We have used this technique successfully on other long-legged birds.

OLD FEMALE GORILLA AT BERGAN MERCY HOSPITAL

Another zoo that had received a female gorilla from overseas called me from their airport and said she had arrived unconscious. With very little gorilla expertise and limited medical facilities they wanted to know if they could forward the gorilla on to Omaha for treatment. We agreed and shortly thereafter met the airplane. The comatose gorilla was severely dehydrated, emaciated and quite old. We took her to the zoo to start her on fluids, antibiotics and steroids. She never came around and died shortly. I called Dr. John Fitzgibbons, a human pathologist at Bergan Mercy Hospital who was interested in gorilla and orang pathology, who told me to bring her over immediately.

We wrapped her in an old army blanket, put her in the back of my station wagon and drove to the Bergan emergency room entrance. John met me with a gurney. I noticed a few raised eyebrows as we hauled the blanketed body through the hospital toward the autopsy room, but since John was head of pathology we didn't meet any resistance. We got her onto the autopsy table and were just beginning to do an external examination when the phone rang and an obstetrician in a delivery room said they had a newborn baby with what might be a slippery umbilical cord. He asked if John could come and do a frozen section to make sure they didn't have a problem.

John said that we would be right up. Since neither of us had had supper we figured we could grab a bite to eat before coming back to do the necropsy on the gorilla. While we were upstairs a representative from a local mortuary came to pick up a human body that was on a gurney against the wall to the left of the automatic double doors. When he entered the deceased human was not visible, but there in the middle of the room was a black, hairy gorilla on the table. He called his office, which immediately contacted the Mother Superior who was the hospital administrator. By the time John and I finally got back to the autopsy room that same Mother Superior was hacked off and looking for an explanation. John's reputation might have saved us. He was a good pathologist but his habit of keeping live rattlesnakes in bags in his desk drawer earned him a somewhat checkered reputation. Additionally, Mother Superior must have been a fan of the zoo, because she finally just shook her head and walked off.

Anyway, this geriatric animal had been shipped to the U.S. having been represented as a breeding-age female from Africa. In fact, she was not just old but ancient. When we got to her internal organs, her primary pathology was a severe pneumonia. Additionally, she had a very pronounced case of anthracosis, which meant that wherever she had spent most of her life it was not in the wilds of Africa but somewhere where she had been subject to breathing heavy coal smoke. Her lungs were absolutely black with carbon particles. She also had some very interesting liver flukes unrelated to having been in captivity. Needless to say, the zoo that had received her did not pay the animal dealer. To this day, when urban legends are exchanged between mortuaries and funeral homes in Omaha, this story lives on.

HIRING AN OPERATING ROOM NURSE

In December 1978 we had a male gorilla born to Casey and Bridget. He was healthy until two months old when he contracted a rotavirus that wiped out the villi of his gut. We called on the staff of Children's Hospital for help, and they responded with advice on basic clinical management. More importantly they provided a pediatric gastroenterologist who helped us put together a treatment protocol and formulated the hyperalimentation formula. We would have to feed the baby intravenously for more than two months.

At the same time the water pipes in our hospital and nursery froze, and in the process of thawing them out a fire started and burned the building down. Our hospital and nursery at that time was a double-wide mobile home. The fire started over the lunch hour when the animal keepers were gone, and the maintenance workers were trying to thaw the pipes with a torch. Due to the construction of mobile homes, particularly the use of plastics, the fire was virtually out of control instantly. As a result, we lost a baby margay and a young female gorilla, both as a result of smoke inhalation. We took the babies to the veterinary emergency clinic here in Omaha, and since we had no experience in treating smoke inhalation we called in pediatricians from Children's Hospital who did. It was a bad day for the zoo that none of us really want to member.

We put the gorilla on a bird respirator and began administering oxygen. One of the pediatricians advised us that a little Smirnov Vodka in the vaporizer of the respirator would help clear the mucus accumulating in the respiratory tract. I went to a nearby bar and ordered a double shot of Smirnov in a "clean glass." I then got to watch the bartender's eyes grow big as I pulled out a large syringe and sucked it up and then left.

The two-month-old male gorilla was spared because his medical problems required 24-hour care, and Maggie Martinez, head of our hospital/nursery, would take him home on her days off. We ultimately named him Murphy because it seemed that anything and everything bad that could happen did happen to him. This left us in the tough position of having to maintain a 24-hour IV line without any hospital or surgical facilities. We eventually ran out of easy veins to insert a catheter and needed to do a cut down to put in a long-term catheter. Our choices were either to do the surgery on a kitchen table or seek help. I made a call to Dr. Rath, our pediatrician, and Otto called his brother-in-law Dr. Schultz, who was a pediatric surgeon at Children's. Dr. Schultz replied that there were no surgeries scheduled on Sundays, and a baby was a baby. He would meet us at the emergency entrance.

We all went up to surgery, and Dr. Schultz, who was obviously very much in command and just a little bit Teutonic, quickly informed the nurses on duty what we needed. After scrubbing the surgical site, we went in and implanted a long-term silicon catheter. The whole thing took less than 30 minutes. Everything would've been fine except that the hospital administrator heard there was something unusual going on in surgery and came up to inquire. The head operating room nurse informed him that he could not come into surgery while a procedure was ongoing. I think if they had let him in he would've been fine with the situation, but as it was he seemed to take offense to the fact that he was excluded. That Monday he fired the head operating room nurse, which was grossly unfair. She had little to do with the matter.

I, of course, was out of reach because I was not on the staff at Children's, and this administrator was certainly not foolish enough to take on Dr. Schultz. We put the nurse on the zoo's payroll for a bit over three months until a group of Children's physicians had a "Come to Jesus" meeting with the administrator. He wisely rehired her, restored all her benefits and wiped her record clean. Many years later when she retired from Children's we hosted her retirement party in the treetops restaurant at the zoo. Head operating room nurses make a lot more than zoo keepers, but it was worth it.

The lining in Murphy's gut re-grew and he became a functioning, normal gorilla. I suppose all that ends well makes the hassle worthwhile. Our next big problem became raising money to build and equip a new hospital/nursery building.

BABY TIGER IN THE ELEVATOR

Having a resource like Children's Hospital was invaluable, but we were very careful not to upset the other patients and their parents. Once with a small tiger cub, we were afraid it had a partial bowel obstruction. I made a discreet call to see if we could slip the cub in for a quick radiograph at the hospital. Following standard operating procedure, we wrapped the cub tightly in a large pink baby blanket, and a keeper drove me to the emergency entrance. Radiology was on the third floor, and as I got in the elevator and punched three a lady got on and punched number two. As the doors closed the tiger cub decided it had had enough of being bound up and started violently trying to break out of the blanket and squalling loudly. The lady backed up to the other side of the car and watched silently as I fought to keep the cub contained and under control, which I did.

As the door for two opened the lady stepped out, paused in the door, turned around and looked at me and said, "I'm not even going to ask." She did an about-face and walked off. Best of all, the tiger cub did not have an obstruction.

LINDSAY PHILLIPS AND THE INTERN

At Omaha's Henry Doorly Zoo we've always believed strongly in training young veterinarians, technicians and curators and passing on any experience and information we have. For most young people starting out in the zoo world, whether in management or zoo medicine, hands-on experience is much more valuable than simply reading about something in a book. Because we had a dormitory and student houses, over the years we have given thousands of students their first hands-on experiences. Dr. Lindsay Phillips was chief veterinarian in Omaha for a number of years and was very good and enthusiastic about aiding these efforts. We always treated students carefully and with respect. We did have one incident, however, that proved to be the exception to the rule, for a few minutes at least.

One of our main immobilizing drugs, as I've mentioned, was M99, a narcotic that's 6,000 times more potent than morphine. One of the interesting characteristics of this drug was that it can be absorbed through mucous membranes or the sclera of your eye. We were very careful with the drug and always had antidote on hand in case somebody was accidentally injected or exposed. The amount of M99 we used to immobilize animals was many times the amount needed to kill a human being.

We had a young female gaur with a bad leg that required periodic re-casting, and it was necessary to immobilize her. One February day while Lindsay was getting ready to immobilize her, a new vet intern showed up at the office. We had someone take him down to where Lindsay was working, and Lindsay said hello. Perhaps more brusquely and with less explanation than usual, Lindsay told the intern to stand back and he would be with him as soon as the procedure was over. As he started to hand inject the gaur the animal simultaneously kicked with a hind foot, sending the injection into the air. Some of it sprayed onto Lindsay's face. Lindsay immediately whirled, ran outside and dove headfirst into a water trough trying to hold his mouth and eyes open while he thrashed his head back and forth to wash off the M99 before it could be absorbed.

The intern, thinking that Lindsay had been kicked by the gaur and was drowning, immediately came to the rescue, grabbing him by the shoulders and dragging him out of the trough. Lindsay shook him off and immediately dove back into the water trough. They repeated this sequence until Lindsay elbowed him in the face and told him to go stand against the wall. He would explain in a minute.

Lindsay then dove back into the water trough. Shortly thereafter they both appeared in my office. Lindsay explained the situation to the intern and told me that he thought he had washed all of the M99 off his lips and eyes, but he would like to sit in the office with me until we were sure. We laid out the antidote and syringes on my desk and then sat and had a long discussion about many aspects of veterinary medicine in zoos while Lindsay tried to decide whether he was feeling any effects from the narcotic. He thought maybe, but I assumed it was imagination helped by being a bit scared. Thankfully we did not have to call a squad or administer the antidote. I'm quite sure the intern will never forget his first day on the job in Omaha. Nor will he likely take the handling of potentially dangerous drugs lightly. Lindsay said the water in the trough was damn cold.

THIOBENDAZOL AND DDVP IN TIGERS

Fairly early on after I became director we had five tigers die suddenly in a matter of 45 minutes. We had just treated them for intestinal parasites with thiobendazol, a product we had used many times before on a wide range of species, including tigers and other big cats. We were able to save one very tame user-friendly tiger by administering a large dose of atropine and oxygen. The cats were gasping for breath, frothing at the mouth and obviously drowning in their own pulmonary secretions.

On postmortem the airways were full of frothy fluid and the pulmonary tissues full of edema. There was no history of thiobendazol ever having caused this. We suspected a toxin such as an organic phosphate, but this was impossible since we had strict protocols for insecticide usage. After questioning everyone and re-examining all of our management we were clueless as to cause. The histopathology showed severe pulmonary edema and edema in other organs but provided no answers. A disaster like this of course makes the newspapers and TV, and a lot of questions were asked of us. We had no answers until two months later when a supervisor observed a keeper spraying Vapona (DDVP) into the exhibits, including over the water bowls. He was an older employee who had been recently hired and had previously worked on a mink farm.

When we questioned him he said, "You young college boys don't know anything about animals. We sprayed this on everything at the mink farm and it never hurt anything." Of course, they had never followed up and stressed the animals by administering an anthelmintic or some other stress factor. The combination had destroyed the animal's ability to make acetylcholine esterase, which destroys and thereby controls the level of acetylcholine in blood and tissue. The accumulation of high levels of acetylcholine had caused the pulmonary edema that killed the animals. We later found out that a tiger had died of this same combination after being treated by veterinarians from the Kansas State Vet School, and that a herd of wildebeest in a Florida zoo had died after their favorite patch of grass had been sprayed with DDVP for sand fleas and later they were given thiobendazol for worms. Unfortunately, neither of these incidents had been published. This helped to cement our policy of publishing all mistakes. And we hired a new keeper.

AN IMPACTION IN TINY

In 1966 we received a young male Indian Rhino named Tiny. He had been orphaned in Nepal when his mother died and had been attacked by a tiger. He was very docile and easy-going. He grew up to be a very handsome animal but unfortunately became the victim of unintended consequences. In 1975 our feed supplier went out of business, and we could no longer get the sweet feed that Tiny was used to. He refused to eat the feed we substituted, and unbeknownst to the keepers he consumed a large quantity of dry prairie hay bedding. We knew we had a problem when he stopped defecating, and we immediately started giving him mineral oil, emulsifying agents and laxatives, just as you would with a horse

Marlin Perkins, right, pictured with me and a bharal, or a blue sheep.

who had a blockage or impaction. We also were very aggressive with high enemas.

For a day or two we thought that we had resolved the problem, but after some initial successes in getting him to pass feces we decided he would need surgery. We sought help from a well-known horse expert at the Iowa State School of Veterinary Medicine. We transported him to Ames, Iowa, and the next morning we tried to get a radiograph, but he was too large for any of their equipment. We prepped him for an exploratory surgery, and after anesthetizing him with M99 we made a vertical incision high on the left side just behind the last rib. Relatively speaking, rhinos have a long rib cage. Wearing sterilized sleeves and working at armpit depth we managed to find a large impaction in the descending colon. By

PHOTO COURTESY OF THE *OMAHA WORLD-HERALD*.

using needles on the end of IV tubing—and without incising the gut—we infused the mass with mineral oil and saline. Taking turns, the equine surgeon and I massaged the mass until we had it softened and broken up into smaller clumps. Assuming we had solved the problem, we closed him up. That night and the next morning he began passing feces.

Unfortunately, he had another large impaction in the transverse colon immediately behind his diaphragm. Because of the sheer size of the animal and the distance to the impaction we had been unable to reach and detect a problem. He lived for another week, but even with aggressive medical support did not survive. In doing a zoo survey I found a number of rhinos who had experienced impac-

Facing page: Tiny, pictured, got into deep trouble when we couldn't supply him the sweet feed he enjoyed.

Don Farst, me, and a bongo, who broke five ribs on my left side.

tions. In retrospect, when he refused his regular feed we should have removed all of his bedding and put him on a diet of chopped fresh vegetables and fruit which he would have readily taken. We could have then gradually acclimated him to a new diet. Hindsight is always 20/20.

A DINING ROOM NURSERY

In our early days in Omaha we didn't have a hospital or nursery facilities for babies whose mothers wouldn't or couldn't take care of them. If they were not very critical or labor-intensive they ended up in the library or sometimes in the shower of the staff men's room. While we could never quite get to Marie's goal of having five children of our own, we made up for it by raising a number of zoo babies in our house.

Anything in need of frequent nighttime and around-the-clock feedings, just like a human baby, came home for Marie to raise. We simply converted the dining room into a nursery. For critical babies like gorillas and orangs we would quarantine the house to outside visitors.

Over the years we had an array of babies that came home for Marie to raise, including orangs, gorillas, leopards, tigers, polar bears, grizzly bears, jaguars, hyenas, and even giant otter pups in the bathtub. The problem, of course, is that exotic animal babies tend to grow and mature much faster than human babies and often develop an "attitude" as they mature.

POLAR BEAR CUBS

Our five little polar bear cubs (two males and three females) grew up and presented us with a litter of cubs before we thought they were old enough to breed. We managed to get one of the cubs out of the communal den alive and proceeded to raise it in an incubator and on a bottle. Despite our successes raising grizzly and black bear cubs on a bottle, polar bear cubs presented a different challenge. In the wild they had to grow rapidly in order to survive, but in captivity they developed slowly and had trouble getting on their feet. It was obviously a case of not having the right formula.

While discussing the problem with Ulie Seal he suggested that we should analyze the milk from a nursing female polar bear. The problem was there were no nursing female polar bears in the United States at that time, but we came up with an alternative plan. One of Dr. Seal's colleagues was doing a study on bone growth on polar bears in the Arctic. His study consisted of injecting a tagged polar bear with tetracycline to stain the current growth ring of the long bones and teeth. Then at a later date he'd collect the bear, remove a tooth and measure the new growth from the date of injection. I had made some equipment for their project, so when Ulie asked his colleague if he could find a polar bear den and collect a milk sample, he readily agreed. However, none of us realized at the time that unlike the grizzly and black bears they had been working with, who were in hibernation in the den and therefore not fully conscious at the time their cubs were born, female polar bears did not hibernate. While the grizzlies and black bears were amenable to blood and milk sampling, this was a different story; they're wide awake when their cubs are born.

After finding a cubing den with the help of local hunters, his first attempt was nearly disastrous. Female Polar bears dig an entrance tunnel in a snow bank and then a cavity in the snow. At the end of this cavity, usually at a right angle, they dig a short tunnel and then a small egg-shaped cavity which they back into. There they lay upside down on their backs to give birth to their cubs. The cubs are therefore born immediately on top of the mother's warm furry belly, covered by her warm furry legs and paws. This is a perfect incubator, and their food supply is right there. They are warm and protected by the female who rests with her nose protruding into the first cavity so that her breath does not condense in the cub's cavity and get them wet. When this scientist crawled into the outer cavity only to find a fully awake, very protective and pissed off mother polar bear he was more than a little surprised. The thing that probably saved him was the fact that in order to attack she would've had to roll over, thus dropping her cubs on the snow to charge out and get him. Her innate maternal instincts probably inhibited her from doing this.

Dr. Seal's colleague was a true scientist who was not deterred easily. He came back with the dart gun and immobilized her so he could get a milk sample and a blood sample. Ulie analyzed the samples and determined that polar bear milk was almost 50 percent fat, with a high percentage of solids and a much higher percentage of calcium than other milk samples. In formulating an artificial diet, the only way we could get the fat content high enough was to use a high concentration of menhaden fish oil. This solved our problem and greatly contributed to the successful rearing of polar bears in captivity.

Ultimately, we constructed cubing dens in a tunnel underneath Interstate 80 so our females had enough privacy to raise their cubs themselves. Three months of quiet isolation without food and with monitoring through a remote video camera does the trick. All together they produced 17 polar bear cubs.

AMUR LEOPARD CUB KIM AND YOUNG LEE

The first zoo baby that came home was a newborn Amur leopard, who had been delivered by caesarian section, named Kim. She stayed with us until she weighed 30 pounds. She still liked her bottle and would

Left: Performing a cesarean section on an amur leopard.

Facing page: Young Lee, pictured with Marie, feeding and playing with "Kim," an amur leopard cub in 1968.

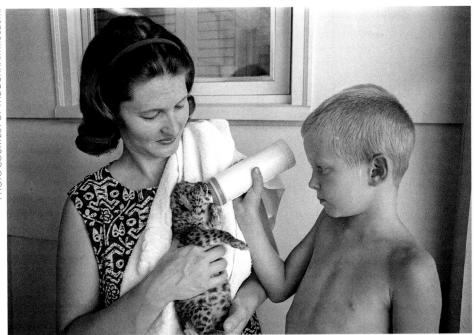

snuggle, but she was practicing her leopard-hunting skills on young Lee, who was about seven years old. She would stalk him down the hallway or lay in ambush on the back of the couch, waiting for him to come into the room. Lee fought back but was becoming more and more wary since she was drawing blood once or twice a week and getting bigger and stronger all the time. She was also becoming increasingly harder on furniture. We were two months away from having our second child when Marie suggested maybe Kim should go back to the zoo. While we were at it, she added, the 11-foot African rock-python in the tank in Lee's room, with the nasty disposition, should go too. Both of these critters in a house with a newborn baby was probably not a good idea.

Our daughter Heather was thus never exposed to a predatory leopard but grew up with the sewer grizzly, and we got to watch while two jaguar cubs who were just barely crawling instantly recognized her as a potential prey species and came at her from different directions. In some species predatory instincts are hard wired from birth.

THREE BABIES IN DISPOSABLE DIAPERS AND ON BOTTLES

When Heather, our oldest daughter, was nine months old and just walking, we brought home a baby female orang. Now Marie had two babies in diapers and on bottles. Heather was initially jealous and exhibited all the baby brother syndrome signs. She even tried to push the orang out of Marie's lap. Our solution was to let Heather give the baby orang her bottle. That seemed to make everything acceptable.

Eight months later we brought home a female baby gorilla. Now Marie had three babies in diapers and on bottles. The baby brother jealousy syndrome started all over again, but this time it was the orang baby objecting to the gorilla baby in Marie's lap. Heather, by then one-and-a-half, thought it was great to have a baby gorilla to care for. We bought disposable diapers by the case, and the refrigerator was full of bottles, each one labeled for a particular baby.

Marie and daughter Heather, getting to know "Rilla," a five-day-old gorilla.

Orang babies are more precocious than human babies, and gorilla babies are much more precocious than both orang and human babies. Within a year they were not only equals but the gorilla had outstripped the other two physically. To say that having three babies in the house was a handful is an understatement. Marie finally figured out that the way to get housework done was to turn a playpen upside down and stuff all three kids underneath with a weight on top. One small problem cropped up when the gorilla started biting the orang and Heather. Marie held the gorilla's arm and bit her and showed Heather how to bite her. Then Heather bit the orang, and the orang bit her back. This solved the biting among our kids, but we soon had a complaint from a neighbor whose kid Heather had bitten. The neighbors had

Over the years, Marie and the kids have been both tolerant and supportive of the zoo babies I brought home.

Facing page: Grandma Webster, pictured holding orang and gorilla babies.

Facing page: Young Lee with "Tye" and "Rilla."

Very rare twin gorilla babies—more precocious than orang babies.

been tolerant, even curious, when Lee and the three girls and our beagle played in the backyard. The only problem was the beagle liked to pull diapers off, but that was a problem with the apes anyway. The good thing was we never a problem finding a babysitter. All the older girls in the neighborhood were more than willing to come along to help. And oftentimes their mothers or other family members were eager to assist.

There are many stories from our days raising kids and zoo babies at home. Once, Marie had the table all set with food on it and decided to go across the street and talk to a neighbor for a minute before calling us to dinner. While she was gone the kids got out of their sleeping enclosure and came upstairs. The orang (we believe) got ahold of the corner of the tablecloth and methodically pulled everything into a pile on the floor. They were selectively eating from the pile when Marie came back. We had to make other plans for dinner.

Another time a little lady in town knitted a pink sweater, bonnet and booties for the gorilla and sent them to us. We put them on her for fun one day and I foolishly let an *Omaha World-Herald* photographer take a picture that was promptly published in the paper. The reaction was mixed, ranging from "That's really cute" to "How dare you insult us by making that gorilla look like a human." Another lesson learned.

Grandmother Webster came to visit and proved to be as enthusiastic about taking care of baby gorillas and orangs as she had been about Young Lee.

CHICKENPOX

When young Lee was eight, the eight-month-old female gorilla named Rilla was scratching herself. Marie examined her and noticed red pustules on her stomach, chest, inner arms and thighs. Dr. Otto Rath came over and examined her and asked me if gorillas ever got chickenpox. I said I didn't know because no one had ever reported it. The next day young Lee came down with the same lesions, and we confirmed it was chickenpox. The two of them suffered together with calamine lotion dubbed over the pustules and scabs. Both recovered completely with no scars. The upside was that the University of Nebraska Medical Center lab confirmed, through electron microscopy, that in fact, both of them had

PHOTO COURTESY OF THE OMAHA WORLD-HERALD.

Young Lee and Rilla were both stricken with chickenpox at the same time.

chickenpox. This was the first-time chickenpox had been confirmed in a gorilla. This was a zoonosis in reverse and made for a nice paper.

GASTRIC DILATATION

A problem with a baby gorilla occurred at 90 days of age when Marie was making her last check at midnight. The baby was gasping for breath, and her abdomen was acutely distended to the point that she could barely breathe. I picked her up and tried to relieve the pressure by burping her. When that didn't help Marie hung her up by her hands and bounced her up and down in a tub of hot water, which did seem to help. I called Dr. Rath who came charging over in his Corvette. We took the gorilla and headed for Children's Hospital in a hurry, Otto driving and me alternating between mouth-to-mouth resuscitation and dangling the baby by her hands.

As soon as we got in the door Dr. Rath called for a stomach tube, which we quickly slid down the baby's esophagus and decompressed her stomach. The acute part of the emergency was over, but we still needed to find out what had caused the acute gastric dilatation. With the stomach tube in place Dr. Rath called the lab and asked the tech on duty to bring down some blood and culture tubes. After midnight at Children's they always had a tech sleeping in the lab in case there was an emergency, so when he came down he was barely awake but he had his shoebox full of tubes and syringes. Otto introduced me as Dr. Simmons and said I would tell him what I wanted. I had the baby partially wrapped in a pink baby blanket, and the first thing I asked for was a culture tube and syringe so I could aspirate some of the stomach contents to see if we had some rare gas-forming bacteria or yeast culture growing. He passed me the tube, I filled it, passed it back to him and then asked him for a syringe and some micro blood tubes since the baby only weighed about eight pounds. He passed me the syringe and tubes, and I filled them and passed them back. About this time, he came out of his partial sleep state and took a closer look at the wiggling hairy black baby in the pink blanket. He just about jumped out of his skin, and I thought he was going to upset his whole shoebox and we'd have to start all over again. It had finally dawned on him that this was not a human baby.

This became a recurring phenomenon exactly every 30 days for the next three months until we begin to ease the baby onto mostly solid food. From then on, we always kept pediatric stomach tubes at home. Marie learned to slide one into the stomach and decompress the baby. We could never culture anything that was not normal stomach flora for a baby, but we ultimately found out the problem was that we were using a high solute, banana-based human baby formula which was prone to rapid gas formation with "normal gut flora."

RESEARCH WORKING GROUPS

One of the problems that most zoos face despite a keen awareness that conservation and research are key parts of our mission is finding the money and people to fulfill that part of their mission. Quite simply, it's hard to come by. Today we have progressed from having virtually no in-house resources to having the Bill and Bernice Grewcock Center for Conservation and Research (CCR) and the Hubbard Research Wing, with a total of 34,000 square-feet that houses veterinary medicine, reproductive physiology, cellular genetics, nutrition and our rare plant micro propagation laboratory. With four full-time practicing veterinarians, a director of conservation, seven Ph.D.-level scientists and a number of interns and graduate students, Omaha has become a very positive contributor to conservation worldwide. Over a period of 20 years we exposed over 2,200 interns from 41 countries to zoo medicine, reproductive physiology, nutrition, genetics, rare plant micro-propagation, and husbandry. Omaha has had a major impact on medicine, research and conservation in the zoo world and in the wild.

This was not always the case. Like many zoos, we talked a good game but didn't have the resources to actually deliver. Soon after I became director we figured out how to become a player by collaborating with zoos and universities that

The world's first test tube tiger was born in Omaha from a collaborative effort with National Zoo scientists.

had the resources and senior scientists available to work on exotic animal projects but no access to animals. We had access to animals. We put together an informal working group that consisted primarily of our staff, vets and scientists from the Smithsonian Institution's National Zoo, The National Cancer Institute and Ulie Seal from the Veterans Administration Hospital and the University of Minnesota in Minneapolis. Omaha had an advantage over many other institutions because we didn't have committees or a bureaucracy to answer to. If we thought a project would advance conservation, breeding or management either in captivity or in the wild we could simply pursue it without committees or bureaucrats second-guessing us.

Over a considerable period of time, until we were able to raise the funds and build our own center, a couple or more times a year we would put together a working group in Omaha to address a conservation or reproductive problem. While the main players were from the aforementioned institutions we welcomed and utilized expertise from other zoos, universities and institutions. Omaha's medical community was a great help, too. The result of all this has been a considerable number of advances in artificial insemination, invitro fertilization, genetics and cryobanking.

ZOO GUESTS IN OUR HOUSE

Since we didn't have the funds to put our partnering veterinarians and scientists up in a hotel they would stay at our house. We would put the kids in sleeping bags in the den in the basement, and as many as 10 or 12 of our visitors would sleep in their rooms, on the living room couch or floor in sleeping bags. Marie would rise at 5 a.m. and cook a big farm breakfast and later dinner for everybody. At the zoo we fed them zoo hot dogs and hamburgers. These working groups would generally be in Omaha for seven to 10 days, at which time everybody would take the data we had collected and return home to write up their reports and share it with the group. This is why so many of the early publications have many co-authors. The primary authors would often be from the Smithsonian or Minnesota, supported by co-authors from their staffs and the staff of the Omaha Zoo.

This system worked very well, for it gave us access to senior scientists, which we could not afford in Omaha. And it gave these scientists access to a working environment that had freedom of action uncommon in their own institution. That's why a number of world-first advancements were actually made here in Omaha, even though logic said that we didn't even remotely have the resources to do this kind of research and conservation work. Additionally, the synergy and stimulation from collaboration on a single project usually expanded the scope of the project and everyone's understanding of the needs and problems.

This routine went on long enough that individual veterinarians and researchers ended up laying claim to specific sleeping quarters in our house. Dr. JoGayle Howard for many nights laid exclusive claim to the sofa in the living room, whereas people who snored got put together in one of the bedrooms. Among the more frequent guests were Dr. Ulie Seal, Dr. Ed Plotka, Dr. David Wildt, Dr. Mitch Bush, Dr. JoGayle Howard, Dr. Janine Brown and Dr. Steve O'Brien. Setting at the dinner table with this mob made interesting childhood memories for our three kids.

Of all our guests, Steve O'Brien, a geneticist from the National Cancer Institute, may have been the most interesting. Steve was a brilliant scientist who liked country-western music, big cigars and to play the piano while solving problems. About two o'clock one morning our kids shook Marie and I awake and said, "Come look." We could hear a piano going, and when we went out into the hall and looked into the living room there was O'Brien, in his underwear, with a big cigar in his mouth, hammering away on our piano while working through a genetics problem. JoGayle Howard and a couple of people sleeping on the floor were peeking out from under their blankets as if to say, "What in the hell is this crazy guy doing?" None of this could have happened without Marie's active participation and a great deal of tolerance. When Mitch Bush became grumpy—due to a diet that omitted beer—Marie told him that if he wasn't going to eat her cooking or drink beer, he should not come back. He came back.

BLACK-FOOTED FERRETS

One of the advantages of not having a bureaucracy or governmental entity to deal with is that we could make quick decisions to react to a conservation problem and carry it out as soon as we could find the money. One such project occurred when it was discovered that that black-footed ferrets, contrary to popular belief, had not become extinct. There was a small isolated population in Meeteetse Canyon, Wyoming. This small population ultimately became threatened with extinction by a canine distemper outbreak, and the last 18 animals were brought into captivity at the Wyoming Fish and Game Department Re-

Five black-footed ferrets, born in Omaha, were part of a ferret recovery program.

search Station in Sybille Canyon, Wyoming. Ultimately only 5 of these survivors would become the founding ancestors of all the black-footed ferrets left on earth.

The station was run by Floyd Blunt and Dr. Tom Thorn (of snake collecting fame), two longtime friends of ours. Along with Ulie Seal, Dave Wildt, JoGayle Howard and a number of other zoo people, we became involved in the project. When enough animals had been bred in captivity in Wyoming it was decided that for safety the population would be distributed among a number of institutions. A quick call to Walter Scott produced the money and built an off-display breeding facility in Omaha. In late 1988 and early 1989 we received 23 ferrets, and the Smithsonian Institution's CRC in Front Royal, Virginia received a smaller number of animals. Our first births occurred in 1990, (the first black-footed ferrets born in a zoo). In the 10 years we actively participated we were able to contribute to the recovery of this species by breeding 305 babies, some of which went to other zoo breeding programs and most of which were released back into the wild.

The first captive bred ferrets to produce offspring after being released back into the wild had been born in Omaha. In 2017 it was estimated that there were over 1,000 black-footed ferrets again living in protected areas in South Dakota, Wyoming and Colorado. After successfully investing 10 years of effort and more than $1 million in Black-Footed Ferret Conservation, we finally discontinued the program when a U.S. Fish and Wildlife Service supervisor attempted to insert himself into personnel decisions at the zoo in a manner that was unacceptable. When I talked to his supervisor about the problem, he said, "You can't tell us what to do, we're the U.S. Government." Well, we did, in fact, tell them what to do!

THE AMPHIBIAN CRISIS AND THE OMAHA RESCUE CENTER

At a 2005 meeting when the zoo world first recognized that the amphibian crisis was caused by the Chydrid fungus and that potentially we could lose one third to half of all amphibian species on earth, it was suggested that we put together a committee meeting to look into solutions. Omaha had 4,200 square feet of space in an elevator lobby and long hallway which was originally to be used as part of the panda exhibit. Not being very good at committees and meetings, we simply went home and began the conversion of this space into 17 biologically isolated and secure amphibian breeding and holding rooms. Each room is isolated with its own HVAC. We have space for approximately 10,000+ amphibians and in addition to currently holding nine species as assurance colonies have bred a substantial number of animals and a number of species for reintroduction back into the wild. These reintroduced species include Wyoming toads, Puerto Rican crested toads, Mississippi gopher frogs and Eastern Hellbenders.

RARE PLANT LAB

Another significant conservation effort occurred as a result of needing a volunteer expert to help us with orchids when we were finishing the Lied Jungle. Marge From was working on an advanced degree developing the technology to micro propagate the Western Prairie Fringed Orchid, the rarest flower in North America. Marge was an atypical student, having graduated many years earlier. She had married and raised a family before returning to graduate school and taking up the cause of the Prairie Fringed Orchid, which amazingly grows in Nebraska, Wyoming, the Dakotas and Canada. It is so rare that in a good year 300 plants could be found, and in a bad year almost none would be found. One thing led to another, and we found space for Marge to continue her work in the basement of the WKP in a little cubbyhole we called "the mushroom hole." Marge was developing the ability to micro propagate orchids from seed, not an easy task. Her work progressed well, and when we constructed the second phase of the Grewcock Center for Conservation and Research, The Hubbard Research Wing, we included space for an office and an honest-to-goodness research lab with a tissue lab, small greenhouse and a culture lab.

We currently have somewhere north of 300,000 rare and endangered baby orchids from Madagascar growing in culture, plus rare orchids from China,

South America and other places. And that's in addition to the Prairie Fringed Orchids and 100,000 or so rare ferns. Marge has sent a number of large shipments of micro propagated orchids back to Madagascar to be reintroduced into habitat. She has trained a number of Malagasy graduate students who are carrying on the work in their home country. We also have millions of seeds stored in liquid nitrogen and -86° C freezers as insurance against extinction.

The ferns are an interesting spinoff to this story. A number of years ago the government of Bermuda, having heard of Marge's work, contacted her because they had two rare species of ferns that were on the verge of extinction. One was the Governor's Fern, which had just five plants left, all in captivity. The other was a larger fern of similar numbers. Marge collected spores from all the plants and brought them back to Omaha. The Governor's Fern became completely extinct, and the other fern is functionally extinct for all intents and purposes. However, we now have more than 100,000 baby ferns growing in culture flasks in our lab. We've sent a number of shipments back to Bermuda where they have been successfully reintroduced back into the wild. Marge has trained technicians from Bermuda. In 2017 Marge began applying the same techniques to an endangered fern from Hawaii.

MADAGASCAR

At a zoo conference a bit over 20 years ago when we were interested in wild cattle, antelope and elephant genetics, I was introduced to a newly graduated veterinarian who was only a month or so from receiving a Ph.D. in cellular genetics. He had done both programs concurrently. Dr. Edward Lewis seemed a perfect fit for the research programs we wanted to expand into. We hired him on the spot and fairly shortly after moving into the CCR Ed was in Thailand collecting the gaur bantang and elephant genetic samples. His next project was in East Africa collecting giraffe and antelope samples. Ed had written his Ph.D. thesis on the genetics of Galapagos tortoises, so at the end of his antelope project he called home and asked if it would be all right to extend his trip to Madagascar since there were two rare tortoise species there. The rule of unintended consequences took over, and when Ed came back he had a fire in his belly to work in Madagascar on lemur and tortoise genetics. One of the things I had realized early on was that when somebody has a real fire in their belly to do good conservation work, the smart thing to do is encourage and support them. The long term benefit to the conservation world will be much greater than if you say, "No, we hired you to work on this and such." The genetics department is now far and away the largest research program at Omaha's Henry Doorly Zoo. For the last 20+ years Ed and his group have spent an average of six to eight months of the year in Madagascar. He has discovered and named 23 new species of lemurs and a number of species of other animals. Additionally over the last 4 years they have produced and planted over 1 million trees to reestablish migration corridors between mountain-

top remnants of Madagascar's forests so that lemurs can maintain better genetic diversity. They have reintroduced a number of lemur species to areas in which they had been exterminated. In 2017 Ed's group planted over 500,000 trees with a goal for 2018 of 650,000 trees. The long-term goal is to maintain this program for at least 10 years with production increasing to 1 million trees per year.

We never have completed our wild cattle and elephant work but the tradeoff has been well worth it.

SALT CREEK TIGER BEETLES

A unique decades-long Nebraska conservation program involves the breeding of the Salt Creek tiger beetle, a critically endangered species found only in one spot—the salt flats of Lincoln, Nebraska. We've seen a nearly extinct species produce more than 3,000 larva that have been introduced back into their environment.

Facing page: Visiting Lake Naivasha in Kenya, 1983.

At an old hunting camp waterfall in Shaba, Kenya, in 1983.

SAFARI LEADERS

One of the good things about working in the zoo world is that Marie and I have had the opportunity to travel around the country and the world. While some trips were to zoo conferences and consulting projects where the pace and the content wasn't appealing to a spouse, on many other trips Marie came along. Fairly early on after becoming director in Omaha we began leading eco-tourism trips and safaris to different places in the world. Over our career I had the opportunity to work and travel in 40 states and 51 countries, plus the Antarctic. Marie has traveled to 35 states and 27 countries, plus the Antarctic. We have had the pleasure of introducing 384 zoo supporters to experience ecosystems and rare animals around the world.

I'm happy to say that the vast majority of groups we took with us were composed of individuals who were either good travelers or tried hard to be good travelers and companions. Over more than 35 years I can only remember a couple of

people who would not have been welcome on the next trip. One was a preacher who didn't believe in buying cigarettes or whisky but smoked and drank everyone else's. He also had a tendency to put his hands on women, including some bare-chested locals in a Maasai kraal. We went behind the kraal and had a very serious discussion about the immediate availability of airplane flights out of Nairobi. On a horseback ride among giraffe, wildebeest, zebras and gazelle at Lewa Downs he made the mistake of kicking his horse just as it climbed out of a deep gully. As he was bucked off and rolled to the bottom the whole safari group cheered and clapped.

That is not to say our trips were entirely incident free. Most of our difficulties involved convincing neophyte travelers how to stay well so they wouldn't miss any days of animal viewing because of "Montezuma's Revenge" or the "Kenyatta Quick Trot." That last phrase, however, is not something you should use in Kenya as I once found out during a rather stern discussion with two armed guards standing in front of the presidential residence.

On most trips, whether to East Africa, Southern Africa, China, India, and Borneo or wherever, you could almost count on the fact that there would be some individuals who missed days due to illness. Usually this was because a salad looked so good that they simply couldn't resist eating it and ignored the fact that they had been warned not to eat anything that wasn't thoroughly cooked or that they peeled themselves. We learned to always take along a fairly complete medical bag. While in the United States it might be frowned upon for a zoo veterinarian to treat human ailments, if you are in the middle of the Serengeti in Tanzania or the Kaziranga Game Reserve in Assam, someone with extra antibiotics and anti-diarrheals was very welcome.

Probably the worst instance I can remember came after a 21-day run in Kenya, during which time Marie and I had carefully mother-henned 16 travelers so that none of them had missed a single day. On our last night we went out for a final banquet, and I made the mistake of leaving the table to visit the men's room before dinner. When I came back I found the whole group guzzling water like they had been lost in the Sahara Desert for a week. When I shouted, "Stop that," they all assured me it was okay because the chef had greeted our group and assured everybody that the hotel water was filtered and safe. Unfortunately, his standards for safe water were considerably different than mine. The next day, 15 out of the 16 had bad cases of the Kenyatta Quick Trot. It was a long ride home. In those days you got on the Pan Am airplane in Nairobi and were on that same plane for 22 hours before landing in New York. It was an airplane ride from hell most would never forget. Many of them became frequent travelers but never made that mistake again.

HE'S CHARGING

Another memorable instance occurred when a fellow traveler offered our driver some M&Ms candy. She explained that they were chocolate, famous for melting in your mouth but not in your hand. After a bit more explanation, he had a small handful clenched in his fist trying very hard to melt them with everyone looking on when suddenly Marie's voice came from the back of the Land Rover saying, "He's Charging." I looked around and a large male cape buffalo was indeed charging the Land Rover. The M&Ms went flying into the air, and our driver was trying frantically to get the Land Rover in gear when the bull hit the left rear corner of the vehicle and bent the sheet metal considerably. Luckily the driver got it in gear and out-of-the-way before the next charge.

HEATHER AND THE RHINO

Luckily most of the charges we experienced were false or, short, charges without ever hitting our vehicle. One I remember well was when our oldest daughter Heather traveled in Marie's place on a safari to East Africa. It was her 16th birthday, and the trip made a great present. We were in the Masai Mara and had been down at a hippo hole in a bend of the Mara River. We had counted 88 heads out of the water at one time. A number of big males had been roaring, grunting and challenging each other and Heather had tape-recorded it. We found that if you played a tape recording of a lion roar around a group of sleeping lions, their heads came up and you could get great photographs. In another part of the Mara we came on a pair of black rhinos with a calf hiding in thick scrub brush on a small flat mound elevated about five feet. Other than seeing one occasionally poke their nose out from the brush to look at us I couldn't really get any good shots.

Our driver was making his very first trip as a driver guide which, in that part of the world, is an elite position that pays well. He had been a mechanic for seven years before moving into a top spot. He was a nice guy but since he didn't yet know a great deal about animal life, I elected to ride in his vehicle every day and rotated everyone else through his and the other two vehicles. After a half hour of frustration, I said to Heather, "Cue up that that hippo recording and see if we can get the rhinos to respond to it." She did and the consequence exceeded both our expectations. We got an immediate dead-on charge from the male, and it was obvious he was not bluffing. He was fully intent on smashing our vehicle. Our driver must have ground every gear in the transmission before he got us out of harm's way. When we were a safe distance away he stopped and shakily said, "Please Dr. Simmons, this is a brand-new vehicle, and if that rhino had damaged it I would be a mechanic for the rest of my life. Please don't do that again." We didn't do it again.

CANOEING THE ZAMBEZI

At one-time Zimbabwe was our favorite place in Africa. We once watched the elephant herd responsible for giving biologists and researchers the first hint that elephants could communicate long distances with ultra-low-frequency infrasonic sound. And there was the time I was left beside the railroad tracks on the Kalahari sands so I could photograph a 100 miles-per-hour, double-ended steam locomotive pull a train out of South Africa to Victoria Falls while the rest of the group went game viewing but I had a tree nearby. We participated in a black rhino relocation project in Hwange where a female rhino with a half-grown calf

chased our Land Rover for more than one-half mile with serious intent. We overnighted in a houseboat on the crystal-clear, 400-foot-deep Lake Kariba and canoed in the shallows where you could see tiger fish and large Nile crocodiles 10 feet below.

Some of our most exciting memories were downstream on the Lower Zambezi River where we made a number of canoe trips and walking safaris. One night a puff adder crawled into the cook tent and caused major pandemonium. I wanted to show our travelers what a puff adder looked like, but after the cooks got through pounding it with anything they could lay their hands on there wasn't a lot to show. On the last day of the trip a few of us wanted one more canoe ride. The plan was for everyone to pack up and drive 20 miles to a little hilltop landing strip. The six of us who wanted to canoe were going to take two canoes 14 miles

Facing page: Our group at Victoria Falls in 2010.

Victoria Falls, Zambia, 2016.

downriver to a pickup point. We wanted to start early because at that time of year, by mid-morning, the wind comes up and blows upstream against the strong current of the Zambezi, making canoeing difficult. We didn't start as early as we wanted, and a wind in excess of 30 miles-per-hour was blowing directly into our faces by the halfway point. It was so strong that if you quit paddling it would actually blow you back upstream against the current. Garth Thompson, our senior guide who had actually been one of the naturalists who helped identify elephant infrasonics, was in the front of the canoe with Marie and I.

Even with two of us paddling I thought my lungs were going to burst. We finally came to an old oxbow where the river channel had changed course. Garth suggested we take it to get out of the wind, even though it would be an extra three miles. It was shallow, had very little current and the high bank sheltered us from the wind. About halfway through we met a very large male hippo who thought he owned the oxbow. He was lunging and short charging in the water and gave every indication that he would be more than willing to chomp a canoe. Rather than turn back we decided to move to the far bank and carefully creep past him. It's worth noting that Garth had a 404-caliber rifle. I paddled quietly while Garth stood ready to fire a round into the water if the hippo charged us in the narrow channel. By keeping both canoes close to the bank we could jump out and run up the bank to safety. Only as a last resort would Garth actually shoot the hippo, since that would cause all kinds of problems with the Zimbabwean government. We followed the plan, and everything worked out fine. The hippo made all kinds of bluffs and

Facing page: The Cape of Good Hope, 2008.

The Simmons family on safari in Tanzania, 2015.

slashed the water with his open mouth but didn't come on. Since I was paddling I could not photograph him, so the only pictures we have are from Marie's instamatic, which were not terribly good without a telephoto. Once we passed the hippo we traversed the rest of the long oxbow safely and exited back into the river channel about a mile-and-a-half from our pickup point.

Once we were on a stretch of the Zambezi—classified as a "braided" river, which means that there are many parallel winding sandbars in between multiple streams of water, much like the Platte in Nebraska, but much bigger, deeper and faster—transiting down one of these streams between two sandbars, in the lead, with Marie in the middle of our canoe and Ruth Poli, a longtime zoo docent, sitting in the front. Ruth was well over 80 and weighed, at most, 90 pounds. We drifted past two large old bachelor cape buffalos when they apparently decided they didn't like being that close to a string of canoes. They both began charging downstream on the sandbar right beside our canoes with a great deal of noise. As they got level with our canoe they abruptly turned left and charged through the shallow water directly in front of our canoe. Marie made some noise, but Ruth sat perfectly still with her hands folded in her lap and simply took it all in. Afterwards, she said, "That was interesting." Since I was paddling I didn't get any pictures. It would have made a great shot with the water splashing up and almost landing on Ruth.

Facing page: Tanzania, 1998.

Marie and I, pictured in 2008, have always loved Victoria Falls.

INDIA

In India we visited castles and walls that rivaled anything in Europe or China. And we camera hunted tigers and Indian rhinos from the backs of elephants. One morning we were quietly slipping through the forest on elephant back when there was a disturbance on another elephant. I heard Sandy, a fellow traveler, say, "Let me down right now." The mahout protested, saying there could be tigers in the tall grass of the glade we were in.

Sandy, who apparently had too many cups of coffee at breakfast, said, "If you don't let me down right now I'm going to pee on your elephant." He brought the elephant to her knees, and I ended up with a great photograph of the top half of Sandy's head peering over a thick clump of elephant grass. So much for friendship and chivalry when you've got a camera in your hand.

Another time in India we treated a young elephant who had been attacked by a tiger. The baby, who was still nursing, had severe bite wounds on its head and visible brain tissue. Without instruments or sutures there was little we could do except round up all the antibiotics we could and hope Mother Nature would do the rest.

For my 50th birthday we saw the sun rise over the Taj Mahal. The game preserves and monuments were spectacular, but the culture shock was significant. At dinner one night at the house of Kailash Sankhala, head of India's "Project Tiger," who had helped arrange our trip, he observed that westerners couldn't really appreciate India until they no longer saw all the poverty, filth and disease. I felt compelled to point out I wasn't sure I could live that long.

In New Delhi one night I had arranged for a birthday cake after dinner. Joe Caggiano, our Zoo Societies' treasurer and longtime friend, immediately said, "Hey, it's somebody's birthday. Come on, we'll all sing happy birthday. Whose birthday is it?"

When no one answered he looked around the table and finally spotted his wife Cathy smiling at him with a wicked gleam in her eye. It was an expensive

Marie, pictured in 2004, during one of our two trips to China.

lapse of memory, and Cathy took Joe out shopping the next day and came back to the hotel with an antique star ruby and emerald bracelet.

In Assam I spotted an ant nest in a small tree that looked exactly like one of our paper hornet's nests. I asked our guide if I could collect it, and he said no problem. I put it in a big plastic bag since it was full of aggravated ants. Three days later when we got back to New Delhi I thought I needed to do something about the ants before bringing the nest back to Omaha, so the hotel let me put it in their freezer overnight to kill the ants. The next morning I put it into a cardboard beer box and hand carried it on board the airplane. I put it in the overhead bin, and about four hours later I noticed a commotion in the seats in front of us. The ants had survived and had come out of the nest and were dropping onto passengers. I decided that discretion was the better part of valor and sat quietly while the stewardesses dealt with the problem. The beer box didn't have my name on it, and they never discovered where the ants were coming from.

CHINA

Marie and I made two trips to China together, and I made two more on my own. On our first trip we led a group of travelers that we had previously taken to Africa and India. The last three trips came as part of our pursuit of acquiring giant pandas for the Henry Doorly Zoo. Unfortunately, like many zoos around the country and the world, we were enticed by the Chinese Diplomatic Corps into pursuing pandas for nearly 10 years. This is a game that the Chinese diplomats have played with many cities around the world.

As in India, there are many incredible things to see in China, and we had many good experiences to remember.

Having been in Tiananmen Square just days before the massacre we were in Kunming when it occurred. We decided to bypass our planned visit to Canton and instead go straight to Hong Kong. Our Chinese guide took us to the airport and waited until we boarded the plane before leaving. After sitting on the plane for over an hour, China Air canceled the flight and we all had to get off. Simultaneously, they closed the airport and we all had to leave the terminal. Unable to

contact our guide, we managed to find someone who said there was an airport hotel down the road. Carrying our luggage, we walked to the hotel and managed to roust out a desk clerk. They had some rooms, and I went up to inspect them. "Bad" and "awful" are not strong enough words to describe the rooms. They smelled like a foul latrine. By the time I came down to tell everyone that we weren't staying it was raining cats and dogs outside. I explained the room situation and the fact that at 1 a.m. there were really no other options. I told everyone to go to their rooms but not to undress and get in bed. I advised spreading their rain coats out on top of the bed and pillow and sleeping on top of them. I paced the halls keeping watch, and at the crack of dawn got everyone up for the walk back to the airport. It was a night in China no one will ever forget. Fortunately, there were a lot of other great memories that more than made up for this one.

Facing page: With Dr. Yong Shi, left, and Dr. Douglas Armstrong, right, in China in 2001.

The Great Wall makes for a wonderful backdrop.

AUSTRALIA

Once we were in northern Australia, and I saw what appeared to be another ant nest hanging in a tree. I asked our driver to stop and got out saying that I wanted to collect it. He wisely drove down the road a ways as I started climbing the tree. I could see the little ants crawling out of it, then all of a sudden they turned out to have wings. These were hundreds of small hornets. Climbing down a tree while being stung by a swarm of hornets is an interesting experience. By the time I made it halfway to the vehicle they quit attacking, and one of our travelers had a bee sting stick which helped quite a bit. After that I lost my enthusiasm for insect houses.

All told, Marie and I made five trips to Australia, two of them with zoo travelers and three conservation working trips.

PERU

On a trip to Peru, we were 60 miles downstream on the Amazon from Iquitos and another 100 miles upstream on the Napo River, when a note came that my dad had died of a heart attack in Dallas. It had taken two-and-a-half days to get the note to us, and it took another two days to get to a satellite phone. All the relatives had gathered and were awaiting word from me on what to do. Since it could easily have been another three or more days to get to Dallas I said go ahead with the funeral. I took a long walk in the dark on the riverbank. A week later I went home by way of Dallas. While sad, the experience taught us to always discuss these kind of contingencies with our travelers in advance, since many places in the world do not lend themselves to getting home quickly.

On this same trip I made the mistake of putting a captured rhinoceros bee-

Facing page: Marie in Australia with a Koala, 2005.

Marie in Cusco, Peru, 2001.

tle in my binocular case. Rhinoceros beetles are perhaps the strongest insects in the world, and in the morning the inside of my binocular case was totally trashed. There was a big hole in the side and the beetle was gone.

Probably the best of the Peruvian trips that Marie and I made, even including the ones to Cusco and Machu Picchu, was the one we were given for our 30th zoo anniversary. We went by ourselves in the rainy season on a relatively small boat to go 200 miles upstream on the Amazon from Iquitos. The Amazon had risen more than 30 feet and flowed for miles back into the rain forest. You could take a small boat or dugout and wander in amongst the trees, seeing orchids and animals at eye level. Freshwater pink and gray dolphins and large fish swam among the trees. From this high water level the monkeys and birds and other animals were much easier to see. It was a great trip, and we had no responsibilities to anyone but ourselves.

ANTARCTICA

Perhaps our most visually spectacular travel was to Antarctica. Descriptions of the grandeur of the glaciers, icebergs and wildlife are simply inadequate. We were on the Akademik Sergey Vavilov, a relatively small, formerly Russian KGB spy ship that had been rented to the Norwegians for tourism. The ship was very sturdy, ice hardened and had been built in Finland. It was very nice but didn't hold many people because it had been designed for intelligence gathering. It seemed the KGB lived quite well.

There were 27 active antennas and another 14 empty antenna mounts, causing us to wonder if the Russian crew was still gathering intelligence. The captain was the original commanding officer and hailed from Vilnius, Lithuania. In the very center of the ship there was a long, narrow moon well open through the bottom of the hull with two huge cable reels, one of which still had a thick cable and some kind of sensor on it. We had 40 guests on board, which was a perfect number for a great trip. On this trip, Sam Cooper, our district attorney, smuggled an

Distance-home signs at Argentine Station, Antarctica, part of which had recently burned down (1996).

old tuxedo under his insulated coveralls, and when we landed on the Antarctic Peninsula to walk among thousands of penguins, he stripped down to his penguin suit.

We went ashore inside the caldera of Deception Island, the flooded caldera of an active volcano. It had been an old whaling station in the days of sail, and the ships could enter through the small opening into a protected warm-water harbor to render their whales into oil. This was our first opportunity to go ashore, and I had been worried about keeping my hands warm enough to handle the cameras, so I had put a couple hand-warming packets in my pockets. It turned out to be an unnecessary precaution since the black sand on the beaches was warm underfoot from the volcanic action. Forgetting that I had activated the packets, I started

On the Antarctic Peninsula, 1996.

taking photographs, and as was my usual custom I took each roll of film as I shot it out of the camera and put it in my right-hand pocket. By the time we got back on the ship most of those rolls were fried as crisp as well-done bacon with all kinds of wrinkles and orange and red stripes running through the film. Needless to say, I modified the procedure for the rest of the trip.

Allow me to back up a bit. During the trip we pulled into the Argentine government research station where the crew normally spent the Antarctic winter until they were replaced in January. When the new crew had arrived they had been unable to find a doctor who would spend the next winter. Everyone else was told to pack up and board the ship, but the "old" doctor would have to stay another year. Well the doctor apparently had seen enough of the Antarctic winter, and while everyone was boarding he went back to the barracks and poured kerosene all over the floor and set it on fire. There was nothing left but a few charred sticks. He apparently had said, "If I can't go home then everyone has to go home."

On the way down to the Antarctic we had crossed the Drake Straits in bad weather. The seas had been so high and rough that they hung vomit bags along the stairways. A number of us were seasick, but as we went further south the weather was calmer. For 10 days we experienced the most incredible scenery of icebergs, glaciers, penguins, leopard seals, crab-eating seals, Weddell seals and whales. Going ashore to walk among the penguins was an experience not to be forgotten. On the way back the Drake Straits were like a millpond and you could see your face in the reflection. We detoured west so that we could then swing around east, and everyone could say they had rounded Cape Horn. We also spent some time in the Straits of Magellan observing sea lions and birdlife.

SOUTH KOREA

I made two trips to South Korea. The first was with Ulie Seal to consult on their efforts to re-masterplan the Seoul Zoo, which is located in a scenic hanging valley in the mountains overlooking Seoul. The third trip was to Busan, Korea, to consult on a new zoological and horticultural park they wanted to build inside five large geodesic domes similar to our desert dome.

JAMAICA

Let me tell you about my wife, Marie the tree smuggler. In January 1993 Ulie Seal decided that CBSG should hold a 10-year futures workshop in Ocho Rios, Jamaica. About 60 of the CBSG steering committee and staff met at the Shaw Gardens Hotel. The old Shaw Gardens Hotel had been up on the hill as part of an extensive botanical garden but was long since gone. The new hotel was on the beachfront. From the standpoint of gauging where worldwide conservation was at the time and attempting to predict where conservation should be 10 years into the future, the workshop was as successful as most workshops are. In addition to providing early morning and late evening opportunities for snorkeling in the lagoon, the conference had one very interesting highlight. Unbeknownst to Ulie, when he had booked the hotel, the beach was divided into two sides. Our long conference room with its big windows was right at the dividing line. To the right was a normal sunbathing beach, and to the left was a "clothing optional," or nude beach. The nude beach was far and away the most populated. The head of the conference room was to the right, but no matter who the speaker was it was hard to keep from periodically looking over your shoulder to the left until Maryalice Seal finally shouted, "ALL RIGHT, ENOUGH OF THIS!" Then she pulled the drapes shut so no one could see outside. We spent the rest of the conference in a closed-in room tending to business.

Our Jamaican trip came just 10 months after we had opened the Lied Jungle in April 1992, and Terry Gouviea, our horticulturist, was still looking for plant species to fill out the collection. When she heard I was going to Jamaica she promptly gave me a list of roots and tubers she wanted plus the USDA permit to import them. We made contact with the head botanist at Shaw Gardens and arranged to meet her at the gardens. She was very helpful and promised to supply as many species as she could, except for the breadfruit tree, which is propagated from a slip cut off the parent tree at just the right time of year. She wasn't sure that this was possible right then. She connected us with one of the garden's horticulturists who agreed to take us up to some small mountain villages where we could to buy some of the rootstock for plant species which they sold for food in the open-air markets.

On the day before we left, Marie and I played hooky and went on a tour of village markets, buying roots and tubers, which they eat like potatoes. Altogether we had more than 60 pounds. I planned to hand carry everything through customs and the inspection stations in Miami. Just as we were ready to leave for the airport the Shaw Gardens botanist showed up carrying a breadfruit tree slip. A large refrigerator had just been delivered to the hotel, and using a pocket knife we commandeered a long piece of corrugated cardboard and made a three-cornered box seven-feet long to fit the breadfruit slip into. We made the airplane, slid our long box lengthwise into the overhead shelf and settled in for the ride back to the States. We had flown in through Miami, where there is a large plant inspection and quarantine station, and everything was going well until the pilot came on the loudspeaker telling us that we would be landing in Tampa. I hadn't paid enough attention to the return ticket and had just assumed that we would be going back the same way. This was a near-fatal mistake since Tampa does not have a quarantine station, only an incinerator to burn plants, vegetables or fruits visitors try to bring into the US. There was no way to sneak 60 pounds of roots and tubers (and a seven-foot breadfruit slip) past customs, so the only thing I could do was throw myself at the mercy of the local USDA agent and ask for help. As soon as we got off the plane and got to customs I asked to see the agent in charge so I could explain my situation. Luckily I had pictures and brochures of the Lied Jungle with me, plus the USDA plant import permits that we had filled out in advance. After considerable discussion and pleading he was sympathetic. He inspected the roots and tubers in our carry-on, and after finding a banned yam species, which he

promptly confiscated, he promised to send the shipment on to be fumigated and then shipped to Omaha. He had just assured me that everything was fine and we could go catch our airplane when I happened to look around to see Marie standing there with the seven-foot long, three-cornered box in her hand and a funny look on her face. We were already close to plane time, so I thought about it for a second then shook my head gently "no." I took her by the arm and proceeded to the plane for Omaha. After being sent to a USDA station in Maryland for fumigation, all the roots and tubers arrived in Omaha. Unfortunately, the breadfruit slip refused to take root and withered. It was the wrong time of the year. This is how Marie became a notorious but happily unindicted plant smuggler.

OVER KILIMANJARO

Possibly one of our most memorable trips occurred while the movie *Kilimanjaro: To The Roof Of Africa* was being filmed. Walter & Sue Scott organized a photographic safari for a small group of board members plus Marie and I to Tanzania and to see the film crew at work. A pair of French Aerospatiale (B2 Squirrel) helicopters had been chartered, and Walter and I—along with our pilot—became the first people to fly over the top of Kilimanjaro in a helicopter. It was forbidden to fly a plane over Kilimanjaro, so our pilot filed a flight plan to sightsee around the mountain. No one paid much attention since everyone knew that helicopters couldn't fly higher than 18,000 feet. That is except this model. With half a load of fuel and just the three of us, we circled and then flew over the caldera at 20,000 feet. I have some great video and still film of the flight. Trying to photograph with an oxygen mask on is interesting. Another experience on this trip was a balloon ride over the Serengeti with a high wind landing and luckily, a crash into an acacia tree that prevented us from going into a deep gully.

ZOO GOOF OF THE YEAR AWARD

If you live long enough and work hard enough you are likely to receive well-deserved recognition and awards. For many years the zoo world presented an annual award at our fall conference that we all looked forward to. The honor was usually well deserved, but none of us actually wanted to be the recipient. To be

Facing page: The B2 Squirrel provided a bird's eye view of Kilimanjaro.

Our balloon crash landing on the Serengeti in 2000—it could have been worse.

the recipient meant that your closest friends and good buddies had ratted you out for something really stupid that you had done or something that had gone remarkably awry. Allow me to recall some of the more notable Zoo Goof of the Year Awards because I was in fact the recipient one year and was later partly responsible for its demise.

One of the more notable awards went to the director of the Oklahoma City Zoo after a keeper making rounds found a small, pink, almost translucent baby in the bedding below the tree kangaroos. Kangaroos give birth at a stage which would be considered premature in other mammals. Their babies, with underdeveloped tails and hind legs, are blind but somehow manage to crawl up through the fur into the pouch and attach to a teat. Their skin is so thin and transparent that you can literally see their blood flow and almost see their heartbeat. The keeper cupped the baby in his hands to keep it warm and rushed it to the zoo nursery where they had an incubator. The zoo's nursery keeper was nationally recognized for having a good touch at hand raising difficult babies. The director, an inveterate publicity hog, immediately called a press conference. Tree kangaroo births in those days were rare. Unfortunately, he also decided to call in pediatricians and neonatologists from the university medical center to consult and give advice.

With the newspapers present and the TV cameras rolling everybody gave their advice and the cameras recorded the wiggling little pink baby. This garnered so much good PR that he called a press conference every day for the next week, but then everything went completely silent. Many people assumed the little thing must not have made it, but in fact what had happened was someone had finally taken a close look at the baby as it developed and realized that they were doing an absolutely spectacular job of hand raising a white lab rat. For many exotic animals, who will only eat live food, a standard diet is newborn mice and rats, commonly called pinkies. Apparently a pinky had fallen out of a keeper's feed bucket on the way to feed something else.

Years later that same zoo director bought a pair of white tiger cubs from a private individual in Texas for a great deal of money. After bringing them back to the zoo everyone got to watch them slowly and inexorably turn yellow as they shed their baby fur and their adult-colored hair came in. It was great fun watching as he tried to explain this to the press. Sadly, by then the Zoo Goof of The Year Award had been discontinued, otherwise he might have been the only two-time recipient.

The award winner who immediately preceded me was Merv Larson of the Arizona Sonora Desert Museum. They had built a new exhibit featuring beavers, otters and desert big horn sheep. It was a fantastic naturalistic exhibit. As their grand opening approached the desert big horn herd had not arrived and only came in the night before. Being cautious, they kept them in their sleeping quarters overnight. On the morning of the grand opening with the governor of Arizona, the mayor of Tucson, board members and the press, they first introduced the otters and beavers and then, with the whole world looking on, they opened the door to let the rare desert big horn herd out. An old ewe, who was the matriarch of the herd, led them out and looked around. She spotted an artistically carved crack running diagonally up the man made rock wall, put her foot in the crack and in front of God and everyone, calmly climbed out. The rest of the herd followed, casually trotting out of the zoo and disappearing into the desert. Merv Larson became the 1974 recipient of the award and automatically went on the committee to select the next recipient.

At that time I had just become chairman of the computer data committee, a largely inactive committee, since very few zoos had computers and no software had been developed. Ulie Seal and I had been working hard on developing and rolling out ISIS (the International Species Inventory System). I handled most of the politicking and fundraising, and Ulie and his graduate students developed software. We had used Omaha as the beta test site since we were a relatively young zoo, and our data, we thought, was very accurate. For the system to be truly useful, all the known data on all known animals, dead or alive, needed to be entered accurately. This included all births, including stillbirths or abortions, and all deaths, no matter the cause or age. At that time the zoo world had a sort of unwritten code to alert the press to successful births or new arrivals and avoid notifying the world of unsuccessful births or deaths. There was a fair amount of angst among the American zoo community about a computer data system that had all this information recorded. It could potentially get breached by a news organization that didn't exactly have the best interest of a particular zoo at heart. It was not an unreasonable apprehension. We all knew that there were many news organizations that prefer to focus on bad news. Three years before The American Association of Zoo Veterinarians (AAZV) had enthusiastically adopted the concept of ISIS and pledged $2,500 per year for four years for development. That same year, Gladys Porter from Brownsville, Texas wrote a check for $10,000. Not so for the zoo directors and curators. As an aside, Ulie would additionally spend the equivalent of approximately $90,000 counting all the resources he had available at the University of Minnesota and the VA Hospital.

In order for ISIS to be successful we needed to get all of the North American Zoos (AAZPA) to buy-in and overcome their apprehensions. At the 1975 AAZPA conference, before bringing it up for a vote, we developed a strategy. We decided to identify the 10 most influential zoo directors who, if they spoke out against the program, could kill it. Ulie and I took them one by one up to my suite to reason with, cajole, beg (or sometimes just plain drink) them into submission. If we couldn't convince them to actively support ISIS we tried to extract a promise not to publicly oppose it, at least until we could demonstrate that our security and confidentiality system was solid. We managed to do exactly that, and after some considerable and sometimes heated discussion in the main meeting, ISIS was adopted as obligatory for all members. AAZPA finally anted up $2,500 for development. About this time, Ulie quietly dropped yet another bombshell. He was absolutely adamant that for ISIS to be successful worldwide it needed to be a totally independent, international organization. If any one zoo, any one regional zoo association or any one country could claim ownership and control there would likely not be universal participation. He was right. After 43 years of data collection, including 62 million records of some 10 million animals, 22,000 species in 1,060 institutions, history has proven Ulie correct. In the beginning, I thought simply getting the U.S. zoos to participate would be a miracle.

Yet, there was still one fly in the ointment. Having used Omaha's Henry Doorly Zoo as the beta test site, we had decided to demonstrate its value to the group by shipping in boxes of large, thick fan-fold printouts that went back to day one when the zoo received its first animals. Unfortunately, we hadn't had time to debug or edit Omaha's database printout. Everyone was duly impressed, except for Marvin Jones, the record keeper from the San Diego Zoo. He actually read the whole report. It must have

Top: Danum Valley, Borneo, 1997.
Right: On the Kinabatangan River, Borneo, 1997.

taken him the better part of two days. According to the print out, Omaha had a 67-year-old golden lion marmoset whose parents were 63-year-old spider monkeys. Of course, he ratted us out to Merv Larson, the reigning Zoo Goof Recipient. This is how I got to be on the committee to select the Zoo Goof recipient for the following year.

The next year was a target-rich environment. Over dinner and drinks a small group of former recipients consolidated the lists of potential recipients. There was a veritable wealth of screw ups to consider, but finally after a lot of laughing and table pounding we narrowed it down to three possibilities. The problem was that we couldn't decide which one was most deserving. Merv Larson gleefully solved the problem by suggesting that we give out three awards, two runners-up and a first-place.

The first runner-up was the director of the Brookfield Zoo, where a master's degree had been granted and a Ph.D. thesis had been submitted on the breeding behaviors of a pair of flat-headed cats when a zoo keeper finally took matters into his own hands. He picked up both cats, looked under their tails, and proclaimed that they were both males. We gave the director a big magnifying glass and a drawing detailing the difference between males and females.

The next runner-up was the San Diego Zoo. As I've said, sometimes revenge is sweet. When their longtime zoo director Dr. Charlie Schroeder retired they were in the midst of some financial difficulties. Instead of hiring another veterinarian or a biologist or zoologist they elected to hire an economist with a Ph.D. from the University of Vienna, who had apparently pulled nine or 10 companies back from the brink of financial disaster. He ran the zoo for about six months until Charlie suspected something was amiss and hired a private detective to investigate him. The man turned out to be complete imposter with no degrees or credentials at all. We gave them an even bigger illuminated magnifying glass with chart of instructions on how to read and vet the fine print in a curriculum vitae.

The final Zoo Goof of the Year Award recipient was The National Zoo, a division of the Smithsonian Institution. They had purchased, at extraordinary expense, a guaranteed breeding herd of Bactrian camels from a private zoo in Canada. A veterinary team from Washington went to Canada to inspect the animals and pregnancy check the females. They pronounced some of them pregnant. The animals were shipped to Washington but then nothing happened, no babies were born. Sometime later, the zoo director was on vacation in Louisiana and there was a little zoo that no one had heard of. Additionally, there in the zoo stood a big male Bactrian camel. The D.C. zoo director asked if they'd be willing to sell the camel. He bought him right on the spot.

He went to town, had a trailer hitch installed on his station wagon and rented a horse trailer. He loaded the camel, drove back to Washington and unloaded him into the pasture with the Canadian camels. Sometime later it occurred to someone to ask if the new male had been TB tested before being introduced into the herd. The answer was no, so now the new animal and the whole herd needed to be tested. While the original and very expensive Canadian male was being injected with tuberculin antigen, a somewhat inexperienced zookeeper innocently asked, "Dr. Bush, are camel testicles internal or external?" Mitch looked, and sure enough they had been sold a castrated male, for a lot of money. So much for being a proven breeder. The Louisiana male in fact tested positive on the TB test (we would later find that the majority of all camels test positive on the intradermal test whether they have ever been exposed or not so he was not tubercular), but at least he had testicles. We gave them an even bigger magnifying glass with a drawing of the external genitalia of a male Bactrian camel.

That year's award ceremony was one of the best ever with a great deal of glee on all sides. Because the National Zoo was involved it made the federal register, and the incident was actually discussed in the U.S. Congress. Thus, I became partly responsible for the death of one of the best traditions the zoo world ever had.

When an individual or organization can no longer laugh at themselves, it's probably the beginning of the end of usefulness.

ZOO AND AQUARIUM DESIGN

Functional, structural, and mechanical design at zoos is often left to outsiders with no hands-on experience with exotic animals. This is almost always a serious mistake, like letting an architect or engineer who was not a surgeon or had never cooked a meal design a surgical suite or restaurant kitchen. This is not to say that architects and engineers are incapable of getting it right, because most of them do. Those that get it right do so by doing their homework and consulting with people with experience in that particular discipline or with that particular species of animals and then listening to what they have to say. We've all seen exhibits that from the outside were grandiose monuments to the designer, but from the inside, and particularly from the behind-the-scenes-working side, were functional abortions for the keepers, medical staff and, unfortunately, the animals.

Experience has taught most of us the hard way that if you are not in firm control of the process, Murphy's Law and the Law of Unintended Consequences will be. We developed a procedure to be used in the early stages of conceptual design called "Playing the What-If Game." Below you can read an excerpt from a paper I wrote and have presented to a number of organizations and conferences around the world. The full paper is presented in Appendix A.

"THE WHAT IF GAME" is an exercise in which you mentally, systematically walk step-by-step through every function from feeding, cleaning, bringing in new specimens, removing specimens, breeding introductions, births, deaths, breaking up fights, escapes, neonatal exams, immobilization and treatments, to washing the windows, taking out the garbage or manure and visitor interactions. While "THE WHAT IF GAME" can certainly be played by one person, and in fact this is usually how most projects start, it should ultimately be played by a team that is used to working together with a purpose in common. This team concept will be touched on later in this paper. If possible, every person who will ultimately work in the project should be included in and encouraged to play "THE

WHAT IF GAME." The perspectives from which architects, engineers, keepers, curators, veterinarians, horticulturists directors and the maintenance tech see a project, are oftentimes dramatically different. These perspectives shape what is perceived to be the function. While institutional and individual management philosophies and practices can and should have bearing on design form and function, these influences should transcend, "All of our buildings have always been red brick." There is seldom only one single, absolute or perfect way to accomplish the desired function.

I am a firm believer that you are highly unlikely to be able to hire an outside expert to design a system or exhibit and expect it to work well for your institution unless you, your staff and the people who will have to live in that facility day in and day out, have played an active part in its functional design. This is particularly true of outside experts who have never been down on their knees with dirty hands working in a similar facility. Ultimately, all outside experts go home, while you must live with the facility. This can seem longer than forever if the facility doesn't work. If at all possible, hire a local architect who lives in your town and who is both knowledgeable enough and intuitive enough to listen and see things from the perspective of your institution. Architects, engineers, zoo directors, veterinarians, curators and other staff involved at the primary design level all need secure egos to effectively play "THE WHAT IF GAME." There is only one acceptable response to any of the players stating, "That won't work." No matter where the idea being discussed originally came from, or if it simply slipped in by default, the only acceptable response is, "Alright, why won't it work and what will make it work?" This is, unfortunately, often followed closely by, "Do we have enough money to make it work?" This is not a democratic committee where everyone votes. The director (say owner), architect, and acknowledged experts—together—should be the final arbitrators of compromises after listening to all ideas. Ultimately, the owner who pays the bills and lives with the results has the final say.

EXHIBITS AND CONSTRUCTION IN THE HENRY DOORLY ZOO

Next to seeing new baby animals born, probably one of the most challenging and fun things a zoo director gets to do is to design and build new exhibits and animal facilities.

OMAHA ZOO RAILROAD

There had been a small narrow gauge kid's railroad in the park for 11 years, but it was closed in 1965 when the Henry Doorly Zoo began construction.

In 1967 the board decided to build the Omaha zoo railway and buy a replica of Union Pacific's #119 steam locomotive, which pulled the ceremonial train to Promontory Point in 1869 for the Golden Spike Ceremony. Through the offices of zoo board member Bob Brown, the U.P. surveyed, designed, and graded three-and-one-half miles of right-of-way. There were many cuts and fills. They then installed 70 pound-per-foot rails 30 inches apart (mining gauge) on shortened mainline ties. This was no mean feat since the zoo is on hilly land and some of our grades were six percent. The theoretical maximum grade that a steel wheel on a steel rail can pull is seven percent.

With help from Bob Brown and Ed Owen and Paxton and Vierling Steel we contracted with the Crown Metal Company of Wyano, Pennsylvania to build a steam locomotive and four passenger cars on a 5/8 scale. It was important to have a locomotive capable of pulling four loaded cars up our steep hills and around our tight curves. The new HDZ #119 was a Classic American 4-4-0 steam locomotive. It had a leading truck with four wheels plus four tall driving wheels and no trailing wheels. The Omaha zoo railway made its inaugural run in July 1968, just short of the centennial anniversary of the Golden Spike ceremony. We made a number of empty test runs with two retired "hogheads" (steam locomotive engineers) the day before to polish the wheels and track and to make sure we could get around. There were no problems except it took a real "touch" to hook up and ease the throttle open just before the pop off valve blew or you wouldn't make it up the first hill out of the station. Being a successful hoghead on the HDZ Railroad was much more an art than a science.

On dedication day we made the inaugural run with Mr. Ed Bailey, chairman of the Union Pacific Railroad, at the throttle in the cab. Other than some slight difficulties getting up our hills everything went well until we were virtually all the way back to the station. Since every seat on the train was occupied by dignitaries and all of the space in the cab taken up, Bob Brown and I and two other U.P. engineers were standing on the platform above the cow catcher, immediately in front of the smoke box door. As we got close to the station the fuel valve was closed too far. As a result the fire in the firebox went out and the locomotive

Steam Locomotive #119, early 1970s.

drifted to a stop short of the station. Bob and I and the other two execs stepped down to walk back to the cab and see what was wrong. We had no sooner cleared the cow catcher when the steam atomizer and fuel valve were turned full open. A cloud of vaporized diesel was blown into the red hot firebox. There was an immediate explosion, which not only blew the firebox door open but traveled all the way through the tubes of the boiler to the smoke box and blew the smoke box door open. It swung in a violent arc on its hinges right through the space where we had been standing moments before and bent a solid five-inch brass post 45 degrees. If we had been a few seconds slower in stepping off the front of the engine there would surely have been some broken backs or worse, that day.

Over the next number of years we sent the 119 into the U.P. shops every winter and tweaked it mechanically so it got progressively more powerful. Initially the valve timing was not quite squared up, and one valve opening had been cut at a slight angle. Because of this the exhaust made a very characteristic sound as the engine went through the zoo. We also insulated and jacketed the firebox and boiler. This had the advantage of making the cab much more tolerable in the middle of summer and increased the steam production of the engine.

An urban legend within the Union Pacific is when, on his first day as its new CEO, Mr. John Kenefick called for a meeting of all his senior staff. When he asked where his chief engineer was he was told he was not in the building. When he asked where he was he was told that he was at the zoo. He asked why he was at the zoo and no one would answer. When Bob returned and Mr. Kenefick asked what he was doing at the zoo Bob replied, "We're building a railroad." He then looked at Mr. Kenefick and said, "Do you want me to tell you everything we are doing or should I just keep on doing what we are doing?"

Mr. Kenefick thought about it for a minute and said, "Just keep on doing what you're doing but don't get us in trouble."

In early 1974 Bob Brown brought a visitor from Austria to the zoo for a tour and to go to lunch. It turned out that the visitor was a Mr. Joseph Theure of the Plasser & Theure mining company of Austria. During the tour Bob casually remarked as we came to the train station that what I needed was another locomotive so that we could pull two trains. Mr. Theure remarked that they had a coal-fired steam locomotive in one of their mines outside of Vienna about that size. They had acquired it during the oil embargo in case they ran short of diesel fuel.

Bob said, "Why don't you give it to Lee." Mr. Theurer replied, "Well, maybe I will."

He asked me for the specifics of our rails and what kind of load our bridge was able to support. I told him what he wanted to know and we finished the tour and went to lunch. It was a casual bar room type of conversation that would obviously lead nowhere. Neither Bob nor I thought anymore about it for six months until I got a call from an individual who identified himself as being from a shipping company based in Norfolk, Virginia. He asked if I was Dr. Simmons of the Henry Doorly Zoo, and when I answered yes he said, "Well, I've got this green steam locomotive on a ship here, with your name on it, what do you want me to do with it?"

I asked him to repeat that and he informed me it had been shipped freight paid from Austria. Now he needed to know what to do with it. When I got over my shock I asked him to give me his number and told him I would call him back. I then called Brown at the UP and told him what was up. Bob's response was slightly profane, and when he stopped sputtering he said the Austrian company was trying to sell the UP some mining equipment and probably thought if they gave us the engine it would influence the deal. He said, "Whatever you do don't tell anybody." He then told me to tell the shipping company to put it on the Norfolk and Western Railroad and ship it to Council Bluffs, Iowa in care of the zoo.

About a week later it arrived in Council Bluffs and we went over to look at it. It was a coal burning 0-6-2 (no leading truck – six driving wheels – two trail-

Marie, visiting the Galapagos Islands, 2001.

ing wheels) saddle tank engine which had been built in Linz, Austria, in 1890 by the Krauss Locomotive Fabrication Company. The saddle tanks located over the wheels alongside the boiler held 700 gallons of water. It had been designed with the last set of drivers having extraordinarily wide lateral movement so that it could navigate tight curves. Given the size and stroke of the pistons and the diameter of the wheels it was obviously a very powerful engine that had been designed to operate on narrow gauge mountain lines. It weighed 27.5 U.S. tons dry or empty. We offloaded it, put it on a lowboy trailer and brought it to the zoo and then ultimately to the U.P. shops in north Omaha. They converted the coal bunker into a 300-gallon diesel tank and installed an air brake system compatible with U.S. standards. We had the maintenance logs dating from the 1950s. All of the other paperwork pertaining to the engine and its early maintenance logs had apparently disappeared.

The Austrian locomotive had a shrill European-style peanut whistle that grated on your ears. Nevertheless, due to its design it was much more powerful than the #119. On large days with a full load and the caboose the #119 still struggled to make it up our hills. The Austrian had enough tractive power to pull the #119 and its train and probably five or six more cars. At nearly 100 years old it had been maintained in good shape. Aside from the conversions necessary to make it safe and compatible with our system it ran well from day one.

As we dug into its history we found that it had been stolen by the Russians during World War II and simply disappeared off of the face of the earth for a period of time before reappearing first in Hungary and then on a Romanian mountain line. This is where the Austrian mining company had found it and purchased it in 1968 during the oil embargo. It had been sitting in one of their rock quarries ever since.

We acknowledged the gift and thanked Mr. Theure, but never knew whether or not the U.P. ever did business with them.

PACHYDERM HILL

Our first new exhibit, after Marie and I arrived in Omaha, came about almost by serendipity. About seven o'clock one morning in early 1967 I was getting ready to check the crew in when a car pulled up. In it was Peter Kiewit, head of the Kiewit Construction Company, which was also our contractor for the zoo. He introduced himself and asked me if I had time to drive around with him and bring him up to date. The answer, of course, was "yes," and as we toured the grounds he asked me a number of succinct questions about how things were working and what our needs and problems were. He asked, "What do you really need, not what do you want?" The last site we visited was the old picnic pavilion down by the lagoon, which had replaced the 1904 classic Greek pavilion. It was a metal roofed open structure that we had boarded in with plywood. We built inside and outside corrals using salvaged telephone poles and bridge planks from the Union Pacific Railroad. At that time there were three rhinos and three young elephants in the building. Every night the young elephants used their short tusks to tear down parts of the corral, and every morning we were faced with repairs. I pointed this problem out to Mr. Kiewit and he asked what it took to hold elephants. I said, "concrete and steel."

"What happens if you don't get your concrete and steel?" he asked. I replied that, "The elephants are growing, and at some point in time we'll be unable to keep them contained and we'll have to get rid of them."

He nodded, and that was the total extent of the conversation. He thanked me and left the zoo. I went back to work and didn't think much more about it. About 9 o'clock that morning a keeper came and said that Warren Thomas, the director, wanted to see me in the office. When I walked in he looked up and said, "What in the hell did you do?"

"What do you mean?" I asked. He said he had just gotten a call from Leo Daly, the head of the Daly Architectural and Engineering Company, who said that we were going to build an elephant house. From what he was told, Peter Kiewit and Leo had coffee that morning and Pete had told him about his tour. Leo said that they had decided we should build an elephant house and told Thomas he should talk to me because I knew all about it and how it was to be constructed. After I got over my surprise I said, "I hope they know where we're going to get the money." As it turned out they did. That's how I got to participate in the design of the Eppley Pachyderm Hill, in Omaha. Peter Kiewit did not tell us how big it was supposed to be. Instead, he told us how much money we had to spend. This fit with what was apparently one of his favorite sayings: "Cut Your Pattern to Fit the Amount of Cloth You Have." This incident illustrates how things often worked in Omaha in those days with a very small but elite group of individuals who generally did not serve on boards or committees but got together quietly, behind the scenes or over coffee, and decided what needed to happen in the city and then saw to it that it happened. This system still works well today.

We decided we could afford a reinforced concrete building submerged halfway underground with three holding pens for elephants and four pens for rhinos. The building was surrounded by three large moated outdoor enclosures. While this was a smaller building than we would've liked at the time, it compared favorably with many other elephant facilities at the time. We did our homework on things like elephant trunk reach distances and minimum celling heights and designed the building. We designed the building so it could be easily modified later on and a new floor could be poured when needed. In fact, when heated floors became the standard for keeping elephant feet dry and in good shape, we were able to easily add another four-inch thick slab with imbedded heating tubes. We then topped the new concrete floor with polyurethane and neoprene to provide a soft warm cushion for the elephants' feet. My one mistake might have been setting the distance between the six-inch vertical pipes of the pens at 16 inches. Elroy politely pointed out that while I could go thru easily not everyone was skinny.

THE LAGOON

Riverview Park and ultimately the Henry Doorly Zoo sits on a wooded-bluff a little more than 40 feet above the bottom lands beside the Missouri River. After the Park was dedicated in 1894, one of the first things that the city did was to dam up the lower end of a deep gully that ran through the park. This became the Riverview Park Lagoon. Then they drilled an artesian well beside the lagoon to supply it with water. They found water at 800 feet but continued drilling. The well was drilled to a total depth of 1,064 feet and free flowed 80 gallons- per-minute.

Directly west of the lagoon and next to the well is where in 1904 the city moved the classical columned Greek pavilion that had been part of the 1898 Trans-Mississippi Exposition. This was a world's fair held in Kountze Park north of town. There had been a succession of three bridges across the middle of the lagoon between the pavilion and the 1916 swimming pool. The first two had been wooden and one of them had apparently burned down. The current bridge in the Henry Doorly Zoo is a concrete arch bridge built in the 1930s by the WPA. A number of years ago we covered it with a roof, and it became a favorite place for visitors to feed the Japanese Koi. In 1966 the lagoon was very shallow and muddy with a population of large carp. During the hot summer months the lagoon would turn black and start to smell. We later learned there was a good reason for this. Soon after I became zoo director in 1970 we decided that something needed to be done about the lagoon, to dredge it out and make it deeper. Bob Brown, one of our board members, was the chief engineer in today's terms the "COO" of the Union Pacific Railroad.

In 1967 and '68 the U.P. had built three-and-a-half miles of 30-inch gauge track through the zoo for our new steam locomotive to pull 4 train cars on. As a result, Bob Brown had adopted the zoo as the railroad's primary philanthropic concern in Omaha. In those days, U.P. was careful not to let it be publicly known when they helped out organizations such as the zoo. The great thing was that they

had all kinds of equipment and skilled engineers, so if we needed something, a phone call to Bob Brown was usually enough to make it happen. In 1970, I made a phone call, and Bob and a couple of his engineers came out to see the problem. Soon we had the lagoon drained, and a causeway of compacted clay was brought in by Union Pacific dump trucks. When the dragline had worked itself to the bottom end of the lagoon the start of the deepening process began. It turned out that there was literally no bottom to the lagoon. It was silted in with a depth of more than 30 feet of slimy, soft, black goo. The only thing that kept the dragline from sinking out of sight were the heavy wooden rafts sitting on top of the compacted clay. As the dragline deepened the lagoon to a depth of 18 feet first it backed up

Facing page: Alaska on the Ice Bear, 2007.

Once a fisherman, always a fisherman.

A 125-pound halibut, caught on the Ice Bear in Alaska in 2008.

toward the shallow upper end of the lagoon, and part of the clay spine was left behind as an island. We couldn't find a hard bottom, so the depth was dictated by the fact that any deeper and the sides would start sloughing in. When it got to the bridge the dragline turned west and backed its way out and up the bank.

We now had two problems to deal with. The first was the discovery at the southeast corner of the lagoon that a sanitary sewer pipe from a small enclave of houses east of the zoo had apparently been emptying directly into the lagoon for years. This explained the black water and foul smell during hot summer months. Luckily this point was not far from the overflow manhole for the lagoon. I suspect that at one time the sewer had connected to that overflow manhole but had been exposed by the bank caving off. We built a crushed rock ledge to stabilize the lagoon bank between the two points, and the city came out and reconnected the sewer to the lagoon overflow.

Another problem was that the Riverview Park Spring suddenly dried up while we had the lagoon drained for our dredging project. The spring had flowed year-round for as long as anyone could remember. It bubbled out of a rock ledge on the far eastern edge of the zoo and ran down a gully into the creek, which then supplied the lagoon with water. The day after the spring went dry, two grinning representatives from the city came into the office and informed us that the spring wasn't actually a spring. In fact, the water came from a four-inch city water pipe. They informed us that they had shut the valve and installed a water meter in the manhole outside the zoo fence. We were welcome to open the valve but would have to pay for the water. The city furnished free water to all the other "springs" in the city parks, but now suddenly and without warning we would have to pay.

For years people had come to the "spring" with bottles and cans to get drinking water because they said it tasted so much better than city water. Some of the complaints from the neighborhood when they had first fenced the zoo grounds was that they had been cut off from their supply of good drinking water. With a total operating budget of $350,000 we certainly didn't have the funds to pay for refilling the newly deepened lagoon with city water. The calculated volume of the lagoon was now 4.5 million cubic feet. We ultimately came up with a devious solution of, shall we say, questionable legality. We borrowed some old fire hose from the fire department and detailed a small crew to connect a line of six-inch hose to the closest fire hydrant at one o'clock every morning. We turned it on and let it run full force for four hours, then we'd disconnect it before daylight so that the neighborhood would have enough water pressure to shave, cook breakfast or flush a toilet. We were feeling somewhat smug that we had outsmarted the city guys, who had deliberately waited until the lagoon was drained to shut off the spring. It was, after all, still a city park. Shortly after we had the lagoon filled those same two city guys showed up and informed us that they had also put a meter on the line to the fire hydrant. Now we owed the city a huge amount of money.

This was money we didn't have, so we told them to go pound sand. We would argue the case in front of the city council and on the front page of the *Omaha World-Herald*. They were not quite ready for that kind of a fight but sent us a bill for the water every year. The problem finally came to the attention of Councilwoman Betty Abbott, who was also on our board. She suggested that we could negotiate the price down if we went directly to the mayor. We did and got a 50 percent reduction in the bill. We later came back to each new mayor and renegotiated it down, so that we ultimately paid the city $3,500 for refilling the lagoon. By then we could afford $3,500.

We now had the problem of keeping the lagoon full. An old city plumber who was nearing retirement told us that in addition to the 1894 artesian well, which had a caved in casing, there had also been an artesian well drilled further up the gully. We dug into the city records and found that it had been drilled in 1908 to a depth of 1,355 feet and free flowed 130 gallons-per-minute. There were no visible signs of the well, but we knew that it was next to the ravine. We set up a search pattern using sharp rods to probe the ground. It took us almost a month to find it. We dug it up, and the casing was still intact. The water level was a little more than 90 feet down. A phone call to Bob Brown at the UP produced a used, long shaft, multistage turbine pump from a well in Wyoming. We installed it and drove it with a flat belt and pulley from the power takeoff of our John Deere tractor. It quickly cleaned the debris and sludge out of the bottom of the well and produced more than 600 gallons of 55-degree good, hard water per minute.

As an aside, for many years to come we enjoyed telling Omaha residents who loved discussing the big carp they'd catch out of that lagoon about the open sewer line.

Years later we would again drain the lagoon during the winter to dredge it and install a crushed rock bottom. When the top crust of the sludge froze deep enough to drive on it with two large excavators we brought the bottom of the lagoon up to about 16 feet at its deepest level by dumping heavy pieces of concrete rubble from the old cat line into the sludge until they stopped sinking. We covered the rubble with two feet of dry clay and then installed heavy overlapping layers of nonwoven Geo cloth over the bottom and part way up sides. Then we laid down two feet of crushed limestone. We did a similar thing under the bridge and in the shallow area north of the bridge. This provided a solid bottom so that the lagoon can, at some future date, be cleaned out with a bobcat and trucks.

SEALION POOL

In late 1970 a board member, who owned a large steel fabrication company, told me he was going to London on business. He asked if there was a zoo there that he should visit. The answer, of course, was Regent's Park. He asked if we might have a contact who could show him around and I said yes.

Not long before Ed Owen had come into the office, I had been grumbling one day that we didn't have a sea lion pool. That same old city plumber who had worked in the park since high school told me, "You do have a pool if you just dig it up." I asked him what he meant and he told us that buried on the east side of the lagoon there was an old swimming pool which had been built in 1916. The city had apparently discontinued using it in 1938 because of the polio epidemic. The city had discontinued use of a number of other swimming pools during that same period. They had poured a new floor in the pool but instead of reopening it, as they did with some others, they ultimately buried it in 1944.

The area was a gentle hillside with no sign of anything ever having been there, but when we examined it we could see a faint yellow convex arc in the grass close to the lagoon where the edge of the pool was just below the grass roots. A faint yellow concave arc in the grass further up the hill was just above the top of a buried retaining wall. We borrowed a front-end loader and two dump trucks from Bob Brown and the UP and dug the pool out. It was oval in shape, sloped from a depth of two-and-a-half feet to eight feet and had a calculated volume of 333,000 gallons. The walls and floor of the pool were in good shape. Now we had to figure out a way to convert a 54-year-old swimming pool into a sea lion pool.

It was right after this that Ed Owen walked into the office inquiring about zoos in London. I tried writing to the London Zoo, but it was during the big English mail strike, so I finally placed a transatlantic call to their director during London working hours. After a bit of discussion it was agreed that someone from their staff would pick Ed up at his hotel and give him a guided tour of Regent's Park Zoo. It just happened that the staff member who picked Ed up was the London Zoo's marine mammal specialist and he just happened to talk about sea lions all day long.

When Ed came back to Omaha he said that turning the old swimming pool into a sea lion pool was a great idea. We were feeling fairly clever, and then the law of unintended consequences caught up with us. Ben Morris and two other board members came to see me and said that Ed wanted to fund the renovation of the old Riverview Park swimming pool into a sea lion pool but wanted to be president while the work was being done. I couldn't see a problem with that. They told me not to say yes too quickly. Ed had a reputation of sometimes being a little difficult to work with. In retrospect, I remember foolishly saying, "For that much money I could stand on my head for a year." That was the normal term of office. Ed stayed three years. To say that he made life interesting would be an understatement. But he and I ultimately became friends. His heart was in the right place. Years later, his widow would say, "Ed was always your friend, you just didn't know it."

With more help from the Union Pacific Railroad and Ed's funding, we converted the old swimming pool. We installed a shallow moat around the pool and installed a new drain with a 24-inch butterfly valve in the deep end to flush the water into the lagoon. We buried a holding building into the hillside. Additionally, we built a concession stand, picnic pavilion and public restrooms. We dedicated the Owen Sea Lion Pavilion in 1972. Ed ultimately became chairman of the board for a number of years. The artesian well, with a new 100-horsepower pump, supplied water to the sea lion pool and lagoon for many years until we drilled a second well near the north gate.

CHRISTINA HIXSON AND THE LIED FOUNDATION

In the summer of 1980 Marie took our kids for a vacation to see her parents in Guthrie, Oklahoma. George Mazanec, who was then president of the Omaha Zoological Society, and his wife Elsa took pity on a couple of temporary bachelors whose wives were taking kids to see grandparents and invited Tyler Gaines and me to dinner. This was greatly appreciated since Elsa had a reputation as a great cook, and George was a connoisseur of fine wines. Toward the end of a great evening, Tyler who was the attorney for the Lied Foundation, said that although Ernie Lied had died and had left a substantial estate, there was actually very little cash in the estate. He estimated that the Lied foundation owned 75 percent of the undeveloped land in the city limits of Las Vegas. He advised George and me that we should start making a case for a gift, even though it would likely be many years before there was available cash to distribute. I stated that the project we wanted to do would be a tropical rain forest. Tyler advised that whatever we did we should not appear to be extravagant or spendthrift in presenting our case since

Ernie Lied had been very frugal. Chris Hixson was following his lead and would not look favorably on an expensive presentation.

This kind of advice was invaluable. Ernie Lied and his parents had owned a Buick dealership and a five-state distributorship in Omaha before the Buick company bought him out. He moved to Las Vegas in 1958 and began investing in land. Chris Hixson had come to Omaha after graduating high school in Clarinda, Iowa, and had gone to business school. After seven months she went to work for the Lied Buick Company. Chris became Ernie Lied's assistant in Las Vegas and ultimately became the sole trustee of the Lied Foundation after his death. She was knowledgeable about events in Omaha and read the *Omaha World-Herald* every day.

I wrote a letter to Chris explaining our goals for the zoo. Taking Tyler's advice, I simply painted a vivid word picture of what the exhibit would look like and how it would provide a rain forest experience for Omaha visitors. The exhibit could educate the public about the importance of conserving these critical habitats and ecosystems. In particular, I stressed the importance of conservation education for children and the effect such an experience would have on them. We got a prompt letter thanking us and pointing out that it would be some time before the Lied Foundation would actually be able to make grants. For the next eight-and-a-half years we wrote a letter to Chris every six months, gradually adding more details, pictures and examples of different kinds of displays and animals that the building would contain, until finally Tyler advised us that the time was right to make a formal request. He advised that the request should be made in person with one or two people and should not have a flashy set of exhibits. Stan How, our architect, agreed to do the conceptual design drawings on the cuff, and with our own, in-house graphics department we produced a number of color renderings to show what the building would look like and feel like as you walked through it. We also produced a God's-eye view of what the building would look like from above, with multiple layers of clear plastic drawings overlaying the architect's drawing. This enabled us to start with a view that contained all of the plants and animals and then peel down through the building until you were at the footprint on the lowest level.

We asked Chris Hixson for an appointment to come to Las Vegas and discuss the project. It had been stressed that people who simply showed up at the foundation's Las Vegas offices cooled their heels and went away without having talked to Chris. Harold "Andy" Andersen, a board member and the publisher of the *Omaha World-Herald*, and I flew into Las Vegas to make an initial presentation. We had selected "Andy" because he was very low key and, while representing a very important Omaha institution, would not come off as overly aggressive, assertive or arrogant. We made our presentation and were careful to point out that all of the materials and conceptual design exhibits had been done in-house. The fact that we were planning something that would be the best in the world, which would also help the public, particularly children, seemed to catch Chris's attention and appeal to her. She agreed to come to Omaha in the near future and see what we had accomplished at the zoo thus far and look at the site.

The site we had chosen was a large tree-filled pit about 50-feet deep and was the head end of one of the two large ravines that had run down through the zoo. Instead of having a huge, tall building sticking up into the air like a sore thumb, we would bury the majority of the building so only a portion of the wall and the roof would be visible from the outside. Visually it would get progressively bigger and bigger and bigger as you walked through it. Our maintenance department cleared out as much of the underbrush as possible. We had Kiewit survey the site and lay out the corners. The building was the shape of a long octagon, covering one-and-a-half acres. Carl Vires, head of our maintenance department, installed 50-foot poles at each of the eight corners. As designed, the maximum height down the center ridgeline of the translucent fiberglass roof was 80 feet above the ground on the lower trail through the jungle. The elevation of the bottom of the ravine corresponded very closely to the lowest elevation of the building.

When Chris arrived she toured the zoo with Stan How and me. She observed the site and asked many questions. She turned out to be very knowledgeable about building maintenance, roof lifespans, repairs and many things which we had not expected. It turned out she was in charge of all of the maintenance and repairs on the offices, buildings and hotels that they owned in Las Vegas. Luckily we had done our homework and had the answers to her questions. She also wanted to see our financial statements for the last 10 years and a list of our board membership. Chris had an acute sense about people and had a number of comments to make about our board. She could get to the bottom line with short, to-the-point, questions faster than anyone I had met, except Peter Kiewit.

We decided to meet for dinner that night for further discussion of the project. Stan was a member at the Omaha Country Club, so we met there, and after dinner and a considerable amount of discussion Chris finally said, "All right, all right, I like what I see. But this looks expensive. Cut to the chase: What will it cost?" I will always remember trying to work up enough moisture in my mouth to say, "$25 million."

When I finally managed to get the number out of my mouth she not only blinked but visibly flinched and said, "That's a lot of money, much more than I had counted on. I'll have to think about it overnight." We agreed to meet for breakfast the next morning.

It was one of those meetings you never forget. Stan and I were already apprehensive from Chris's reaction the night before, and after coffee and some cinnamon rolls Chris looked up and said, "I didn't sleep at all last night. I came to town with my mind made up about what I was going to give you, and you asked me for $25 million. That's too much money, and I'm just not going to do it."

I looked at Stan, and it was obvious that his stomach was in his throat. So was mine. Neither one of us knew what to say, so luckily we just didn't say anything. After a few moments of silence, Chris went on to say, "I came to town with my mind made up to give you $5 million dollars, but I'm willing to compromise.

I'm willing to give you three times what I intended, that's $15 million. But I want everything you have shown me in the jungle. I don't think we need the big orientation building out front. I'm not interested in selling hotdogs, so let someone else build the restaurant. You'll have to get someone else to build the support greenhouses, and I want the Omaha Zoological Society to raise a minimum of $5 million for a permanent endowment to support the building."

She looked Stan and me up and down. Then, looking directly at me, she said "Now boy, do you think you can do that?" I took a deep breath and looked at Stan and said, "Yes ma'am." Chris very quickly got to the bottom line on how the grant would be administered while reinforcing the fact that she expected everything that we had shown her in the main jungle building.

Neither Stan nor I were absolutely sure we could deliver everything I had just promised. We decided that whatever it took we would just have to make it happen. Then we went to talk to Walter Scott, our zoo board chairman and happily then chairman of Peter Kiewit Construction Co. With Walter, we got all of the stakeholders together for a "Come to Jesus" meeting. After explaining the situation, we stressed that no matter what it took we had to deliver the exhibit fully planted and populated with animals on time and within the $15 million we had to spend, "period." And we still weren't there. With Walter leading our meeting, he pointed first to Stan How and then to each stakeholder in turn and asked each one to agree to contribute 10 percent of their fees to the project. It was also agreed that the zoo's workers could work alongside the union trades and would do anything they were capable of and that nobody would try to change order their way to profitability. Chuck and Marge Durham stepped up to fund the Treetops Restaurant and our education facility for $3.5 million. The result was a much larger restaurant and education facility than originally planned. During the two-and-a-half-year construction of the Lied Jungle and the Durham Treetops Restaurant we only issued three formal change orders. That is not to say that we only made three changes, but we either traded them out for equal value or found better and more economical ways of doing things. The precedents set for bringing this project in on time and on budget carried over to every successive project and benefited us for many years to come.

We took a deep breath and decided to break ground as soon as we could, completing the drawings as we built.

Three months later with only the foundation drawings totally complete we broke ground on the building with all of the board and dignitaries present. The mayor was thanking Chris for this great gift to the city of Omaha when she looked at him and said, "I don't give money to cities or institutions. I give money to people who I think will spend it wisely, as I want them to." It was a lesson we remembered for the future.

We opened the Lied Jungle in April 1992 to huge crowds. Our attendance increased from 870,000 to 1,300,00. It was our first world-class exhibit and set the stage for many world-class exhibits to follow. We had delivered everything we promised.

THE LIED JUNGLE

The Lied Jungle was to be a total immersion exhibit where the visitor is immersed in the same environment as the animals. By comparison to the freedom given to some animals like free flying birds or marmosets, the visitor is more constrained in their movements. We wanted the visitor to actually experience the jungle: to smell the leaf mold, feel the humidity, to get wet in the mist from waterfalls and to view the jungle from both high in the canopy level and walking on a dirt path on the floor. Our goal was to make the building as inconspicuous as possible. The idea was to create the illusion of a jungle environment that was so realistic it would give visitors the feeling that they were actually there.

To create that kind of experience you must pay close attention to details in all of the vistas so that the visitor can go with the illusion and not be suddenly or constantly be jerked back to reality when they see something obviously man made. We wanted people to enter not having a concept of how big the undivided 62,000 square-foot exhibit space actually was. The idea was that as they walked counterclockwise through the building at the mid-canopy level progressing from one vista to the next jungle habitat it would get bigger and bigger until they finally realized, "Wow, this is a really big jungle." Most of the more formal views into animal habitats, particularly those in which the animals were contained by a moat, glass or bayonet wire barrier, would be experienced from the upper boardwalk. The building was designed around three geographically correct tropical rain forests, starting with Asia and progressing through Africa and then South America until you were back at the beginning of the small orientation area. From there you descended one level down to the jungle floor to progress through those same three geographical areas up close and personal but in a clockwise pattern. A little disorientation helps keep the illusion alive. I think we were successful. We've had many Vietnam veterans over the years tell us that they experienced déjà vu, sometimes so strongly that it was not necessarily a pleasant experience.

The long octagon of the concrete ring wall, which extended 20 to 25 feet above the level of the formal canopy walkway, was covered with man-made rock wherever possible. Some spots were painted out with jungle murals to give the illusion of greater depth and space. Most of the animal barriers were water moots that incorporated waterfalls and aquatic displays such as small-clawed otters, giant arapaima fish or aquatic Asian saddleback tapirs. Virtually all of the exhibits would display multiple species of animals in addition to the birds, which were allowed to roam freely. While we tried to make sure that all of the plants and animals were geographically correct to their area, you could however be in Asia or Africa and have a South American bird sitting on the rail close by. The top of the building was 80 feet above the jungle floor so that very quickly as the canopy closed over the walkways the translucent fiberglass roof disappeared. This greatly enhanced the illusion.

One of the great things about designing a new exhibit such as the Lied Jungle is that you almost always have to go back to school and do your homework. This is both challenging and a lot of fun because you want to incorporate all of the good experiences from other exhibits while avoiding bad visitor experiences from around the world. Everyone is more than willing to tell you the good parts. The mistakes frequently only come to the surface over an after-hours dinner and a few drinks. Our solution to this was to visit the two best tropical jungle exhibits in zoos in the U.S., first with zoo people and then later with our design and construction team. Since this building would contain many species of plants, we visited many of the best botanical garden conservatories in the country. I had the opportunity to spend three-and-a-half days at Kew Gardens in London, possibly the largest botanical facility in the world. A number of their Ph.d. research and

Baby Gorilla, 2005.

scientific staff took me through their tropical conservatory and behind the scenes, and I compiled a long list of innovative techniques and new ideas. Happily, for part of the last day I toured the facility with the staff member who actually ran it and made it work. He very quietly but candidly told me which innovations worked and which did not or had been abandoned.

Terry Strawser, a longtime friend and a former colleague from the Columbus Zoo, was in the Imagineering department at Disney World in Florida. While scouting for plants in southern Florida, Danny Morris and I stopped by on two occasions. Terry was careful about adhering to the Disney corporate rules on disclosing insider information when discussing problems. He always prefaced every statement with, "You understand that we don't have any personal knowledge or know anything about this but you should read this or not do such and such." The insights gained from these visits was extremely valuable and saved us from many mistakes. Animal people and plant people have very different perspectives on the environments necessary for their favorite species. You need to understand both sides of the issue if you're going to be successful with a mixed animal and plant facility. We designed the building with no floor under the large central exhibit area to allow tree roots to go deep. Five feet down we installed a network of perforated drainage pipes so that over-watering would not over-saturate the earth and suffocate the roots or make a swimming pool out the exhibit.

Taking a lesson from two existing jungle buildings and three large botanical gardens, where the only way to get new trees in was through a man-sized door, we put in two sets of large overhead doors so that we could back a semi-trailer truck full of plants right into the building. Additionally, if it ever became necessary we would be able to bring in a hydra crane with a 100-foot boom. In a couple areas we buried heat coils in the dirt, but in retrospect we should have put heat under the entire building since tropical plants and trees like warm feet. It took a year to heat the soil deep enough so they were happy. For all of the animal species such as tapirs and primates in moated exhibits and viewed from the upper walkway, we put in ramps and stairs so the animals and keepers could come and go from the basement holding areas into the display. For every square foot of animal display area we had 1.5 square feet of animal holding and management area in the basement. You can drive into the basement level with a small truck and completely circumnavigate around the outer edge of the entire building. Servicing filters, pumps and other equipment is therefore easy.

Populating the building with enough plants of the size and density to create the illusion we wanted from day one was going to be another thing. If we planted small trees like other conservatories it would be five or six years before the illusion of being immersed in a jungle begin to take place. Finding trees large enough to make an immediate impact in a building the size of the Lied Jungle would be difficult in view of our budget. One problem was in finding African species of plants and trees. Our solution was to make contact with as many tropical growers and nurseries as possible while compiling our want lists. Our next move was a road trip. Terri Gouveia, Danny Morris, Carl Vires and I flew to Miami and visited almost every nursery in the area south to the sea.

The National Zoo had been acquiring trees for their tropical rain forest, "Amazonia," and almost every commercial grower we visited seemed to have plants they were holding for them. They were due to open their exhibit in April 1992, the same time we were opening. The trees they had warehoused under shade cloth were perfectly shaped specimens with a price tag totally out of our reach. Some of them had been held for three years already. The National Zoo's plant budget was $2.5 million.

We explained our situation to everyone and asked if they had or knew of any trees that were too big, misshapen, lightning struck or windblown that might be available cheap. A significant number of the growers had trees still growing in their fields that had gotten too big or damaged and were imperfect, symmetrically speaking. We also compiled a substantial list of properties where trees were growing but the owners were not commercial nurseries. Four decades earlier there had been a very enthusiastic cycle of starting tropical tree nurseries in southern Florida. Many of these had not panned out and the remaining trees had gotten too large and had been sold to private individuals who were not in the nursery business. We drove the back roads of Florida, going from lead to lead. We bought trees out of fields, out of front yards, out of backyards, out of a roadside ditch along a state road (the farmer said he owned it and surely he wouldn't lie). We knocked on a door at 11 o'clock one night and bought half of a bamboo clump out of a front yard. We were always asking the owners if they knew of any other trees. We mapped the location of every tree and then later hired locals to dig them up and load them on trucks for transport to Omaha or we sent Carl Vires and our maintenance crew to Florida to bring them back.

As the word got out we had a number of calls from growers and nurseries offering to donate trees that they couldn't sell. In one instance we had a 40-foot truck with more than 20 feet of a South American Ciba sticking out of the back when a Georgia Highway patrolman pulled our guys over. There was no question we were bending the rules and no amount of explanation or pleading would convince him to let us just transit across the state. They had to cut the top of the tree off. He let us keep eight feet sticking out the back. It was painful, but we still had a 48-foot-tall tree to plant in Omaha.

We acquired enough trees and plants to heavily populate the exhibit for $250,000. We did virtually all of this with our own crew because we simply couldn't afford to hire it done. Since they were much larger and more misshapen than the bilaterally symmetrical trees planted in most conservatories, the exhibit had the look and feel of a real jungle from day one. The illusion was everything we had wanted.

THE SUZANNE AND WALTER SCOTT AQUARIUM

On the day we dedicated and opened the Lied Jungle in early April 1992, as the crowd was streaming into the building, Walter Scott and I were standing

Walter and Sue Scott, joining me in the aquarium tunnel, March 1995.

PHOTO COURTESY OF THE *OMAHA WORLD-HERALD.*

outside watching. Walter looked at me and said, "Well, maybe you'd better start thinking about the next thing you want to build."

My answer was quick and simple: a full-fledged marine aquarium. Our first saltwater aquarium had been hugely successful, both from the visitor standpoint and from the standpoint of the fish. For eight-and-a-half years we had had the lowest mortality rate of any aquarium in North America. The problem was that there were only seven exhibits, totaling 70,000 gallons of saltwater, in our systems. Our biggest system had 32,000 gallons in it with 20,000 of that being on display in an hourglass shaped exhibit. This configuration allowed our sharks to make the turn at each end with a short glide in between each turn. We had deliberately kept our systems simple with airlifts to circulate water and no pressure sand filters. To do a full-fledged modern saltwater aquarium we went back to school and did our homework. We picked out eight of the best aquariums and visited them, touring both the visitor side and the behind-the-scenes side with aquarium staff. We asked a lot of questions and kept notes on good ideas and bad ones. Then we revisited some of the more pertinent aquariums with our construction team to give them first-hand insight and understanding of the things we wanted to accomplish and the things that we wanted to avoid. Ultimately, we revisited a number of these institutions with Walter and Sue Scott, Mike and Gail Yanney, John and Lynn Boyer and Marie and I. Somewhere along the way, Sue Scott asked, Couldn't we have penguins?" The answer was simple: penguins are very difficult to acquire, but why not? All it takes is money.

Everyone was on the same page, and we set about establishing the parameters of the building and exhibits. It would not be a grandiose architectural statement soaring into the sky but would focus on function with large exhibits with the best husbandry and life-support systems in the country. A maximum of one half of each system's water would be on display with the off display volume providing a large biological dilution factor. All pumps, filters, ozone generators, air compressors and other equipment would be redundant. All the water used in the exhibits would be formulated using deionized water from a reverse osmosis system. All filter backwash would be captured, filtered, sterilized and reused. We designed the water turnover to be able to recycle each system in either 30 minute, 45 minute or 60 minute cycles, depending on the needs, clarity and water quality. This meant that we would have three pumps or banks of pumps and filters on each system. We would have backup emergency generation capable of running our life-support systems at minimally one-half capacity. Again, the project was larger than our budget. I will always remember the day when Walter said we are going to have to "cut our pattern to fit our cloth." It was painful to cut a 40-foot section out of the building. At 1.3 million gallons, it is still the largest aquarium in any North American Zoo.

DESERT DOME

In 1999 when we decided to construct the Desert Dome (the world's largest exhibit of three deserts of the world) under the world's largest glazed geodesic dome, the process was much faster and simpler. After developing a conceptual design and an estimate of costs, Gene Mahoney and I had dinner with Allan and Dianne Lozier with our design concept, a five-foot diameter carved Styrofoam model of the desert and a geodesic model. Allan was interested, asked questions about the dome and said they would think about it. The next morning Allan called, and we had over half of the funding. Again, this was to be a total emersion experience featuring the Namib, Central Australian and Sonoran Deserts with visitors, animals and plants all sharing the same space wherever possible.

We opened the Desert Dome in April 2002. That was followed in April 2003 by the Eugene Mahoney Kingdoms of The Night (the world's largest nocturnal exhibit) 15 feet below the Desert Dome.

These openings were the beginning of an incredible chain of exhibits and buildings:

- 2004 – Hubbard Gorilla Valley

- 2004 – The Elevator Tower and Orangutan Quarters

- 2005 – Hubbard Orangutan Forest

- 2006 – Hubbard Research Wing addition to Grewcock Center for Conservation and Research

- 2006 – Guest Services Building

- 2007 – Mutual of Omaha's Exploration Station

- 2008 – Bernice Grewcock Butterfly and Insect Pavillion

- 2009 – Skyfari aerial tram

- 2010 – Hubbard Expedition Madagascar

RETROSPECTION

After 4 decades as zoo director I became chairman of the Omaha Zoo Foundation in 2009. Looking back on more than 65 years of zoo experience, 54 of them as an active staff member in the zoo world and more than 50 years at Omaha's Henry Doorly Zoo, there are, I think, some observations to be made.

The Omaha community is probably one of the best and most unique cities worldwide to build a zoo in. Marie and I have had an incredible run. In addition to raising three great kids we have worked and traveled in 51 countries and the Antarctic. While most of our trips have been professional or working conservation projects, we have also had the pleasure of leading individuals and zoo supporters on safaris to many parts of the globe to introduce them to the wonders of the natural world. These trips change the way you see the world and support conservation. They are also responsible for many lifelong friends.

Zoos are addictive! People are drawn to work and volunteer in zoos because they have a fascination for animals, habitats and how our ecosystem works. They develop a fire in their bellies to make a contribution but generally not to get rich. This is partly due to the fact that the only totally predictable thing about wild animals is unpredictability. You never know on any given day what you will be faced with. It is challenging, exciting and also fun. Additionally, there is frequent positive feedback as you successfully breed and manage endangered species. Watching the birth of a giraffe calf or a gorilla baby is an experience almost equal to watching your own children come into the world. You have the opportunity to make positive contributions to conservation of rare species insitu and exsitu and additionally to their habitats in the wild. Feeling like you and your institution are making a difference keeps you pedaling.

For Marie and me, coming to Omaha was a great decision because the community is quite unique in the way it supports its cultural and educational institutions. Being a 501(c)(3) has meant that there is no comparison between the way we have been able to do business versus the way a city, county, state or federal zoo does business. For the vast majority of my career in Omaha, the zoo board has had a solid sense of its management and fiduciary responsibilities. There has been little or no micromanagement. In addition to some very good board presidents who early on served one-year terms—and later served three-year terms—we've had very little turnover in our board members. Additionally, we've had two board chairman who served much longer. Both of these individuals have had considerable influence in the community, and when it was known that they had blessed a project it made things infinitely easier to raise funds.

Ed Owen of Paxton and Vierling Steel served as either president or chairman for 11 years. Walter Scott, former chairman and president of Kiewit Construction Company, with 41 years of zoo service, has been either president or chairman of the board of the Omaha Zoological Society for the last 36 years. While in some institutions short terms of office and an active board turnover rate are considered the healthy norm, in our instance just the opposite has been true. Having long-term consistency in governance from the leaders of our business community has meant that we have been able to operate much more like a for-profit company than a nonprofit charitable or government institution.

In 1973, a prospective board member asked me how much endowment the zoo had. The answer was none, but it was high on our list to establish an endowment. He promptly said, "Okay, I'll give you $50,000 so the next time someone asks you if you have an endowment you can say 'yes,' but I won't come on the board." That was when $50,000 was a lot of money. Peter Kiewit followed this up by leaving us $1 million for our endowment. This ultimately led to the formation of the Omaha Zoo Foundation, an independent nonprofit organization. For the first three-plus years, Sue Singer, who was ultimately to become Sue Scott, was our first executive director in 1985. Eugene Mahoney followed her in that role in

Jean Bressler, front row, far left, was among our second class of zoo docents in 1971.

1989. Calvin Sisson came along in 2005, then Tina Cherica in 2012. Over the years, working with both the Omaha Zoological Society and the Omaha Zoo Foundation, we have raised $450,000,000 in private sector donations for new construction, endowment and conservation. By any measure, this is an example of the incredible generosity and support of a community of 450,000 people—at least within its city limits.

That early pronouncement from Ben Morris to "balance the damn budget, and we will probably let you do anything you want," has proven prophetic, although over time it morphed into, "We'll let you do anything you can raise the money for." We have routinely been able to take risks that no government or typical eleemosynary would dare do. Early on we developed an understanding that once we got to the halfway point in our fund raising we could just take a deep breath, jump off the end of the pier and start construction. The assumption was that the community would come through with the funds to cover the last half by the time we finished. It worked out this way, probably because everyone knew that once our board chairman backed something it would be made to happen, no matter what.

In addition to his background as an engineer and having the Kiewit philosophy, Walter Scott is an outdoorsman. He likes to hunt and fish. He is fascinated by animals and has supported conservation projects in Omaha and in Nebraska, and in many other parts of the world. He once rousted the whole family out in the wee hours one morning to watch a giraffe born. We developed an iron-clad philosophy of always finishing every project on time and on budget, no matter what it took. During almost every project there was usually a point where we were unsure if we could finish on time and on budget. Our solution was always to simply put our heads down and peddle harder. Happily, we always succeeded. Marie and I traveled the world together with Walter and Sue, and they became good friends.

Considering the depth of our ignorance when we started in the zoo world—

we used intuition to formulate diets, had almost no good immobilizing drugs, our knowledge of physiological norms and exotic animal medicine was limited to extrapolating and comparing them to their closest domestic relative and we only talked a good game on conservation—we have come light years. Today the world's zoos and their related organizations are without question possibly the most effective force for conservation on earth.

All three of our children, Lee III, Heather Ann and Heidi Marie grew up with animals at home and worked summers at the zoo. The zoo is a great place for a kid to develop a good work ethic.

No retrospective would be complete without acknowledging the importance of our many mentors and of the staff and crew that actually makes things work. Early on, we were such a small family that anyone and everyone did anything and everything that needed doing. We accomplished many projects just by shear guts and willpower—and the fact that we weren't smart enough to know we couldn't. We developed a culture that when a project was identified, every department would send part of their crew for part of the day to accomplish what we couldn't have accomplished otherwise. Much like our governance, we have been blessed with a long lived, dedicated staff, many of whom have worked for more than 40 years at the Henry Doorly Zoo.

While it is not possible, with our current 1,000+ peak season employees, to recognize everyone who ever worked at the zoo over the last 50 years, a significant number of individuals have been mentioned in these stories. There is an additional group, I'll call the "Dirty Dozen++," who could be counted on to make things work, often by just shear guts and willpower. The world was a smaller and simpler place in those days. Notably among these people was Elroy Cleghorn, the zoo's very first keeper, who came right off of the streets to become hoof stock supervisor. More importantly, he imparted a sense of responsibility for the welfare of the animals in all our keepers, including much of our senior staff, who started their zoo careers under him.

Carl Vires, head of our maintenance department for 40 years, could build anything or take a piece of old, warn-out government surplus equipment and accomplish miracles.

Of two 14-year-olds who started as Explorer Scouts and volunteers, Danny Morris ultimately became our chief operating officer. Dan Cassidy ultimately became general curator. Sue Lions, who had lied about her age at 13 so she could work concessions, would ultimately manage our membership drive and all of our profit centers. Kathy Vires ran many zoo departments and the aquarium. Randy Wisthoff, who started driving the garbage truck, was our first curator of education, then assistant director. Randy is now director of the Kansas City Zoo. Dan Houser became curator of large mammals. Johnny Martinez went on to become director of three other zoos. Alan Holst had what it takes to get tigers and other big cats together to produce babies. Steve Cundiff keeps our life support systems working and the animals alive. Terri Gouveia not only populated the jungle with plants but transformed the whole zoo. Garry Pettit stepped forward as a young man to become superintendent of the safari park. Dr. Douglas Armstrong, director of medicine, was also our longest-serving veterinarian. Last but not least is Sharon Sklenar, secretary and executive assistant, who for more than 35 years really ran the place and kept me on the straight and narrow and where I was supposed to be.

To the dirty dozen and all of the countless other staff members over the years who made good things happen, we couldn't have done it without you!

◆ ◆ ◆

From left: Dottie, Lynette, Lee, Lee Sr., Barbee, and Dorothy Simmons.

Youngest sister Cindy, standing behind young Lee, celebrated a birthday at the Henry Doorly Zoo Museum.

Christmas with family, 2003.

At Ak-Sar-Ben Ball, 2009.

ZOO AND AQUARIUM DESIGN

Functional, structural and mechanical design at zoos is often left to outsiders with no hands-on experience with exotic animals. This is almost always a serious mistake, like letting an architect or engineer who were not surgeons or had never cooked a meal design a surgical suite or restaurant kitchen. This is not to say that architects and engineers are incapable of getting it right, because many of them do. Those that get it right do so by doing their homework and consulting with people with experience in that particular discipline or with that particular species of animals and then listening to what they have to say. We've all seen exhibits that from the outside were grandiose monuments to the designer, but from the inside, and particularly from the behind-the-scenes-working side, were functional abortions for the keepers, medical staff and unfortunately the animals.

Early on we developed the policy of doing our own conceptual design in-house, in-town and not bringing in outside hired guns to try to sell us the same designs they had already pitched to five or six other zoos. After seeing what had happened in a number of other zoos it became my firm belief that the drivers of design philosophy should be the individuals who have the animal experience and who will have to care for those same animals after the exhibit is built. It also became my firm belief that you should work with a local architect and local engineers who live in your town and who will either take credit or assume responsibility for the final outcome and function of the building or exhibit. Another very strong belief is that form should follow function and not the other way around.

Experience has taught most of us the hard way that if you are not in firm control of the process, Murphy's Law and the Law of Unintended Consequences will be. We developed a procedure to be used in the early stages of conceptual design called "Playing the What-If Game," and it goes something like this. This is a paper I wrote and have presented to a number of organizations and conferences.

PLAYING THE WHAT IF GAME
Lee G. Simmons, DVM
Director, Omaha's Henry Doorly Zoo

Designing a zoo building or animal exhibit is easy! Designing one that WORKS for the animals, plants, staff and visitors is, sometimes, slightly more complicated. A facility for a single hardy mammal species, not on public display, is easier to design AND TO OPERATE than one for multiple species of marine invertebrates on public view. The greater the number of species and families, let alone kingdoms, you mix under one roof, the more complicated the task. FUNCTION should always dictate FORM and take precedence over esthetics. Different functions may dictate dramatically different forms. A clinical lab functions differently than a jelly fish exhibit even though both have volumes of liquid contained in glass and plastic vessels. The jump distance for a langur is different than for a Tasmanian devil, even though they both can bite like hell. That a truly successful design should function for all concerned is a given. However, this is not always recognized by an outside designer who has not lived with a similar exhibit species or facility. Can you accomplish a functionally successful design? That is the question to be answered.

Once the need and funding for a new facility has been agreed upon by all concerned and that first basic flash of inspiration is past, the starting point for answering the questions necessary to successfully complete any project, large or small, should be a series of lists and counter lists. These lists identify the prime objectives of the project, its parameters and potential problems. These lists should be prepared by individuals with relevant expertise in similar exhibits. They are then expanded upon by the design and engineering team members to address each identified objective. In Omaha, we believe strongly that this set of lists should include both those positive objectives and as many negative possibilities and worst case scenarios as can be thought of. Whether lists are committed to paper or with enough experience kept in your head the process is the same.

Additionally, never assume that the exhibit functions and or species represented on opening day are cast in stone forever. Part of the design process should be to identify and imagine possible future uses 5, 10 or 15 years down the road. You need to combine individual staff and institutional expertise, experiences gleaned from other zoos, as much outside technical expertise as can be found or purchased, and a liberal dose of "THE WHAT IF GAME" in order to compose an effective set of lists from which to design, build and OPERATE a new exhibit.

"THE WHAT IF GAME" is an exercise in which you mentally, systematically walk step-by-step through every function from feeding, cleaning, bringing in new specimens, removing specimens, breeding introductions, births, deaths, breaking up fights, escapes, neonatal exams, immobilization and treatments, to washing the windows, taking out the garbage/manure and visitor interactions. While "THE WHAT IF GAME" can certainly be played by one person, and in fact this is usually how most projects start, it should ultimately be played by a team that is used to working together with a purpose in common. This team concept will be touched on later in this paper. If possible, every person who will ultimately work in the project should be included in, and encouraged to play "THE WHAT IF GAME." The perspectives from which architects, engineers, keepers, curators, veterinarians, horticulturists directors and the maintenance tech see a project, are often times dramatically different. These perspectives shape what is perceived to be the function. While institutional and individual management philosophies and practices can and should have bearing on design form and function, these influences should transcend, "All of our buildings have always been red brick." There is seldom only one single, absolute or perfect way to accomplish the desired function.

I am a firm believer that you are highly unlikely to be able to hire an outside expert to design a system or exhibit and expect it to work well for your institution unless you, your staff and the people who will have to live in that facility day in and day out, have played an active part in its functional design. This is particularly true of outside experts who have never been down on their knees with dirty hands working in a similar facility. Ultimately, all outside experts go home while you must live with the facility. This can seem longer than forever if the facility doesn't work. If at all possible, hire a local architect, who lives in your town and who is both knowledgeable enough and intuitive enough to listen well enough to see things from the perspective of your institution. Architects, engineers, zoo directors, veterinarians, curators and other staff involved at the primary design level all need secure egos to effectively play "THE WHAT IF GAME." There is only one acceptable response to any of the players stating: "THAT WON'T WORK." No matter where the idea being discussed originally came from, or if it simply slipped in by default, the only acceptable response is: "Alright, why won't it work and what will make it work?" This is, unfortunately, often followed closely by, "Do we have enough money to make it work?" This is not a democratic committee where everyone votes. The director (say owner) and architect, and acknowledged experts, together should be the final arbitrators of compromises after listening to all ideas. Ultimately, the owner who pays the bills and lives with the results has the final say.

Specific lists should start with:

1. type and function (hospital, quarantine station, exhibit, mixed exhibit, aquarium, etc.)

2. number and species of animals and plants

3. budget range and monetary constraints to be considered

4. time constraints to – start – construct – open

For each function or species or exhibit, these lists should include those things which:

A. absolutely must be accomplished (NO COMPROMISES ALLOWED)

B. should be accomplished if at all possible

C. would like to accomplish (if the world were perfect and money is no object)

D. absolutely must be prevented (NO COMPROMISES ALLOWED)

E. should be prevented if at all possible

F. would like to prevent (if the world were perfect and money is no object)

The order in which each set of the above lists should be examined, satisfied and solved is:

First – animal and plant needs and considerations

Second – staff needs and considerations

Third – public needs and considerations

Last – esthetics

At first blush, placing animal and staff needs first and second would seem to short change the public, but in reality, by the time you have solved the animal and staff needs, the exhibit side of the facility is invariably larger and much better designed than if it was designed for the public first.

Nothing should be cast in stone until all of the above have been carefully taken into consideration and examined from all perspectives. The reward for this kind of attention to detail is a facility that usually costs less in build time, change orders, and money, and FUNCTIONS BETTER.

Lastly, all of the above must be accomplished within the constraints of existing budget, fund raising abilities and your willingness to take risks.

An Exhibit and/or Educational facility should:

- Create an experience so strong and realistic it will help to educate the public on the diversity of the species and their ecosystems, and the consequences of their extinction.

- It should make a positive contribution to conservation for these species and habitats.

- Provide display and management space for rare and endangered species of plants and animals.

- Have a design flexible enough to support current and future inhabitants and functions:

  - This is oftentimes simpler to say than to do when the facilities inhabitants may include:

    PLANTS – woody, succulent, dryfooted, wetfooted, aquatic +

    MAMMALS – apes, leaf monkeys, pygmy hippos, tamarins +

    BIRDS – hornbills, hook bills, soft bills, seed eaters +

    REPTILES – crocodilian, lizards, poisonous snakes, non poisonous snakes, turtles +

    AMPHIBIANS – frogs, toads, salamanders etc. +

    FISH – freshwater, saltwater, cold water, tropical +

    INSECTS – butterflies, ladybugs, praying mantis, assassin bugs +

    GRUMPY OLD ZOO VETS – who just want a little quiet and a cup of coffee.

In today's world, environmental and life support systems are often computer controlled for labor saving and ease of operation. However, all controls must have manual overrides for safety in emergencies and for when Murphy's Law catches up with you, as it surely must and periodically will. Assume all pumps, valves and life support systems will ultimately fail and decide in advance how you want each to fail. A three way valve controlling water temperature should fail differently for a cold water aquarium than for a tropical exhibit pool. Everyone should understand what you are trying to accomplish for each species or exhibit, and pay close attention to detail throughout both design and build phases. There should be manual override valves on both hot and cold water lines so that you can continue to function when the computer fails. For instance, in a cold water aquarium the three way valve should fail in the closed or the cold position so that when a lightning strike fries the computer you will not make 60,000 gals of boiled fish soup. Some of us have learned this small detail the hard way, and I can personally assure you, the lesson is a lasting one.

All critical systems should be redundant at two, and preferably three, levels. Instead of depending on one large boiler (almost guaranteed to be inefficient during the spring and fall) heating can be provided by multiple, small, high-efficiency natural gas boilers fed from a looped main. Electrical power for fans, pumps and lights supplied by a public or private utility should have the potential to be supplied from two different area circuits. If at all possible, and if you can afford it, the switch over gear should be automatic. Additionally, back-up electrical generation supporting at least 50 percent of the critical life support systems should be in place. The public can survive without filters, heat or air conditioning, but some plants and animals can't.

For many institutions, the requirement to always accept the lowest bid, almost guarantees a new, green team of potentially adversarial strangers for each new project. Omaha's Henry Doorly Zoo, as a society operated 501 (c)(3), is very fortunate in this respect. For over 40 years we negotiated virtually all projects.

The result of this was a team composed of the zoo director and staff, the same architect, mechanical engineer, and general contractor. The first obvious advantage, even with the inevitable personnel changes, is to greatly lessen the need to educate each new team on the basics of animal care, safety, containment, air changes, sanitation, that drains should where possible be outside the animals exhibit, and that floors should actually slope to these drains, etc. Additionally, the zoo part of the team develops a good sense of the fact that some fantastic ideas may cost more money than you have. Sometimes the most difficult thing you must do is to collectively commit to "cutting your pattern to fit the size of your cloth." Having a non-adversarial team, well inoculated to the institutions culture of making things work, really pays off. While wildly fantastic ideas may cost a lot more, great ideas often save money and give you a better product.

Good ideas aren't limited to zoo directors or architects. Some of our best ideas have come from keepers, job superintendents, engineers, electricians or plumbers whose experience says there may be a better, faster, stronger or less expensive way to do something. Once a week we would sit down as a team to review the past week, project the next, solve problems and listen to ideas. One key to Omaha's success has been negotiated contracts with the architect and general contractor which establish a set or maximum fee. The removal of economic incentives, other than finishing on time or early, coupled with the concept of trading out instead of writing conventional change orders, and a clear understanding with the subcontractors that problems will be solved without writing change orders, if at all possible, helps you stay within budget. Additionally, a reputation for strongly resisting change orders that increase the cost and the fact that a sub who bids low and tries to change order their way to more profit, meets a stone wall and is likely never invited to bid again helps you stay within budget. Having a negotiated contract also means that the zoo has a say about who the subs are. Another absolutely essential part of a successful project is for key zoo staff to look at the project everyday and three or four times a day during critical construction phases, like exhibit work and glass installation. The result for the Omaha Zoo has been increasingly larger, better projects, that are built faster for less money, and establish a track record for the team that makes past, present and future donors feel good and leads to more projects.

Playing "THE WHAT IF GAME" will hopefully make possible stable ecosystems that function, supporting plants, animals, keeper staff, enthusiastic zoo visitors and grumpy old zoo veterinarians.

◆ ◆ ◆

Projects, designs and Exhibits I had the opportunity to participate in:

1968 – Omaha Zoo Railroad

1968 – Eppley Pachyderm Hill

1971 – Lagoon deepened and islands built

1971 – 1908 well discovered and reconditioned

1971 – First Veterinary Hospital and Nursery

1972 – Owen Sea Lion Pavilion

1972 – Ak-Sar-Ben Waterfall and Swan Valley

1973 – Primate Research Building

1974 – First Diet Kitchen and Educational Classrooms

1974 – Flamingo Pool

1974 – Austrian Steam Locomotive

1977 – Largest Cat Complex in North America

1980 – Second Veterinary Hospital and Nursery

1981 – Giraffe Complex and Hoofstock Pastures

1983 – Lee G. Simmons Free-Flight Aviary

1984 – First Saltwater Aquarium

1985 – Owen Primate Valley renovation (gorilla and orangs)

1986 – World Herald Square and First Tier Wolf Woods

1987 – Mutual of Omaha's Wild Kingdom Pavilion and New Main Entrance

1987 – US West Plaza, Maintenance Building and Diet Kitchen

1988 – Black Footed Ferret Building

1989 – Greenhouse

1989 – Doorly's Pride Lion Sculpture

1989 – Durham Family Bear Canyon

1990 – Dairy World and Red Barn Concession Stand

1991 – Durham Family Birthday House

1992 – Simmons Plaza

1992 – Lied Jungle, Durham's Treetops Restaurant and Education Center

1994 – Union Pacific Engine House

1995 – Walter and Suzanne Scott Kingdoms of the Seas Aquarium

1996 – Bill and Bernice Grewcock Center for Conservation and Research

1997 – Zebra Barn

1997 – Lozier IMAX 3D Theater

1998 – Lee G. Simmons Conservation Park and Wildlife Safari

1998 – Garden of the Senses

1999 – Necropsy, Pathology Lab and Keepers Lounge

1999 – Sue's Carousel

2000 – New North Entrance, Gift Shop and Plaza

2001 – Cheetah Valley

2002 – Desert Dome

2003 – Eugene T. Mahoney Kingdoms of the Night

2004 – Hubbard Gorilla Valley

2004 – Elevator Tower and Orangutan Night Quarters

2005 – Hubbard Orangutan Forest

2005 – Amphibian Rescue Center

2006 – Hubbard Research Wing of Grewcock CCR

2008 – Berniece Grewcock Butterfly & Insect Pavilion

2009 – Skyfari

2010 – Hubbard Expedition Madagascar

APPENDIX C

CURRICULUM VITAE

Name   Lee Guyton Simmons Jr.

Date of Birth   February 20, 1938, Tucson, Arizona

Marital Status Married
Wife, Marie Annette (Giem)
Son, Lee Guyton III
Daughters, Heather Ann, Heidi Marie

Education   Central State College, Edmond, Oklahoma, Pre-Veterinary
studies, 1957-1959

Oklahoma State University, Stillwater, Oklahoma
Degree – Doctor of Veterinary Medicine, 1963

Organizations American Association of Zoo Veterinarians (AAZV)

American Veterinary Medical Association-Life Member

American Zoo and Aquarium Association (AZA) *formerly*
(AAZPA) The American Association of Zoological Parks
and Aquariums

Captive Breeding Specialist Group (CBSG) of the IUCN

Global Conservation Network (GCN)

International Species Inventory System (ISIS)

Nebraska Academy of Veterinary Medicine

Nebraska Veterinary Medical Association

Nebraska Wildlife Federation

Ohio Veterinary Medical Association

Rotary

United States Animal Health Association

World Association of Zoos and Aquariums (WAZA) *formerly* (IUDZG) The International Union of Directors of Zoological Gardens

Zoological Association of America (ZAA)

Professional Experience

Columbus Municipal Zoo, 9990 Riverside Drive, Powell, Ohio 43065, June 1963 – December 1966 – Mammals Curator, Resident Veterinarian, Assistant Superintendent.

Omaha's Henry Doorly Zoo, 3701 South 10th Street, Omaha, Nebraska 68107. Resident Veterinarian – December 1, 1966. Associate Director – March 1, 1967. Acting Director – March 3,1970, Director – May 1, 1970-March 15, 2009

Omaha Zoo Foundation, 3701 S. 10th St., Omaha, NE 68107. Chairman – March 16, 2009 - Present

Areas of Specialization

Aquarium Design and Life Support Systems

Chemical Immobilization of Wild Animals

Design of Functional Zoological Exhibits, Facilities and equipment

Inventor and Manufacturer of: Patented Simmons Pole Syringe, Zoolu Arms – Variable Range Dart Rifles, Blow Guns and Dart Tail Pieces. These devices are used by many U.S. and foreign zoos and field biologists.

Management of Great Apes to include Diagnosis and
Treatment of Tuberculosis

Management and Husbandry of Wild Animals in Captivity

Reproduction of Wild Animals in Captivity

Wildlife Medicine

Wildlife Photography

Zoological Fundraising

Appointments and Elections

American Association of Zoo Veterinarians – Board of
Directors, Secretary, Treasurer, Vice President, 1984-
1985-986

American Association of Zoo Veterinarians – President, 1987

American Association of Zoos, Parks and Aquariums –
Board of Directors, 1985-1988

American Zoo and Aquarium Association – Quarantine
Specialist Committee, 2000

The Community Discovered – Board of Advisors

Conservation Breeding Specialist Group (CBSG) Steering
Committee, Acting Chairman 2002 - 2003

Creighton University School of Dentistry – Associate Clinical
Professor of Oral Biology, 1989

Global Conservation Network (GCN) – Founding Board
Member 1991-Present

International Crane Foundation, Baraboo, Wisconsin –
Advisory Board

International Species Inventory System (ISIS) – Founding
Trustee

International Species Inventory System (ISIS) – Policy
Advisory Group (PAG)

International Wildlife Institute – Board of Scientific
Advisors, 2003

National Fish & Wildlife Foundation – Save the Tiger
Fund, sponsored by Exxon Corporation, 1995-1999

Nebraska Academy of Veterinary Medicine – President, 1980

Nebraska Veterinary Medical Association – Board of
Directors

Nebraska Wildlife Federation – Founding Trustee,
Secretary, Treasurer and Vice President

North American Species Coordinator (SSP) for Gaur
1981-2009

Offutt Air Force Base Advisory Council – Board of Directors
& 55TH Wing – Co-commander in Civil Engineering

Ohio State University, College of Veterinary Medicine Guest
Lecturer, 1963-1966

Omaha Zoo Foundation – Board of Directors and
Treasurer, 1982-2009; Chairman of the Board, 2009-
Present

Omaha Zoological Society – Executive Board, 1970-2009

Omaha's Henry Doorly Zoo (Omaha Zoological Society) –
Executive Director, 1970-2009

Omaha's Henry Doorly Zoo – Animal Research Committee
Chairman

Platte River Whooping Crane Maintenance Trust, Inc.
National Advisory Board

University of Nebraska Medical Center – Associate
Instructor, Department of Internal Medicine

V.A. Hospital Omaha, Nebraska – Chairman, Animal
Research Committee, 1980-1990

V.A. Hospital Omaha, Nebraska – Research Consultant,
1967-1990

The Salvation Army – Advisory Board – 2009-Present

**Awards,
Honors,
Recognition**

Lions Club of Omaha Nebraska – "Citizen of the Year"
Award, May 1978

City of Hope – National Idealism Award, 1979

Nebraska Veterinary Medical Association – Veterinarian of
the Year, 1979

American Association of Zoological Parks and Aquariums
Propagator's Certificate for Recognition of the Sustained
Captive Breeding of Gaur, May 1981

Omaha Kiwanis – Recognition of Long and On-Going
Achievements, April 1984

American Association of Zoos, Parks, and Aquariums Board
of Directors – Resolution of Appreciation for Efforts that
Greatly Assist "in the Strengthening of our Association
and the Body of Professional Knowledge made available to
our Members," April 1984

Face on the Ballroom Floor – Omaha Press Club, May 1988

Big Brothers Big Sisters – "Man of the Year" Award, 1991

Omaha World-Herald – Midlander of the Year, 1991

Chamber of Commerce – Headliner Award, 1992

University of Nebraska at Omaha – Omicron Delta Kappa National Leadership Honor Society, 1993

Creighton University – Honorary Doctor of Zoological Science Degree, May 1993

American Association of Zoological Parks and Aquariums Outstanding Service Award, 1993

Nebraska Society of Washington, DC – Distinguished Nebraskan Award, 1994

Nebraskaland Foundation – Wagonmaster Award, 1994

Sons of Italy Nebraska State Lodge – Humanitarian for the Year, 1995

State of Nebraska – Prestigious Vision Award, 1995

Fremont Area Art Association – Pathfinder Award, 1998

University of Nebraska at Omaha – Honorary Doctor of Science, December, 2002

Nebraska Division of Travel and Tourism – Henry Fonda Nebraskan Award, Governor Mike Johanns, Oct 14, 2003

Greater Omaha Chamber of Commerce Business Hall of Fame Inductee, April 2004

Knights of Aksarben, Court of Honor Inductee, October 2005

Governor Dave Heineman proclaimed Oct. 28 2006 "Dr. Lee G. Simmons Day" in the State of Nebraska.

"Microcebus simmonsi" Simmons' Mouse Lemur named by Dr. Edward E. Louis, 2006

Childrens Square USA – Lee and Marie Simmons – Jason Award Oct 16, 2007

Oklahoma State University – Center for Veterinary Health Sciences Distinguished Alumnus – November 2, 2007

Governor Brad Henry proclaimed October 4, 2008 "Dr. Lee G. Simmons Day" in the State of Oklahoma.

"Dr. Lee Simmons St." in front of Jones High School, Jones, Oklahoma, named October 4, 2008.

Suburban Rotary, Man of the Year Award, April 2009

Midland Lutheran College, Doctor of Science Honoris Causa, May 23, 2009

Knights of Aksarben – King of Quivira 113th – October 10, 2009

The Salvation Army – D.J.'s Hero Award – May 3, 2010

Nebraska Chamber of Commerce, Business Hall of Fame, Inductee Feb. 7 – 2013

Ulysses S. Seal, Innovation In Conservation Award – CBSG – October 13, 2013

Boy Scouts of America – Mid-America Council – Citizen of the Year – April 21, 2014

West Point Society of Nebraska and Western Iowa – Distinguished Citizen Award – March 21, 2015

Voted #132 out of the 150 Notable Nebraskans since Nebraska became a state in 1867 by the Lincoln Journal Star (Lincoln, NE) Jan 11, 2017

Military Service

United States Army Reserve – Four years active reserve duty – Military Police

Oklahoma National Guard – Four years active reserve

duty – Medical Assistant to the 179th Battle Group Surgeon, Discharged, 1963

Have had the privilege of spending time at sea on the nuclear carriers USS George Washington and USS Theodore Roosevelt and the nuclear submarine USS Nebraska

Other Activities

Traveled and worked in 50 countries and Antarctic – Fishing, Working in Basement Machine Shop, and Wildlife Photography

Publications

Autopsy findings of two jungle born female lowland gorillas J. F. Fitzgibbons, Warren Thomas, and Lee Simmons, The Journal of Zoo Animal Medicine, 03/1971; Vol. 2, No. 1.

Picorna virus in an epidemic of rhinotracheitis in cheetahs. Lee G. Simmons, The Journal of Zoo Animal Medicine, 12/1971; Vol. 2, No. 4.

Chickenpox in young anthropoid apes: clinic and laboratory findings. R. J. White, PhD., Lee Simmons, DVM; R. B. Wilson, M.D., Journal of the American Veterinary Medical Association, Vol. 161, No. 6, September, 1972.

Fatal shigellosis in a two year old gorilla. Dr. Lee Simmons, Combined Proceedings of the American Association of Zoo Veterinarians, 1972 & 1973.

Frostbite in antelope horns. Lee G. Simmons. Combined Proceedings of the American Association of Zoo Veterinarians, 1972 & 1973.

Observations on three gastro intestinal problems encountered in baby gorillas. Dr. Lee Simmons, Combined Proceedings of the American Association of Zoo Veterinarians, 1972 & 1973.

Fatality in an infant gorilla due to acute gastric dilation. Dr. Lee Simmons. Combined Proceedings of the American Association of Zoo Veterinarians, 1972 & 1973.

Autopsy findings of a three month old zoo born female lowland gorilla. John F. Fitzgibbons, M.D., Lee Simmons. Journal of Zoo Animal Medicine, 03/1974; Vol. 5, No. 1.

Autopsy findings of a seven year old male lowland gorilla. John F. Fitzgibbons, M.D., Lee Simmons, DVM. The Journal of Zoo Animal Medicine, 03/1975; Vol. 6, No. 1.

United States Patent # 3,880,162: Pole Syringe for Injecting from a Remote Distance. Lee G. Simmons (Inventor); April 29, 1975.

International Species information system (ISIS): A Computerized Record System for the Management of Wild Animals in Captivity. U. S. Seal, D. G. Makey, D. Bridgewater, L. Simmons, and L. Murfeldt, International Zoo Yearbook 17, 1977.

Impaction in a great Indian rhinoceros. Lee G. Simmons, DVM, and Bruce Jenke, DVM, Proceedings of the American Association of Zoo Veterinarians Annual Conference, 11/1977.

G-band patterns hemoglobin and transferrin types of the Bharal (*Pseudois nayaur*) with emphasis on mechanisms of karyotype evolution and speciation. T. D. Bunch, D. F. Nadler, and Lee Simmons; Journal of Heredity, 01/1978; 69(5) 613-30.

Restraint, anesthesia and practice tips for commonly encountered exotic animals. Lee Simmons, DVM. Proceedings of the Illinois State Veterinary Medical Association Conference, 01/1978.

On the extent of genetic variation of the African cheetah (*Acinonyx jubatis*). S.J. O'Brien, D.E. Wildt, J.M. Simonson, D.J. Brand, H. Ebedes, A. van Dyk, D. Metltzer, L.G. Simmons, and M. Bush. Proceedings of the American Association of Zoo Veterinarians, 1981; pp. 74-77.

Gonadotropin regime for inducing ovarian activity in captive felids. L.G. Phillips, L.G. Simmons, M. Bush, J.G. Howard and D.E. Wildt. Journal of American Veterinary Medical Association. 12/1982; 18(1) 1246-1250.

Adrenal response to anesthesia and surgical manipulation in female felids. L.G. Phillips, L.G. Simmons, D.E. Wildt, M. Roelke, J.G. Howard and M. Bush. Proceedings of the American Association of Zoo Veterinarians, 1983; pp. 78-79.

The South African cheetah: A multidisciplinary approach reveals a provocative genetic status and natural history. S.J. O'Brien, M. Roelke, L. Marker, F. Hart, D.G. Goldman, C. Merril, J.G. Howard, D. Meltzer, A van Dyk, H. Ebedes, D.J. Brand, J.M. Simonson, L.G. Simmons, M. Bush, and D.E. Wildt. Proceedings of the American Association of Zoo Veterinarians. 1983; p. 87.

Comparative evaluation and ejaculate characteristics in nondomestic Felids with emphasis on sperm morphology. J. G. Howard, M. Bush, L. G. Simmons, and D. E. Wildt.

Proceedings of the American Association of Zoo Veterinarians, 1984; pp. 168-170.

Radio-triggered anesthetic-dart collar for recapturing large mammals. L. David Mech, R. C. Chapman, W. W. Cochran, Lee Simmons, Ulysses S. Seal. Wildlife Society Bulletin, 1984; 12(1).

Biochemical genetic variation in eight endangered or threatened felid species. A. Newman, M. Bush, D. E. Wildt, D. Van Dam, M. Th. Frankenhuis, L. G. Simmons, L. G. Phillips, and S. J. O'Brien, Journal of Mammalogy, 1985; Vol. 66, pp. 256-267.

Hydraulic squeeze for African bull elephants. Lee G. Simmons, Carl Vires, Proceedings of the American Association of Zoo Veterinarians, 1986.

Yohimbine hydrochloride reversal of ketamine hydrochloride and xylazine hydrochloride immobilization of Bengal tigers and effects on hematology and serum chemistries. U. S. Seal, D. L. Armstrong, and L. G. Simmons. Journal of Wildlife Diseases 04/1987; 23(2).

Seminal-endocrine characteristics of the tiger and the potential for artificial breeding . D. E. Wildt, L. G. Phillips, L. G. Simmons, K. L. Goodrowe, J. Howard, J. L. Brown, and M. Bush. In: Tigers of the World: The Biology, Biopolitics, Management, and Conservation of an Endangered Species. R. L. Tilson and U. S. Seal, (Eds.). Noyes Publishing, Park Ridge, NJ. 1987; pp. 255-279.

Hormonal responses to GnRH and serum cortisol levels in two species of wild Felidae. J. L. Brown, K. L. Goodrowe,

D. Armstrong, L. G. Simmons, and D. E. Wildt. Proceedings of the Society for the Study of Reproduction, Biology of Reproduction, Suppl. 1987; 1; 36: 129.

A comparative analysis of ejaculate and hormonal characteristics of the captive male cheetah, tiger, leopard and puma. D.E. Wildt, L. G. Phillips, L. G. Simmons, P. K. Chakraborty, J. L. Brown, J. G. Howard, A. Teare and M. Bush. Biology of Reproduction. 04/1988; 38: 245-255.

Evaluation of pituitary-gonadal response to GnRH, and adrenal status, in the leopard (*Panthera pardus japonensis*) and tiger (*Panthera tigris*). J. L. Brown, K. L. Goodrowe, L. G. Simmons, D. L. Armstrong, and D. E. Wildt. Journal of Reproduction and Fertility; 02/1988; 82(1): 227-236.

Ovarian function in the elephant: luteinizing hormone and progesterone cycles in African and Asian elephants. E. D. Plotka, U. S. Seal, F. R. Zarembka, L. G. Simmons, A. Teare, L. G. Phillips, K. C. Hinshaw, and D. G. Wood. Biology of Reproduction, 04/1988; 38(1); 309-314.

Progress on in vitro fertilization of banteng (*Bos javanicus*) and gaur (*Bos gaurus*) . W. H. Eyestone, J. M. E. Balke, B. Read, W. Boever, E. Miller, R. Junge, L. Simmons, D. Armstrong and N. L. First, Proceedings of the Fifth World Conference on Breeding Endangered Species in Captivity, 1988.

Validation of a radioimmunoassay for luteinizing hormone in gaur (*Bos gaurus*) serum and observations of behavior around estrus. R. W. Godfrey, D. D. Lunstra, L. Simmons, D. L. Armstrong, J. Schwartz and J. A. French. Proceedings of the Fifth World Conference on Breeding Endangered Species in Captivity, 1988.

An evaluation of supplementing bacterial filtration with algae scrubbers in a recirculating marine aquarium. Warren W. Pryor, Daniel J. Morris, and Lee G. Simmons. Zoo Biology, 01/1988; Volume 7(3); 281.

Techniques for collection and cryopreservation of gaur (*Bos gaurus*) semen. S.M. Junior., L.G. Simmons, D.L. Armstrong, S.H. Hopkins, S.K.C. Hummel, and T.S. Gross. Proceedings of the American Association of Zoological Parks and Aquariums. Proc. Central Regional Conference, 1989.

Post-thaw viability and acrosomal integrity of gaur (*Bos gaurus*) sperm following comparative cryopreservation. M.C. Schiewe, S. Junior, D.L. Armstrong, T.S. Gross, L.G. Simmons, S. Hopkins and D. E. Wildt. Proceedings of the American Association of Zoo Veterinarians. 1989; pp. 62-65.

A chute management system for gaur (*Bos gaurus*). Simmons L.G., Armstrong D.L., Vires C. Regional Proceedings: American Association of Zoological Parks and Aquariums. 1989.

Hormonal induction of ovarian activity and in vitro fertilization in the tiger (Panthera tigris). A.M. Miller, L. A. Johnston, U. S. Seal, D. L. Armstrong, L. G. Simmons, P. Gross, R. L. Tilson, P. Wolf, K. Petrini and D. E. Wildt. Proceedings: Soc. Stud. Reprod., Biol. Reprod., 1990; Suppl. 1, 42: 128.

Semen cryopreservation and the first successful artificial insemination of gaur () S.M. Junior, D.L. Armstrong, S.H. Hopkins, L.G. Simmons, M.C. Schiewe, T.S. Gross Theriogenology 01/1990; 33(1): 262-262.

Conception, design and implementation of new exhibits and the "What If" game. Lee G. Simmons, Proceedings: of the American Association of Zoological Parks and Aquariums (AAZPA) – (AZA) Conference, 1990; p. 47.

In vitro fertilization and embryo development in vitro and in vivo in the tiger (*Panthera tigris*). A.M. Donoghue, L.A. Johnston, U.S. Seal, D.L. Armstrong, R.L. Tilson, P. Wolf, K. Petrini, L.G. Simmons, T. Gross and D.E. Wildt. Biology of Reproduction 12/1990; 43: 733-747.

United States Trademark # 1,648,765: ZOOLU ARMS. Lee G. Simmons (Inventor) June 25, 1991.

Estrous synchronization in the gaur (*Bos gaurus*): behavior and fertility to artificial insemination after prostaglandin treatment. R. W. Godfrey, D. D. Lunstra, J. A. French, J. Schwartz, D. L. Armstrong, L. G. Simmons. Zoo Biology. 1991; 10(1): 35-41.

Gaur semen cryopreservation: comparison of cryodiluents and freezing procedures. Gross, T.S., T. Tharnish, M. Patton, D.L. Armstrong and L.G. Simmons. Proceedings of the Wild Cattle Symposium, Henry Doorly Zoo, Omaha, NE, 06/13-16/1991.

Ability of thawed tiger (*Panthera tigris*) spermatozoa to fertilize conspecific oocytes and bind and penetrate domestic cat eggs in vitro. A.M. Donoghue, L.A. Johnston, U.S.

Seal., D.L. Armstrong, L.G. Simmons, T. Gross, R.L. Tilson and D.E. Wildt. Proceedings of the American Association of Andrology, Journal of Andrology, Suppl. 1992; p. 34.

Ability of thawed tiger (*Panthera tigris*) spermatozoa to fertilize conspecific oocytes and bind and penetrate domestic cat eggs in vitro. A.M. Donoghue, L.A. Johnston, U.S. Seal., D.L. Armstrong, L.G. Simmons, T. Gross, R.L. Tilson and D.E. Wildt. Journal of Reproduction and Fertility 11/1992; 96(2): 555-564.

A clinical trial using three regimens for immobilizing gaur. Wilson SC, DL Armstrong, LG Simmons, et al. Journal of Zoo and Wildlife Medicine 1993; 24: 93-101.

Birth of a Siberian tiger cub (*Panthera tigris altaica*) following laparoscopic intrauterine insemination. A.M. Donoghue, L.A. Johnston, D.L. Armstrong, L.G. Simmons and D.E. Wildt. Journal of Zoo and Wildlife Medicine, 1993; 24(2): 185-189.

Animal escapes in zoological institutions – a simplistic guideline for the inevitable. Lee G. Simmons. Proceedings of the American Association of Zoological Parks and Aquariums Regional Conference (AAZPA), 1993; p. 329.

Animal Escapes in Zoological Institutions – A simplistic guideline for the inevitable. Lee G. Simmons, American Association of Zoo Veterinarians Disaster Preparedness and Response Guide, 1993; pp. 28-32.

Oocyte maturation, fertilization and embryo development in vitro and in vivo in the gaur (*Bos gaurus*). L.A. Johnston,

J.J. Parrish, R Monson, L. Leibfried-Rutledge, J.L. Susko-Parrish, D.L. Northey, J.J. Rutledge, L.G. Simmons. Journal of Reproduction and Fertility. 1994; 00(1): 131-6.

Gaur sperm cryopreservation trial: analysis of packaging and rapid freezing method for potential field application. Schiewe, M.C., N.M. Loskutoff, B.S. Durrant, L.A. Johnston, D.L. Armstrong and L.G. Simmons. 1994; Theriogenology 41: 291.

Oocyte recovery and maturation in the American black bear (Ursus americanus): a model for endangered ursids. L.A. Johnston, A.M. Donoghue, W. Igo, L.G. Simmons, D.E. Wildt, J. Rieffenberger, Journal of Experimental Zoology 06/1994; 269(1): 53-61.

Techniques for collection and cryopreservation of gaur (Bos gaurus) semen. Junior, S.M., L.G. Simmons, D.L. Armstrong, S.H. Hopkins, S.K.C. Hummel, and T.S. Gross. Proceedings of the American Association of Zoological Parks and Aquariums Central Regional Conference, 1994.

Transvaginal egg retrieval and in-vitro embryo production in gaur (Bos gaurus) with establishment of interspecies pregnancy. Armstrong, D.L., C.R. Looney, B.R. Lindsey, C.L. Gonseth, D.L. Johnson, K.R. Williams, L.G. Simmons, and N.M. Loskutoff. Theriogenology, 12/1994; 43(1): 162.

Longevity in vitro and glycerol toxicity of epididymal sperm recovered from a white rhinoceros (Ceratotherium simum). K. R. Williams, W. K. Dyche, J. Brinders, F. Molteno, M. van der Lanken, D. L. Armstrong, L. G. Simmons. Theriogenology; 1995; 43(1): 353-353.

Gonadotrophin induction and its importance to successful intrauterine insemination in the tiger (*Panthera tigris*). Donoghue, A., A. Byers, L. Johnston, D. Armstrong, and D. Wildt. Journal of Reproduction and Fertility. 1996; 107: 53-58.

Species and individual variations in cryoprotectant toxicities and freezing resistances of epididymal sperm from African antelope. Loskutoff, N.M., Simmons, H.A., Goulding, M., Thompson, G., De Jong, T. and Simmons, L.G., Animal Reproduction Science 04/1996; 42(1): 527-535.

Semen characteristics of a western lowland gorilla determined by manual and computer-assisted motion analysis. Kurz S. G., A.M. Barnes, J.W. Ramey, C. Brown, N.M. Loskutoff, L.G. Simmons, D.L. Armstrong, and C.J. De Jonge. Proceedings: of the 29th annual meeting of the Society for the Study of Reproduction, Fort Collins, Colorado. 1996.

The successful recovery of the abscessed foot pad of an African elephant (*Loxodonta africana*), with particular attention given to two treatment elements: the use of a sandal and topically applied chitosan. D. Houser, L. Simmons and D. Armstrong. First North American Conference on Elephant Foot Care and Pathology, Portland, Oregon, March 20-21, 1998.

Transvaginal ultrasound-guided oocyte retrieval and the developmental competence of in-vitro produced embryos in vitro and in vivo in the gaur (*Bos gaurus*). Loskutoff N.M., Armstrong D.L., Ohlrichs C.L., Johnson D.L., Funk D.J, Van Roekel P.V., Molina J.A., Lindsey B.R., Looney C.R.,

Bellow S.M., Hammer C.G., Tyler H.D. and Simmons L.G., Theriogenology 2000; 53: 337.

The right way to save endangered species. Lee G. Simmons, Hillsdale College, Center for Constructive Alternatives Conference, 2000.

Zoo and aquarium design – playing the "What If" game. Lee G. Simmons. Proceedings of the American Associations of Zoo Veterinarians Annual Conference, 2000.

Temporal bone anatomy in *Panthera tigris*. Edward J. Walsh, Darlene R. Ketten, Julie Arruda, Douglas L. Armstrong, Thomas Curro, Lee G. Simmons, Lily M. Wang, Joann McGee. The Journal of the Acoustical Society of America. 2000; 115: 2485-2486.

Compromised development of calves (*Bos gaurus*) derived from in vitro generated embryos and transferred inter-specifically into domestic cattle (*Bos taurus*). C.J. Hammer, H.D. Tyler, N.M. Loskutoff, D.L. Armstrong, D.J. Fund, B.R. Lindsey and L.G. Simmons. Theriogenology, 05/2001; 55(7): 1447-55.

Post-thaw viability of wild cattle (*Bos gaurus*) and buffalo (*Syncerus caffer*) sperm cryopreserved using a novel, non-animal protein cryodiluent. Janesch L., Rohr J., Volenec D., Grobler D., Puffer A., Prokupek A., Armstrong D., Dankoff S., Curro T., Simmons L., Crichton E., Hamilton J., Rasmussen L., Zimmermann D., Lomneth R., Wood R., Wood D. and Loskutoff N. 2001; Theriogenology, 55: 387.

Shift training the Philippine crocodile at the Omaha's Henry Doorly Zoo. Krebs J., Morris D. J., Simmons L. G., Animal

Behavior Management Alliance 3rd Annual Conference Proceedings (2001); 01/2001.

Treatment of an abscessed foot pad of an African elephant using a sandal and topically applied chitosan. Houser, D., L.G. Simmons, and D.L. Armstrong. In: The Elephant's Foot: Prevention and Care of Foot Conditions in Captive Asian and African Elephants. B. Csuti, E.L. Sargent, and U.S. Bechert (Eds.). Iowa State University Press, Ames, Iowa. 2001; pp. 3-7.

Acoustic communication in *Panthera tigris*: a study of tiger vocalization and auditory receptivity. Edward J. Walsh, Lily M. Wang, Douglas L. Armstrong, Thomas Curro, Lee G. Simmons, Joann McGee. Journal of the Acoustical Society of America. 2003; 113: 2275-2275.

Bioacoustics in *Panthera tigris* – hearing and voice in a solitary hunter. Proceedings of the First International Conference on Acoustic Communication by Animals. University of Maryland, College Park, MD, USA. Walsh E.J., D.R. Ketten, L.M. Wang, D.L. Armstrong, T. Curro, L.G. Simmons and J. McGee. 07/2003; 27-30.

Bioacoustics in *Panthera tigris*. Society of Neuroscience, 33rd Annual Meeting, New Orleans, LA, U.S.A., E.J. Walsh, D.R. Ketten, L.M. Wang, D.L. Armstrong, T. Curro, L.G. Simmons and J. McGee, 11/2003; 8-12.

Xylazine-midazolam-ketamine versus medetomodine-mid azolam-ketamine anesthesia in Captive Siberian Tigers (*Panthera tigris altaica*) Thomas G. Curro, DVM, MS, Danelle Okeson, DVM, Dawn Zimmerman, DVM,

Douglas L. Armstrong, Lee G. Simmons, DVM. Journal of Zoo and Wildlife Medicine; 2004; 35(3):320-327. Erratum published in: Journal of Zoo and Wildlife Medicine 10/2004; 35(3): 320-7.

Notes on reproduction of the zebra shark, *Stegostoma fasciatum*, in a captive environment. Kay Kunze and Lee Simmons. Elasmobranch Husbandry Manual: Captive Care of Sharks, Rays and their Relatives, 2004.

A novel and effective procedure for removing HIV-RNA from human semen. In: International Congress Series; Species Issue: Research Papers in Fertility and Reproductive Medicine. Loskutoff N,. Huyser C., Singh R., Simmons L., Walker D., Thornhill A., Smith M., Morria L. and Webber L. Proceedings of the 18th World Congress on Fertility and Sterility. Daya, S., Pierson, R. and Gunby, J. (Eds.) 2004; 1271C, pp. 200-204, 2004.

Dynamics of intrafamily aggression and social reintegration in lion tamarins Betty J. Inglett, Jeffrey A. French, Lee G. Simmons, Kathy W. Vires. Zoo Biology. 05/2005; 8(1): 67-78.

The use of a venomous reptile restraining box at Omaha's Henry Doorly Zoo. Krebs J, Curro T G, Simmons L. G. Journal of Medical Toxicology, 2006.

Venomous snake shift training at the Henry Doorly Zoo. Krebs J, Morris D J, Simmons L G, Journal of Medical Toxicology, 2006.

Madagascar orchid conservation. From M.M., L.G. Simmons, T. Gouveia. Symposium for Malagasy Scientists, United

States Embassy, American Culture Center, Antananarivo, Madagascar, 2006.

In vitro strategies for conservation of Madagascar's endemic orchids. From M.M., L. Simmons, T. Gouveia. Society for In Vitro Biology National Conference, 2006.

Orchid conservation at Omaha's Henry Doorly Zoo. From M.M., L.G. Simmons and T. Gouveia. Mid-America Orchid Congress Annual Conference, 2006.

Influence of diet and time on fat and retinol concentrations in adult feeder crickets. Cheryl L. Dikeman, PhD, Sara D. Plesuk, Darlene L. Klimek, Sarah L. Burke, Kara J. Jorgensen, Lee G. Simmons, DVM.. Proceedings of the American Association Zoo Veterinarians, Nutrition Section. Knoxville, TN, 10/2007.

Preliminary data for comparison of carfentanil-xylazine and thiafentanil-medetomidine in electroejaculation of captive gaur (*Box frontalis gaurus*). Napier J.E., N. M. Loskutoff, S.M. Dankof, L.G. Simmons, and D.L. Armstrong. Proceedings of the American Association Zoo Veterinarians, 2007; pp. 49-50.

Treatment of an abscessed foot pad of an African elephant (*Loxodonta africana*) Using a Sandal and Topically Applied Chitosan. Daniel Houser, Lee G. Simmons, Douglas L. Armstrong. In: The Elephant's Foot: Prevention and Care of Foot Conditions in Captive Asian and African Elephants, 02/2008; pp. 107-113.

An outbreak of avian mycobacteriosis caused by *Mycobacterium intracellulare* in little blue penguins (*Eudyptula minor*). Napier J., S. Hinrichs, F. Lampen, P. Iwen, R. Wickert, J. Garrett, T. Aden, E. Restis, T. Curro, L. Simmons and D. Armstrong. Proceedings of the American Association of Zoo Veterinarians and the American Association of Reptile and Avian Veterinarians Joint Conference, 2008; p. 133.

Ultrasounding gorilla thyroid glands to investigate causation in human thyroid nodularity. The American Head and Neck Society. Coughlin A.M., D. Armstrong, J. Napier, L. Simmons, W.M. Lydiatt. Proceedings of the 7th International Conference on Head and Neck Cancer. 07/2008; 19-23.

Acoustic communication in *Panthera tigris*: A study of tiger vocalization and auditory receptivity revisited. Walsh, E., D.L. Armstrong, J. Napier, L.G. Simmons, M. Korte and J. Mcgee. Acoustical Society of America, 06/2008; 123(5): 3507.

Nutrient digestibility and fecal characteristics are different among captive exotic felids fed a beef-based raw diet. Brittany M. Vester, Sarah L. Burke, Cheryl L. Dikeman, PhD., Lee G. Simmons, DVM and Kelly S. Swanson. Zoo Biology 04/2008; 27(2): 126-136.

Nutrient digestibility, fecal metabolites, and fecal characteristics of exotic and domestic felids fed beef based or horse meat based diets. Vester B.M., S.L. Burke, A.N. Beloshapka, C.L. Dikeman, L.G. Simmons and K.S. Swanson. Proceedings of the Comparative Nutrition Society. 2008; 7, 2412.

Fecal microbial diversity of exotic and domestic felids fed beef based or horse meat based diets. Vester B.M., I.S. Middelbos, S.L. Burke, C.L. Dikeman, L.G. Simmons and K.S. Swanson. Proceedings of the Comparative Nutrition Society. 2008; 7, 243-4.

Diet transition affects serum calcium, phosphorus, and fatty acids in captive giraffe. Koutsos E.A., D. Armstrong, R. Ball, C. Dikeman, J. Hetherington, L. Simmons, E. Valdes and M. Griffin. Proceedings: of the European Zoo Nutrition Centre, 2008.

An outbreak of avian mycobacteriosis caused by *Mycobacterium intracellulare* in little blue penguins (*Eudyptula minor*). Julia E. Napier, D.V.M., Steven H. Hinrichs, M.D., Francois Lampen, B.V.Sc., Peter C. Iwen, Ph.D., Robert S. Wickert, M.S., Jodi L. Garrett, B.Sc., Tricia A. Aden, B.Sc., Eva Restis, D.V.M., Thomas G. Curro, D.V.M. M.S., Lee G. Simmons, D.V.M., and Douglas L. Armstrong, D.V.M.. Journal of Zoo and Wildlife Medicine, 12/2009; 40(4): 680-686.

Influence of feeding raw or extruded feline diets on nutrient digestibility and nitrogen metabolism in African wildcats (*Felis lybica*). Vester, B.M., S.L. Burke, K.J. Liu, C.L. Dikeman, L.G. Simmons and K.S. Swanson. Zoo Biology, 2010; 29(6): 676-86.

Evaluation of nutrient digestibility and fecal characteristics of exotic felids fed horse- or beef- based diets: use of the domestic cat as a model for exotic felids. Vester, B.M., I.S. Middelbos, S.L. Burke, C.L. Dikeman, L.G. Simmons and K.S. Swanson. Zoo Biology, 10/2009; 29(4): 432-48.

Nutrient digestibility evaluations of four raw meats using avians, domestic cats and captive exotic felids. Kerr K.R., A. Beloshapka, C. Dikeman, S. Burke, L.G. Simmons, and K.S. Swanson. Comparative Nutrition Society, 2010.

Nitrogen metabolism of four raw meat diets in domestic cats. Kerr K.R., A. Beloshpaka, C. Dikeman, S. Burke, L.G. Simmons, and K.S. Swanson. Proceedings of the Waltham International Nutritional Sciences Symposium, 2010.

Discovery of a new cryptopus (*Orichidacea*) species in Madagascar, M.M. From & L.G. Simmons Phelsuma, 2011; 19: 115-116.

Preliminary Data for Comparison of carfentanil-xylazine and thiafentanil-medetomidine in electroejaculation of Captive Gaur (*Bos gaurus*). Julia E. Napier, D.V.M., Naida M. Loskutoff, Ph.D., Lee G. Simmons, D.V.M., and Douglas L. Armstrong, D.V.M. Journal of Zoo and Wildlife Medicine, 2011; 42(3): 430-436.

Influence of diet transition on serum calcium and phosphorus and fatty acids in zoo giraffe (*Giraffa camelopardalis*). Koutsos, E.A., D. Armstrong, R. Ball, C. Dikeman, J. Hetherington, L. Simmons, E.V. Valdes, and M. Griffin. Zoo Biology, 10/2010; 30(5): 523-531.

Snakebites in the new millennium: Proceedings of a state-of-the-art symposium. Oct. 21 2005. Audi J., S.A. Seifert, J.F. Gennaro, J.W. Skimming, L.H. S. Van Mierop, C.S. Kitchens, M.D. Cardwell, S.P. Bush, R.T. Clark, E.A. Dugan, R.C. Dart, S.R. Rose, B.S. Poulson, E.R. Waring, K.S. Whitlow, K.L. Wiley, J.R. Harrison, S. Shum, J.E.

Jaramillo, R. Franklin, M. Fernandez, C.P. Lintner, D.E. Keyler, E.F. Bilden, D.P. Pandey, B.G. Fry, D.A. Warrell, J. Krebs, D.J. Morris, L.G. Simmons, L.V. Boyer, L. Boyer, S.L. Kipp, T.G. Curro, E.E. Sánchez, J.C. Pérez, J.A. Galán, J.E. Biardi, L.M. Salgueiro-Tosta, S. Eedala, A.M. Garcia, J. Martinez, F.A. Rodríguez-Acosta, R. Straight, J. Estévez, A. Olvera, B. Ramos, H. Vázquez, G. Odell, J. Paniagua, A. de Roodt, R.F. Olvera Mancilla, M. Salas, A. Zavaleta, R. Stock, A. Alagón, K. O'Donovan. Journal of Medical Toxicology; official journal of the American College of Medical Toxicology, 2006; 2(1): 29-45.